MW00568403

anu

Perspectives: Key Concepts
for Understanding Curriculum 1

The Falmer Press Teachers' Library

Series Editor: Professor I.F. Goodson, Warner Graduate School, University of Rochester and Centre for Applied Research in Education, University of East Anglia, Norwich, UK.

The Falmer Press Teachers' Library: 11

Perspectives: Key Concepts for Understanding Curriculum 1

A Fully Revised and Extended Edition

Colin J. Marsh

RoutledgeFalmer
Taylor & Francis Group

LONDON AND NEW YORK

First published in 1997
By RoutledgeFalmer
2 Park Square, Milton Park, Abington, Oxon, OX14 4RN

Transferred to Digital Printing 2006

A catalogue record for this book is available from the British Library

Library of Congress Cataloging-in-Publication Data are available on request

ISBN 0-7507-0683-X cased
ISBN 0-7507-0587-6 paper

Jacket design by Caroline Archer

Typeset in 10/12pt Times by
Graphicraft Typesetters Ltd., Hong Kong.

Contents

Contents

Contents

Contents

List of Tables

List of Figures

Preface

The diversity and pace of change in curriculum policy and implementation continues unabated in many countries in the Western world. In addition, the players who are taking leading roles in policy formulation are changing, with increasing pressures coming from politicians and employer groups, as well as from community interest groups, parents, teachers and students.

A number of these individuals and groups have very limited understanding of curriculum theories, principles and processes, even though they are prepared to commit enormous amounts of energy to advance their preferred solutions to specific curriculum problems.

Despite the rhetoric and the ambitious programs, schooling has remained remarkably unchanged. The numerous efforts of school reform have been generally unsuccessful. Have we been addressing the wrong factors? Do we need to be better informed about probable futures? What are the challenges ahead for schooling?

The books are (Volume 1 — Perspectives: Teachers, Students, Parents, Politicians and Volume 2 — Planning, Management and Ideology) intended especially for those who will be commencing full-time careers in schools, namely students who are taking teacher education degrees (BA (education), Bachelor of Education, Diploma of Education, Diploma of Teaching and PGCEs). Another major group who are likely to be very interested in the books include those practising teachers who are embarking upon professional development programs. Parents and community members involved as school governors and members of school councils, boards and districts, will obtain considerable assistance from the succinctly stated commentaries about major curriculum concepts.

The books provide details about forty-four major concepts in curriculum.

In Voume 1 Perspectives: Teachers, Students, Parents, Politicians readers are given advice about how to use the key concepts. The four sections of the volume include key concepts which reveal the respective contributions and influence of students, teachers, parents and politicians. However, readers are advised to use the book selectively and flexibly rather than reading it through from cover to cover.

Readers may wish to rearrange the order in which they read the chapters, in keeping with alternative curriculum ideologies and orientations.

The nineteen concepts in Volume 1 cover a wide range of important topics in curriculum. In such a small space each chapter cannot provide an exhaustive treatment of each concept, but every attempt has been made to highlight major features, controversies, strengths and weaknesses. In particular, the follow up questions challenge the reader to reflect further upon specific issues relating to each concept and the listing of recent references at the end of each chapter (including an enormous range of Falmer Press publications), facilitates this task.

I acknowledge various colleagues in curriculum, both within Australia, and in the United Kingdom, United States of America, and Canada, who have helped me hone my ideas over the decades about curriculum. They include Michael Fullan, Gene Hall, Paul Klohr, Michael Huberman, Elliot Eisner, Bill Reid, Helen Simons, Kerry Kennedy, Eric Hoyle, Ray Bolam, Michael Connelly, Christine Deer, David Smith, Noel Gough, Chris Day, Ivor Goodson, Brian Caldwell, Paul Morris, David Tripp and Malcolm Skilbeck.

The second edition (Volumes 1 and 2) has been enlarged considerably upon the first edition and includes a number of new concepts which are having considerable impact during the late 1990s. As a consequence, there are many new chapters and all existing chapters have been extended and updated.

For permission to reproduce figures and tables I am most grateful to Patricia Broadfoot, Brian Caldwell, Chris Day, Stephen Kemmis and Barry Fraser. A special word of thanks is due to Dawn Booth for her expert secretarial assistance in the preparation of the manuscript.

Colin Marsh

To Glenys, Ross, Jenny and Alison

Part I

Introduction

1   What Is Curriculum?

Introduction

Numerous scholars have commented upon what they perceive to be curriculum. For example, Goodson (1994), describes curriculum 'as a multifaceted concept, constructed, negotiated and renegotiated at a variety of levels and in a variety of arenas' (p. 111).

Longstreet and Shane (1993), consider that 'curriculum is an historical accident — it has not been deliberately developed to accomplish a clear set of purposes. Rather, it has evolved as a response to the increasing complexity of educational decision making' (p. 7).

It is certainly the case that curriculum has been a matter of intense debate during the twentieth century. There have been all kinds of priorities put forward including citizenship demands, personal development priorities and vocational training pressures. There have also been various pressures ranging from practical, school-focused approaches to curriculum and curriculum development; theoretical perspectives of different kinds and technical, scientific management approaches.

Some Definitions of Curriculum

Over the decades many definitions of curriculum have been provided but because key players in education represent a diversity of values and experience, it is extremely difficult to get wide public or professional consensus. Consider the following selection of definitions of *curriculum*:

- Curriculum is that which is taught in school.
- Curriculum is a set of subjects.
- Curriculum is content.
- Curriculum is a set of materials.
- Curriculum is a set of performance objectives.
- Curriculum is that which is taught both inside and outside of school and directed by the school.
- Curriculum is that which an individual learner experiences as a result of schooling.
- Curriculum is everything that is planned by school personnel.

To define curriculum as 'what is taught in schools' is of course, very vague. Persons often talk about the 'school curriculum' in this general way and they tend to mean by this the range of subjects taught and the amount of instruction time given to each in terms of hours or minutes.

Curriculum defined as 'content' is an interesting emphasis and brings into question another term, namely the 'syllabus'. A 'syllabus' is usually a summary statement about the content to be taught in a course or unit, often linked to an external examination. This emphasis on *what* content to be taught is a critical element of a 'syllabus' but a 'curriculum' includes more than this. For example *how* you teach content can drastically affect what is taught. Also, the extent to which students are sufficiently prepared and motivated to study particular content will affect very greatly what is learnt.

Curriculum is quite often defined as a product — a document which includes details about goals, objectives, content, teaching techniques, evaluation and assessment, resources. Sometimes these are official documents issued by the government or one of its agencies and which prescribe *how* and *what* is to be taught. Of course it is important to realize that a curriculum document represents the *ideal* rather than the *actual* curriculum. A teacher may not accept all aspects of a written curriculum and/or be unable to implement a curriculum exactly as prescribed due to lack of training and understanding. There can be gaps between the intended, ideal curriculum and the actual curriculum. It may be that the level and interests of the students, or local community preferences, may prevent a teacher from implementing a curriculum as prescribed.

Defining a curriculum as a 'set of performance objectives' or student learning is a very practical orientation to curriculum. This approach focuses upon specific skills or knowledge that it is considered should be attained by students. Proponents of this approach argue that if a teacher knows the targets which students should achieve, it is so much easier to organize other elements to achieve this end, such as the appropriate content and teaching methods.

Few would deny that another strength of this approach is the emphasis upon students. After all, they are the ultimate consumers and it is important to focus upon what it is anticipated that they will achieve and to organize all teaching activities to that end. Yet it must also be remembered that this approach can lead to an overemphasis upon behavioural outcomes and objectives which can be easily measured. Some skills and values are far more difficult to state in terms of performance objectives. Also, a curriculum document which is simply a listing of performance objectives would have to be very large and tends to be unwieldy.

To define curriculum as 'that which is taught both inside and outside school, directed by the school' indicates that all kinds of activities that occur in the classroom, playground and community, comprise the curriculum. This emphasis has merit in that it demonstrates that school learning is not just confined to the classroom. However, it should be noted that the emphasis is upon 'direction' by the school which seems to indicate that the only important learning experiences are those which are directed by school personnel. Few would accept this statement and so it is necessary to look at other definitions.

To define curriculum in terms of 'what an individual learner experiences as a result of schooling' is an attempt to widen the focus. The emphasis here is upon the student as a self-motivated learner. Each student should be encouraged to select those learning experiences that will enable him/her to develop into a fully-functioning person. However, it should be noted that each student acquires knowledge, skills and values not only from the *official* or *formal* curriculum but also from the *unofficial* or *hidden* curriculum (see also Chapter 4). As noted by Pollard and Tann (1987) the hidden curriculum is implicit within regular school procedures, in curriculum materials, and in communication approaches and mannerisms used by staff. It is important to remember that students do learn a lot from the hidden curriculum even though this is not intended by teachers.

The definition which refers to curriculum as 'everything that is planned by school personnel' is yet another orientation which emphasizes the planning aspect of curriculum. Few would deny that classroom learning experiences for students need to be planned although some unplanned activities will always occur (and these can have positive or negative effects). This definition also brings to bear the distinction that some writers make between curriculum and instruction. Some writers argue that curriculum is the *what* and instruction is the *how*, or another way of expressing it — 'curriculum activity is the production of plans for further action and instruction is the putting of plans into action' (Macdonald and Leeper, 1966).

Although it can be important to separate out the two functions of *what* and *how*, it tends to obscure the interdependence of *curriculum* and *instruction*. Classroom teachers do not separate out the two functions because they are constantly planning, implementing and monitoring in their respective classrooms. That is, it is not practical to separate out intentions from actions — there is really a fluid movement of interactions between plans, actions, change of plans, different actions.

It might be argued that for a curriculum definition to be of value to practitioners and scholars it must accommodate different values and perspectives and should not be overly prescriptive. Walker (1990) contends that if a definition is to have some potential use, it should be couched in terms of:

- matters that teachers and students attend together;
- matters that students, teachers and others recognize as important to study and learn;
- the manner in which these matters are organized.

The definition which the author has advanced elsewhere (Marsh and Stafford 1988; Marsh and Willis, 1995) is also relatively generic, namely 'curriculum is an interrelated set of plans and experiences which a student completes under the guidance of the school'. This definition needs amplification and illustration (see Figure 1.1). The phrase 'interrelated set of plans and experiences' refers to the point that curricula which are implemented in schools are typically planned in advance but, that inevitably, unplanned activities also occur. Therefore the actual curricula which are implemented in classrooms consist of an amalgam of plans and experiences (unplanned happenings). The curriculum as experienced in the classroom is not a one-way transmission of ideas and information from the teacher to a group of passive recipients but a series of communications/reactions/exchanges between both groups.

Figure 1.1: An illustrative definition of curriculum

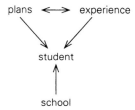

The phrase 'which a student completes under the guidance of the school' is included to emphasize the time element of every curriculum. That is, curricula are produced on the assumption that students will complete certain tasks and activities over a period of time. 'Under the guidance of the school' refers to all persons associated with the school who might have had some input into planning a curriculum. It might normally include teachers, school councils and external specialists such as advisory inspectors.

Above all, the definition presupposes that some conscious planning is possible, and indeed desirable, and that there are some important elements which are common to any planning activity, regardless of the particular value orientation. It also assumes that the learning activities experienced by students in classroom settings are managed and mediated by teachers so that intended outcomes can be reconciled with practical day-to-day restrictions.

Not all readers will be satisfied by this definition of curriculum but it does at least cater for a number of perspectives and value orientations. As noted by Pinar *et al.* (1995) it is to be expected that a complex field such as curriculum will inevitably lead to central terms being used in complex and even contradictory ways: 'The multiplication of definitions is not an urgent problem to be solved. It is rather, a state of affairs to be acknowledged. In a field comprised of various and autonomous discourses, it is inevitable' (p. 26).

It is also possible, according to Jackson (1992) to note definitional shifts over the decades going from 'fixed courses of study' terminology to broader terms such as 'learning opportunities' and 'experiences which a learner encounters'. Thus, it might be argued that these shifts in definition over the decades represent 'conceptual progress' (Tanner and Tanner, 1980).

Characteristics of Curriculum

Some curriculum experts, such as Goodlad (1979) contend that an analysis of definitions is a useful starting point for examining the field of curriculum. Other writers argue that there are important concepts or characteristics that need to be considered and which give some insights into how particular value orientations have evolved and why.

Walker (1990) argues that the fundamental concepts of curriculum include:

- content: which may be depicted in terms of concept maps, topics and themes, all of which are abstractions which people have invented and named;
- purpose: usually categorized as intellectual, social and personal; are often divided into superordinate and subordinate purposes; stated purposes are not always reliable indicators of actions;
- organization: planning is based upon scope and sequence (order of presence over time); can be tightly organized or relatively open-ended.

Tripp (1994) refers to determining characteristics of curriculum, specifically:

- intentions: to produce a curriculum;
- planning: extent to which a curriculum is planned;
- explication: extent to which the curriculum details are made explicit;
- harmony: extent to which the parts of a curriculum are complementary;
- relations: the extent to which the parts of a curriculum are related.

Other writers such as Beane, Toepfer and Alessi (1986) produce principles of curriculum but they are more value-oriented and less generic. For example, they list five major principles about curriculum:

- concern with the experiences of learners;
- making decisions about both content and process;
- making decisions about a variety of issues and topics;
- involving many groups;
- decision-making at many levels.

It is evident that these authors have a particular conception of curriculum, perhaps a combination of student and society-centred. Inevitably, if specific principles are given a high priority, then a particular conception of curriculum emerges. Longstreet and Shane (1993) refer to four major conceptions of curriculum:

- society-oriented curriculum: purpose of schooling is to serve society;
- student-centred curriculum: the student is the crucial source of all curriculum;
- knowledge-centred curriculum: knowledge is the heart of curriculum;
- eclectic curriculum: various comprises are possible including mindless eclecticism!

The conceptions or orientations of curriculum produced by Eisner and Vallance (1974) are often cited in literature, namely:

- a cognitive process orientation: cognitive skills applicable to a wide range of intellectual problems;

- technological orientation: to develop means to achieve prespecified ends;
- self-actualization orientation: individual students discover and develop their unique identities;
- social reconstructionist orientation: schools must be an agency of social change;
- academic rationalists: to use and appreciate the ideas and works of the various disciplines.

These conceptions of curriculum are useful to the extent that they remind educators of some value orientations that they may be following, whether directly or indirectly. Yet others, such as Pinar *et al.* (1995) argue that these conceptions are stereotypes and are of little value.

Who Is Involved in Curriculum?

Curriculum workers are many and include school-based personnel such as teachers, principals, and parents and university-based specialists, industry and community groups and government agencies and politicians.

Jackson (1992) suggests that a large number of those working in the curriculum field are involved in serving the daily and technical needs of those who work in schools. This has been the traditional role over the decades where the focus has been upon curriculum development for school contexts.

Pinar *et al.* (1995) refers to the 'shifting domain of curriculum development as politicians, textbook companies, and subject-matter specialists in the university, rather than school practitioners and university professors of curriculum, exercise leadership and control over curriculum development' (p. 41). It is certainly the case in most OECD countries that a wider range of interest groups are now involved in curriculum development (see Chapter 14).

For those working at the university level there are many divergent priorities in curriculum although all have a central goal of understanding curriculum. Some of these priorities include:

- historical scholarship: the study of curriculum history in terms of theoretical and practical developments;
- political scholarship: analyses of the struggles for influence and power;
- autobiographical scholarship: curriculum as an individual's personal experiences;
- feminist theory: understanding curriculum as gender text;
- phenomenology: a form of interpretative inquiry which focuses upon human perception and experience;
- aesthetic perceptions of curriculum: the role of the arts in curriculum;
- racial discourses: understanding curriculum as racial text;
- poststructuralism and postmodernism: cultural breaks with modernism;

- theological and international dimensions of curriculum: the moral and ethical elements of curriculum.

A number of these developments are discussed in subsequent chapters, especially chapters 39–44 in Part VII, Curriculum Ideology.

Curriculum in the 1990s is indeed moving in many directions and some would assert that this reflects a conceptual advance (Jackson, 1992) and a more sophisticated view of the curriculum. Others would argue that curriculum as a field of study is still conceptually underdeveloped (Goodlad and Su, 1992).

Reflections and Issues

1 'If the curriculum is to be the instrument of change in education, its meanings and operational terms must be clearer than they are currently.' (Toombs and Tierney, 1993, p. 175)
   Discuss.

2 Rather than attempting to define 'curriculum', Tripp (1994) prefers to focus upon the term 'curriculum studies' which he defines as 'a recently developed field of educational knowledge which is primarily concerned with the description, explanation and critique of curriculum texts, their participants, and their practices.' (p. 26)
   Is this a more practical solution? What problems still remain?

3 'The written curriculum is subject to renegotiation at lower levels, notably the classroom.' (Goodson 1994, p. 18)
   If this is the case, is it ever possible to have successful implementation of national curriculum programmes as described in Cox and Sanders (1994) and Ahier and Ross (1995)?

4 Trying to clarify central concepts by proposing definitions for them has been popular in many fields (Portelli, 1987). Have these concepts and definitions proven useful in the field of curriculum?

5 'The future of curriculum studies is uncertain; weaknesses persist in the very nature of curricular discourse.' (Milburn, 1992, p. 302)
   Provide arguments for and against this statement. What have been/are problems in curricular debates and discourse?

6 'The term "social subjects" rarely occurs in the current formulations of the National Curriculum or the whole curriculum in the United Kingdom; indeed the very work "society" is notable by its infrequency.' (Campbell, 1993, p. 137)
   Does this indicate deficiencies in the conceptions of curriculum incorporated into the National Curriculum?
   Discuss.

7   'Analysis of the National Curriculum and its associated testing procedures in the United Kingdom shows that ethnic-minority learners are almost entirely overlooked.' (Pumfrey and Verma, 1993, p. 19)
    Discuss.

8   'The struggle over the definition of curriculum is a matter of social and political priorities as well as intellectual discourse.' (Goodson 1988, p. 23)
    Reflect upon a particular period of time and analyse the initiatives, successes and failures which occurred in terms of curriculum development or policy development.

References

AHIER, J. and ROSS, A. (1995) *The Social Subjects within the Curriculum*, London, Falmer Press.

BEANE, J.A., TOEPFER, C.F. and ALESSI, S.J. (1986) *Curriculum Planning and Development*, Boston, Allyn and Bacon.

CAMPBELL, R.J. (1993) (Ed) *Breadth and Balance in the Primary Curriculum*, London, Falmer Press.

COX, T. and SANDERS, S. (1994) *The Impact of the National Curriculum on the Teaching of Five Year Olds*, London, Falmer Press.

EISNER, E. and VALLANCE, E. (1974) (Eds) *Conflicting Conceptions of Curriculum*, Berkeley, CA, McCutchan.

GOODLAD, J. (1979), *Curriculum Inquiry: The Study of Curriculum Practice*, New York, McGraw Hill.

GOODLAD, J. and SU, Z. (1992) 'Organisation of the curriculum', in JACKSON, P. (Ed) *Handbook of Research on Curriculum*, New York, Macmillan.

GOODSON, I.F. (1988) *The Making of Curriculum*, London, Falmer Press.

GOODSON, I.F. (1994) *Studying Curriculum*, New York, Teachers College Press.

JACKSON, P. (1992) (Ed), *Handbook of Research on Curriculum*, New York, Macmillan.

LONGSTREET, W.S. and SHANE, H.G. (1993) *Curriculum for a New Millennium*, Boston, Allyn and Bacon.

MACDONALD, J. and LEEPER, R. (1966) (Eds) *Language and Meaning*, Washington, DC, ASCD.

MARSH, C.J. and STAFFORD, K. (1988) *Curriculum: Practices and Issues*, 2nd edition, Sydney, McGraw Hill.

MARSH, C.J. and WILLIS, G. (1995) *Curriculum: Alternative Approaches, Ongoing Issues*, Columbus, Ohio, Merrill.

MILBURN, G. (1992) 'Do curriculum studies have a future?', *Journal of Curriculum and Supervision*, **7**, 3, pp. 302–18.

PINAR, W.F., REYNOLDS, W.M., SLATTERY, P. and TAUBMAN, P.M. (1995) *Understanding Curriculum*, New York, Peter Lang.

POLLARD, A. and TANN, S. (1987) *Reflective Teaching in the Primary School*, London, Cassell.

PORTELLI, J.P. (1987) 'On defining curriculum', *Journal of Curriculum and Supervision*, **2**, 4, pp. 354–67.

PUMFREY, P.D. and VERMA, G.K. (1993) *The Foundation Subjects and Religious Education in Secondary Schools*, London, Falmer Press.

TANNER, D. and TANNER, L. (1980) *Curriculum Development: Theory into Practice*, 2nd edition, New York, Macmillan.

TOOMBS, W.E. and TIERNEY, W.G. (1993) 'Curriculum definitions and reference points', *Journal of Curriculum and Supervision*, 8, 3, pp. 175–95.

TRIPP, D. (1994) 'Putting the Humpty into curriculum', Unpublished paper, Murdoch University.

WALKER, D. (1990) *Fundamentals of Curriculum*, San Diego, Harcourt Brace Jovanovich.

2   Introducing Key Concepts

Introduction

We make sense of our world and go about our daily lives by engaging in *concept building*. We acquire and develop concepts so that we can gain meaning about persons and events and in turn communicate these meanings to others.

Some concepts are clearly of more importance than others. The *key concepts* provide us with the power to explore a variety of situations and events and to make significant connections. Other concepts may be meaningful in more limited situations but play a part in connecting unrelated facts.

Every field of study contains a number of key concepts and lesser concepts which relate to substantive and methodological issues unique to that discipline/field of study. Not unexpectedly, scholars differ over their respective lists of key concepts, but there is nevertheless, considerable agreement. With regard to the curriculum field there is a moderate degree of agreement over key concepts.

Searching for Key Concepts

To be able to provide any commentary on key concepts in curriculum assumes of course that we have access to sources of information that enable us to make definitive statements.

A wide range of *personnel* are involved in making curriculum including school personnel, researchers, academics, administrators, politicians, and various interest groups. They go about their tasks in various ways such as via planning meetings, informal discussions, writing reports, papers, handbooks, textbooks, giving talks, lectures, workshops.

To ensure that a list of key concepts is comprehensive and representative of all these sources would be an extremely daunting task. A proxy often used by researchers is to examine textbooks, especially *synoptic textbooks* (those books which provide comprehensive accounts and summaries of a wide range of concepts, topics and issues in curriculum).

Schubert (1980) undertook a detailed analysis of textbooks over the period 1900–80 and this volume provides a valuable overview of curriculum thought over major historical periods. Marsh and Stafford (1988) have provided a similar historical analysis of major curriculum books written by Australian authors over the period 1910–88.

Rogan and Luckowski (1990) undertook an analysis of nine major synoptic curriculum texts produced by American authors. Their purpose in undertaking this analysis was to portray major concepts within the curriculum field. They noted that all texts included an analysis of four major themes, namely paradigms, conceptions of curriculum, history, and politics, but that there was little consensus on preferred positions within each of these topics. This diversity of stance within topics may reflect the nature of the curriculum field compared with the apparent singularity of purpose and methodological procedures followed in some science disciplines.

An Analysis of Synoptic Texts

In the first edition of this book a sample analysis was undertaken of six major curriculum texts that were used widely at the college/university level, namely two from the USA, two from the UK and one each from Australia and Canada.

In the intervening period since the first edition was completed, it is evident that synoptic texts have continued to be very popular in the USA and Australia, there has been no significant increase in number in Canada and in the UK they have largely disappeared.

Table 2.1 depicts details of seven USA synoptic texts and one Canadian text. The American texts are very comprehensive and the majority cover similar topics and key concepts within the broad categories of:

- conceptions of curriculum/models/approaches;
- curriculum history;
- curriculum policy and policy makers, politics of curriculum;
- curriculum development procedures/change/improvement/planning steps;
- issues and trends/problems/future directions.

The majority of those selected tend to provide a balanced account of key concepts across all these five broad categories (Longstreet and Shane (1993), Marsh and Willis (1995), Ornstein and Hunkins (1993), Schubert (1986) and Walker (1990)).

Yet there are other authors who provide very detailed accounts of some categories, to the exclusion of other categories altogether. Pinar *et al.* (1995) provide an extremely thorough analysis of conceptions of curriculum and curriculum theorizing and curriculum history but minimal attention is given to the other categories. Posner and Rudnitsky's (1986) book focuses almost entirely on curriculum development procedures (instruction) as does the Robinson *et al.* (1985) text. The Longstreet and Shane (1993) text has a major emphasis upon future studies in addition to covering the other categories.

By contrast, the Australian/Asian synoptic texts are smaller volumes and do not provide a balanced account across the categories, with the exception of Marsh and Stafford (1988). The most recent synoptic texts (Brady, 1995; Print, 1993) concentrate predominantly on 'curriculum development procedures' with some limited analysis of 'conceptions of curriculum'. Smith and Lovat (1990) provide a detailed analysis of 'conceptions of curriculum' and a limited coverage of 'curriculum

Table 2.1: *Analysis of synoptic curriculum texts in the USA and Canada*

	USA	USA	USA	USA
Major emphases	Longstreet and Shane (1993) 398pp	Marsh and Willis (1995) 379pp	Ornstein and Hunkins (1993) 2nd edition 416pp	Pinar et al. (1995) 1143pp
Conceptions of curriculum	Concepts Design principles Philosophical bases	Planning Theorizing	Foundations Theories	Understanding curriculum Racial text Gender text Phenomenological text Postmodern text Autobiographical text Aesthetic text Theological text
Curriculum history	Educational past Social and historical perspectives	Curriculum history	Historical foundations	Historical discourses Historical text
Curriculum policy	Politics of Curriculum	Decision making		Political text Institutionalized text
Curriculum development procedures	Learners Evaluation Schools curriculum	Curriculum development Planning in action Implementation Evaluation	Aims, goals, objectives Design Development Implementation Evaluation	
Issues and trends Future directions	Futures studies Future relevance Futures-based design	Past, present and future	Issues and trends Future directions	International text Problems and possibilities

Table 2.1: (Cont.)

	USA	USA	USA	Canada
Major emphases	Posner and Rudnitsky (1986) 3rd edition 210pp	Schubert (1986) 478pp	Walker (1990) 511pp	Robinson et al. (1985)
Conceptions of curriculum	Framework	Curriculum domains Philosophies and theories Models	Studying curriculum Curriculum thought Theory The Practical Deliberation	Psychological model
Curriculum history		Curriculum history	Curriculum	
Curriculum policy		Policies Policy makers Contexts and interest groups	Policy making School and community National Curriculum	
Curriculum development procedures	Intended learning outcomes Rationale forming units Organizing units Teaching strategies Evaluation	Purposes/objectives Content Planning phases Evaluation	Curriculum in classrooms Planning Plans and materials curriculum change	Objectives Organizing sets Concepts and beliefs Inquiry skills Growth schemes Motivational dynamics Teaching strategies Assessment Curriculum materials
Issues and trends Future directions		Curriculum problems Promising directions		

Table 2.2: *Analysis of synoptic curriculum texts in Australia and Asia*

	Australia	Australia	Australia	Australia	Hong Kong
Major emphases	Brady (1995) 5th edition 322pp	Marsh and Stafford (1988) 2nd edition 329pp	Print (1993) 2nd edition 260pp	Smith and Lovat (1990) 233pp	Morris (1995) 158pp
Conceptions of curriculum	Contributing disciplines Models	Planning approaches Theories Models	Curriculum presage Models Curriculum design	Disciplines of education Models	Planning approaches
Curriculum history		Historical background			
Curriculum policy		Decision makers			Decision makers
Curriculum development procedures	Situational analysis Objectives and outcomes Selecting content Selecting methods Evaluation Management Programme development Curriculum evaluation School evaluation	Curriculum development Situational analysis Approaches to planning Evaluation Implementation	Situational analysis Curriculum intent Content Learning activities Evaluation and assessment Implementation and change	Procedural approach Critcal reflection Assessment and evaluation Curriculum change	Intentions Content Methods Assessment Evaluation Implementation
Issues and trends Future directions	The system The school	Contemporary issues Future directions		Curriculum futures	Priorities and policies Influences

development procedures'. Morris (1995) provides an analysis of most categories but the emphasis is upon 'curriculum development procedures'.

In the UK it appears that no synoptic curriculum texts have been published since the 1970s and 1980s. As noted in the first edition, Kelly (1977) and Lawton (1986) produced texts which focused upon two of the categories, namely 'conceptions of curriculum' and 'curriculum development procedures'. Both authors also examined the 'common curriculum' in some detail, a topic not covered by most other texts.

Since the mid-1980s UK authors have concentrated upon specific topics such as the National Curriculum (especially assessment); Vocational Curriculum; and Politics of Curriculum. These developments possibly reflect the substantial decline in general curriculum courses at university level and also the overwhelming impact of national curriculum requirements in the UK. Examples of these publications include:

National Curriculum
Cox, T. and Sanders, S. (1994) *The Impact of the National Curriculum on the Teaching of Five Year Olds*, London, Falmer Press.
Daugherty, R. (1995) *National Curriculum Assessment*, London, Falmer Press.
Gipps, C.V. (1994) *Beyond Testing*, London, Falmer Press.

Vocational Curriculum
Burke, J. (1995) (Ed) *Outcomes, Learning and the Curriculum*, London, Falmer Press.
Jessup, G. (1991) *Outcomes: NVQs and the Emerging Model of Education and Training*, London, Falmer Press.
Lawton, D. (1992) *Education and Politics in the 1990s*, London, Falmer Press.

Categories of Concepts Included in This Volume

After examining a wide range of synoptic curriculum texts, including those described above, a decision was made to include material relating to the following categories:

- student perspectives;
- teacher perspectives;
- collaborative involvement in curriculum.

For each category a number of brief chapters were developed. Each chapter focuses upon a *key concept* in terms of its major characteristics, strengths and weaknesses. Follow-up questions and references are also included in each chapter.

Student-centred Perspective

This is the first section in the book and includes five chapters dealing with the following topics:

Figure 2.1: *Concepts included in a student-centred perspective*

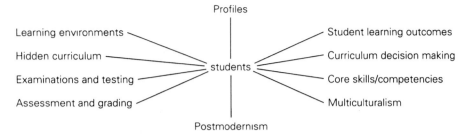

- learning environments (Chapter 3);
- hidden curriculum (Chapter 4);
- student learning outcomes (Chapter 5);
- student's role in curriculum decision-making (Chapter 6);
- examinations and testing (Chapter 7);
- core skills and generic competencies (Chapter 8).

'Learning environments' (Chapter 3) can facilitate or hinder learning, in terms of the physical arrangement of furniture and resources and appropriate levels of noise and temperature. Some open planned classrooms can provide a liberating atmosphere for students whereas some traditional architectural forms can be sterile and forbidding.

The 'hidden curriculum' (Chapter 4) of the classroom, in terms of its rituals and rules, can exacerbate the problems for individuals and can discriminate markedly against minority groups.

'Student learning outcomes' (Chapter 5) have become a vogue term in the mid-1990s with the focus upon student entitlements and identifiable performance standards needed to ensure success for all students.

In some schools there may be opportunities for 'students to participate in curriculum decision-making' (Chapter 6) and where this occurs, more cooperative and satisfying learning can result for both students and teachers.

However, 'examinations' (Chapter 7) often loom large and this can limit the opportunities for creative planning and cooperation between students and teachers. Examinations can also have the effect of encouraging didactic forms of teaching.

'Core skills and generic competencies' (Chapter 8) have been developed in many OECD countries and advocated for all students, whether continuing with their education or going directly into the workforce.

In addition there are other chapters which incorporate student-centred foci (see Figure 2.1). These include:

- multiculturalism and inclusive curriculum (Chapter 13);
- profiles, records of achievement and portfolios (Chapter 7, Volume 2);
- assessment, grading and testing (Chapter 16, Volume 2);
- postmodernism (Chapter 27, Volume 2).

'Multiculturalism and inclusive curriculum provisions' (Chapter 13) are important elements of the curriculum in terms of celebrating diversity and eliminating inequities for minority groups.

Many schools are now broadening the types of evidence they use in assessing students, and to this end, 'profiles, records of achievement and portfolios' (Chapter 7, Volume 2), are proving to be very successful, especially since it gives students more responsibility in the assessment process. In commonly used 'assessment' techniques (Chapter 16, Volume 2) there are also opportunities for student involvement, especially in diagnostic and formative modes.

'Postmodernism' (Chapter 27, Volume 2), involves teachers and students in reflecting upon the uncertainties, doubts and questions about traditional teaching.

The concepts included in these chapters emphasize student interests and problems of unequal power relationships between students and teachers. Questions are raised about functions of schools, about schools as a source of conflict for students and about the legal and moral rights of students as clients and consumers.

Teacher Perspectives and Collaborative Involvement Perspectives

Teacher responsibilities are multifaceted and need to be systematically explored. Collaboration between teachers can be especially powerful and can lead to an enhanced sense of professionalism. Each school needs to establish a collaborative culture that encourages teachers, principals and administrators to work together. These two themes are examined in the next two sections of the book and are included in the following eleven chapters, namely:

- teacher empowerment (Chapter 9);
- teacher competencies and curriculum (Chapter 10);
- collaborative teacher planning (Chapter 11);
- teacher appraisal (Chapter 12);
- multiculturalism and inclusive curriculum (Chapter 13);
- decision makers, stakeholders and influences (Chapter 14);
- parent collaboration (Chapter 15);
- teachers as researchers/action research (Chapter 16);
- curriculum reform (Chapter 17);
- national goals and standards (Chapter 18);
- vocational education and curriculum (Chapter 19).

It can be argued that 'empowerment' (Chapter 9) is one of the most contentious issues facing teachers today. Some writers maintain that teachers are taken too much for granted, that they are only permitted to undertake technical tasks and that over recent years they have become deskilled and disempowered.

'Competency-based standards for teachers' (Chapter 10) are very evident in the mid-1990s and are being widely supported by government and industry groups. There are a growing number of 'collaborative activities between teachers' (Chapter

11) which are having a marked impact in breaking down the traditional culture of individualism.

Some writers contend that 'teacher appraisal' (Chapter 12) is providing opportunities for teacher empowerment. Teacher appraisal schemes can provide opportunities for teacher self-monitoring and for staff members as a collectivity, to systematically develop and build upon their strengths and interests.

'Multicultural' backgrounds (Chapter 13) and interests of students places additional responsibilities upon teachers to ensure that they recognize and support diversity and take positive steps to eliminate inequities for minority and disadvantaged groups.

A classroom teacher's work is affected by many individuals and groups and it is important the he/she is aware of internal and external 'decision-makers and stakeholders' (Chapter 14). 'Parents' (Chapter 15) in particular are one such group who have specific rights and there are increasing pressures and initiatives to ensure that parents are given opportunities to be involved in collaborative planning with teachers and principals.

'Action research' (Chapter 16) is a powerful tool for teacher collaboration and empowerment. It can enable teachers to solve their own classroom problems and to improve practice.

'Curriculum reforms' (Chapter 17) are frequently announced as top–down initiatives but teachers are directly involved in implementing reforms and ensuring their success or failure. Recently, 'national goals and standards' (Chapter 18) have been developed collaboratively by various interest groups, including teachers — it is truly a cross-national phenomenon in the mid-1990s.

'Vocational education' (Chapter 19) developments are another major cross-national phenomenon. Although initiated for political/economic reasons there are important pedagogical implications for teachers.

Figure 2.2: Concepts included in teachers and teacher collaboration perspectives

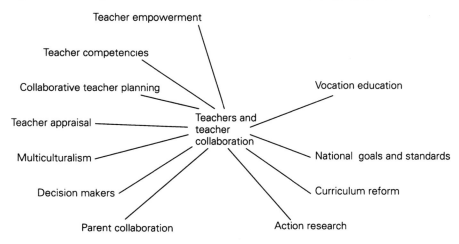

Alternative Groupings of Concepts

A theme which is very evident in the curriculum literature relates to 'politics of curriculum'. According to Longstreet and Shane (1993),

> Politics of every sort and at every level of society affect the processes of curriculum, complicating many times over what appear at first glance to be no more than a simple process of translating the overall curriculum design into a practical plan for students learning. (Longstreet and Shane, 1993, p. 93)

The chapters which incorporate a strong political emphasis include:

- teacher empowerment (Chapter 9);
- teacher appraisal (Chapter 12);
- decision makers, stakeholders and influences (Chapter 14); } in Volume 1
- curriculum reform (Chapter 17);
- centrally-based curriculum development (Chapter 13);
- decentralized curriculum development (Chapter 14); } in Volume 2
- leadership and the school principal (Chapter 18)

Another theme which is also frequently cited in the literature is 'Future Studies and the Curriculum'. As we cross the threshold of a new millennium there are new emerging pressures and priorities. Various predictions have been made about likely issues for teachers and students in the twenty-first century. Yet the most daunting aspect of all is the profound uncertainty of the future and the need to make decisions despite the uncertainty.

Several chapters which allude to future orientations include:

- postmodernism (Chapter 27);
- feminist pedagogy (Chapter 26);
- curriculum theorizing and the reconceptualists (Chapter 24); } in Volume 2
- innovation and planned change (Chapter 17);
- technology as a school subject (Chapter 10);
- curriculum reform (Chapter 17) in this Volume.

Many other themes might be also described but these two examples are sufficient to illustrate the combinations that can be formed. There are benefits for the readers in reflecting upon each concept and considering examples from their teaching experiences which tend to support or do not support the statements included in a chapter. The questions at the end of each chapter should also stimulate the reader to ask probing questions and to explore matters further, perhaps by making use of the references included at the end of each chapter.

There are no simple answers or recipes for major issues in curriculum. However, the time spent in reflecting extensively over curriculum matters can be most rewarding. It is to be hoped that the key concepts presented in this volume provide an accessible entry-point for readers embarking upon this journey.

References

BRADY, L. (1995) *Curriculum Development*, 5th edition, Sydney, Prentice Hall.

KELLY, A.V. (1977) *The Curriculum: Theory and Practice*, London, Harper and Row.

LAWTON, D. (1986) *Curriculum Studies and Educational Planning*, London, Hodder and Stoughton.

LONGSTREET, W.S. and SHANE, H.G. (1993) *Curriculum: A New Millennium*, Boston, Allyn and Bacon.

MARSH, C. and WILLIS, G. (1995) *Curriculum: Alternative Approaches, Ongoing Issues*, Columbus, Ohio, Merrill.

MARSH, C.J. and STAFFORD, K. (1988) *Curriculum: Practices and Issues*, 2nd edn, Sydney, McGraw Hill.

MCNEIL, J.D. (1985) *Curriculum: A Comprehensive Introduction*, 3rd edn, Boston, Little, Brown and Company.

MORRIS, P. (1995) *The Hong Kong School Curriculum*, Hong Kong, Hong Kong University Press.

ORNSTEIN, A.C. and HUNKINS, F. (1993) *Curriculum: Foundations, Principles and Theory*, 2nd edition, Boston, Allyn and Bacon.

PINAR, W.F., REYNOLDS, W.M., SLATTERY, P. and TAUBMAN, P.M. (1995) *Understanding Curriculum*, New York, Peter Lang.

POSNER, G.J. and RUDNITSKY, A.N. (1986) *Course Design: A Guide to Curriculum Development for Teachers*, New York, Longman.

PRINT, M. (1993) *Curriculum Development and Design*, 2nd edition, Sydney, Allen and Unwin.

ROBINSON, F.G., ROSS, J.A. and WHITE, F. (1985) *Curriculum Development for Effective Instruction*, Toronto, OISE Press.

ROGAN, J.M. (1991) 'Curriculum texts: The portrayal of the field', Part II, *Journal of Curriculum Studies*, **23**, 1, pp. 55–70.

ROGAN, J.M. and LUCKOWSKI, J.A. (1990) 'Curriculum texts: The portrayal of the field', Part I, *Journal of Curriculum Studies*, **22**, 1, pp. 17–39.

SCHUBERT, W.H. (1980) *Curriculum Books: The First Eighty Years*, New York, University Press of America.

SCHUBERT, W.H. (1986) *Curriculum: Perspective, Paradigm, and Possibility*, New York, Macmillan.

SMITH, D.L. and LOVATT, J. (1990) *Curriculum: Action on Reflection*, Sydney, Social Science Press.

WALKER, D. (1990) *Fundamentals of Curriculum*, New York, Harcourt Brace Jovanovich.

Part II

Student Perspectives

3 Learning Environments

Introduction

Classroom environments are an integral part of the learning process and no teacher or student can be unaffected by their presence. In any school, the class teachers and students have to adjust to the building architecture — the overall space, the position and number of doors and windows, the height of ceiling and the insulation qualities of the walls.

Yet, as Bennett (1981) reminds us:

> this does not indicate architectural determinism. Architecture can certainly modify the teaching environment, but teachers determine the curriculum and organisation. (Bennett, 1981, p. 24)

Teachers and students have the opportunity to 'express their "personalities" through the arrangement and decor of the environment and the arrangement of space' (Ross, 1982, pp. 1–2). However, creative arrangements need to be undertaken in the knowledge that specific physical conditions and space allocations can have important consequences on the attitudes, behaviours and even the achievements of students.

Use of Space in Teaching–Learning Environments

The use of space in teaching situations is of major importance, but often overlooked. The particular pattern of juxtaposing furniture and spaces within the confines of a classroom (or open teaching area) is done for a purpose, often for many purposes. In some instances the teacher arranges a particular pattern because he/she is convinced that a particular configuration aids learning. For example, single rows of desks might be preferred for expository teaching but a circle of chairs with the desks pushed to one side might be better for a literature lesson.

Although classrooms can vary considerably in size and shape, the typical classroom is twelve metres long and eight metres wide and is designed to accommodate approximately thirty students. One wall is typically taken up with blackboards or whiteboards and another wall often contains several pinboards. The teacher's table is usually at the front of the room and students' desks are arranged in four rows of seven/eight.

In this relatively formal classroom situation it is likely that the 'action zone' (Brophy, 1981) for interaction between the teacher and students will be in the front and centre. That is, students seated near the front and centre desks facing the

Table 3.1: Checklist to evaluate the use of classroom space

- Is there too much furniture?
- Is the best use made of the whole space of the school?
- How does the use of space reflect the range and nature of different activities?
- How effectively is shared space used?
- How attractive and stimulating is the space?
- How does the grouping of tables and work areas reflect the needs of the students and the tasks?
- How well do students understand the classroom organization?
- How appropriately and effectively are the resources deployed?
- How accessible are resources and spaces?
- How easy is pupil and teacher movement?
- How effectively does the organization of space promote pupil interaction?

Source: Morrison and Ridley, 1988

teacher are more likely to be the focus of the teacher's attention, than the students seated on the margins or at the rear of the room.

The interactions between the teacher and students can be increased with small class numbers. Reviews of class size (Glass and Smith, 1978) indicate that class size is an important factor affecting student learning. It is evident that smaller numbers, for example 22–5, enable the teacher to direct more attention to individual students. It also results in less desk space and therefore more free space available for informal activities or for specialist equipment.

Many teachers are able to devise very 'different', creative patterns of use within the confines of the standard classroom. Small group activities are facilitated by clusters of desks. A common area formed by the combination of 5–6 desks may be ideal for spreading out documents and charts as well as providing close physical contact between a small group of students. The desks can still be oriented toward the blackboard and the teacher or they can be located at points in the room which maximize space between groups.

Large items of furniture such as cupboards can be used as dividers within a room. Pieces of pegboard can be used to cover the sides of a cupboard and thereby provide additional display space. It is also helpful to have one or two large tables in a classroom even though they take up a lot of space. These tables can be used for a multitude of purposes including storing audio-visual materials, storing unfinished work or for displays of completed projects/units.

The task for each teacher is to work out how to make the best use of available furniture and facilities. It is often amazing how the rearrangement of particular desks or cupboards leads to unforeseen increases in space/access. The checklist above (Table 3.1) includes some useful reminders about how space might be utilized in a classroom.

Organizing Rooms Based on Territory or Function

In classrooms organized by 'territory', the major decision is how to allocate and arrange student desks and chairs. It is assumed that each student has his/her own domain/work space and that this is the basis for considering how certain learning activities will occur. The teacher may produce some rather different configurations of desks in his/her efforts to encourage particular kinds of interactions between students, but the focus of each activity segment and the location of the desks will be such that the teacher remains as the central figure.

Classrooms organized on the basis of 'function' are commonly found in junior grades in primary schools and in specialist subject areas (for example, media, science, woodwork) in many secondary schools. In this case, the allocation of space is based upon what specialist materials/activities can be accommodated in a given area, and the matter of the location of desks is only of minor consideration. If several different functional areas are to be included in the one room, then additional considerations need to be made about how each area should be arranged in relation to the others.

Learning stations are examples of functional areas which are often established in primary schools. A learning station is simply an area in a room where a group of students can work together at well-defined tasks. Usually, all resource materials are provided at the one location and tasks are included on colour-coded cards so that individuals or groups can involve themselves with minimal supervision by the teacher. Sometimes a room might contain three or four learning stations, located so that there is sufficient space between each to minimize noise interruptions and provide convenient access to other support areas, such as a 'conference' section where the teacher can discuss completed work units with students. In addition to the traditional specialist rooms in secondary schools such as manual arts centres, home economics, science laboratories, this has been extended over the last decade to include sophisticated language laboratories, media centres and computer laboratories (Parker, 1983).

Students' Needs and Classroom Space

Students have a number of needs with regard to classroom patterns of use and these include:

- A need for them to be seated at points in the classroom where they can comfortably undertake the learning activities. This might include being close to the teacher to see and hear him/her clearly without straining; to be able to read the blackboard/whiteboard/overhead projector in comfort; to be close enough to the teacher and centrally located to ensure that they will be fully engaged in the interactions (questioning, discussions) with the teacher.
- A need for them to be located with peers and with whom they have a close and mutually positive relationship (Woods, 1990).
- A need for them to have learning goals and value orientations consonant with those adopted by the classroom teacher (and which would be reflected in the teacher's use of classroom space and activity segments).

Some students will make a conscious effort to be seated close to the teacher so as to ensure that they are able to interact verbally and non-verbally with him/ her. Other students may, of course, have no such intention and will do their utmost to ensure that they distance themselves from the teacher. The teacher has to ensure that as many students as possible are located at appropriate positions in the room so that they gain maximum participation in the ongoing activities. Ideally, the teacher and students should plan together the physical arrangements of desks and chairs which will provide the kinds of behaviour intended.

Interaction with peers is of importance at the primary school level and even more so with secondary school students. Students do prefer to work closely with their friends and the location of the furniture should provide for these preferences, if at all possible. The use of single rows of desks lessens the possibility of close interactions between students, except for those seated adjacent to each other. Other desk combinations, especially block clusters of five or six and U and H patterns do enable far more opportunities for student interaction.

Recent research on teacher effectiveness has provided very clear evidence that a teaching approach which is successful with some students is not necessarily effective with all students (Bangert *et al.*, 1983). It is important therefore for a teacher to provide a range of different teaching styles, where possible, and to be alert to the fact that he/she will be disadvantaging some of the students at least some of the time.

Any data which can be obtained about teachers' styles of teaching (including learning goals and value orientations) and students' preferences provide valuable information in any endeavours to provide a better 'person-environment fit' (Fraser and Walberg, 1991). At the primary and secondary school levels students can be surveyed to get data on their present levels of personal satisfaction and adjustment and their respective teachers can then use this information to make adjustments where appropriate. A number of student inventories have been developed which provide this information. *The Classroom Environment Scale Manual* (Moos and Trickett, 1974) has been widely used in the USA. This instrument measures nine different dimensions of the classroom environment including students' interpersonal relationships, personal growth, and teacher control.

In a study by Nielsen and Moos (1978) who used this instrument with high school classes, it was found that those students who were not high on coping style (anxious, conforming, not explorative in trying out new ideas) reached higher levels of satisfaction in structured classrooms. However, the data also revealed that students who had high coping styles expressed far more dissatisfaction at being in highly structured classrooms than students with low coping styles who were located in little structured classrooms. One conclusion which the authors drew from this information was that it might be better for all classrooms to be low on structure because it doesn't disadvantage the high coping student and the low coping student isn't too troubled either way. But as Nielsen and Moos (1978, p. 10) point out:

> Yet adjustment and satisfaction are not the only (not even perhaps the most important) objective of schooling. Student achievement must also be kept in mind in evaluating education treatments. (Nielsen and Moos, 1978)

This conclusion points to the complexity of the classroom environment for the student. Although it might be considered desirable to provide a classroom environment which best fits personal satisfaction levels of individual students, this environment may not be the most conducive for high achievement. In fact, some studies [for example, Javor (1986)] have found that highly structured classrooms produced highest levels of achievement for students, regardless of students' level of anxiety. It may be necessary therefore for teachers to consider a trade off between personal satisfaction for students and high achievement levels.

'My Class Inventory' is an instrument developed by Australian researchers, Fisher and Fraser (1981) and is used to gain information about primary school students' perceptions of classroom goals and value orientations. The items require students to make ratings on actual classroom environments as well as preferred environments. This information can be of great interest to class teachers who are concerned about providing instructional environments which are more in accord with those preferred by students.

Fraser, Seddon and Eagleson (1982) used the Individualized Classroom Environment Questionnaire (ICEQ) to examine the environment of a secondary school classroom. The class consisted of thirty-one seventh year boys of mixed ability who were studying English, mathematics and history with the same teacher. From feedback received from the initial testing, the teacher used a series of intervention strategies to enhance interaction between students and to encourage greater involvement in group planning and decision-making. The post-test results revealed that students had gained on all five dimensions of the ICEQ. The ICEQ has subsequently been used very successfully within Australia and in a number of overseas countries (Fraser, 1990), Fraser and Walberg (1991).

Interrelationships between Physical Environment Factors and Affective States of Students

Research evidence indicates that relationships between the physical environment and students are far from clear (Fraser, 1981). There are some patterns emerging related to crowding, privacy and territoriality (Sebba, 1986), but few conclusive studies relating to specific physical environment factors. In fact, it is very difficult to disentangle the physical from the psychological factors. The research studies which have provided conclusive results are those which have demonstrated particular interrelationships between the two, such as the density of students in a classroom with student attitudes of dissatisfactions. The examples which follow, indicate the interrelationships between physical environment factors and affective states of students rather than direct influences on achievement measures.

Colour

The communications media are very aware of the use of colour and it is little wonder that colour television, colour inserts in daily newspapers, glossy colour magazines and colour computer games are so popular. So it is in classrooms. The list of items which can add colour to a classroom are endless. Newspaper clippings, pamphlets and photographs are an integral part of many classrooms and they can add to the visual impact. So too can three dimensional models (for example, of landscapes, buildings and animals) and dioramas. Even the latest nooks and cubicles for microcomputers found in many classrooms add to the diversity of colours in the typical classroom.

Noise

Sounds are all around us but when certain sounds are unwanted it is generally termed 'noise'. Bell, Fisher and Loomis (1976) make this point when emphasizing that noise involves a physical component (by the ear and higher brain structures) but also a psychological component when it is evaluated as unwanted.

As far as the classroom is concerned, it is important that the physical environment provides acoustics which enable participants to hold discussions in a normal conversational voice. The level of desirable noise will vary in different settings such as a manual arts workshop with noisy lathes and electric drills to an extremely quiet library. Each instructional setting has its own noise level requirements to the extent that each person can hear clearly what is needed to be heard and not to be distracted by other noises (Eriksen and Wintermute, 1983).

Every classroom has a background noise level due to the operation of various ventilation and audiovisual appliances (for example, oscillating fans, recorders, computer keyboards, calculators). Background noise level (BNL) is typically measured in decibels. According to the Department of Education and Science (1975) in the United Kingdom, a teacher can communicate clearly in a quiet voice when BNL rises to 35 dB. A normal voice will carry quite well over a BNL of 40 dB, but once a BNL of 45 dB or 50 dB is reached a teacher (or student) has to speak in a very loud voice. Inevitably the exchange of conversation in a loud voice can lead to irritation, stress and fatigue. Of course the irritation is generated by disagreements over what is being said as well as the level of noise which is being created by the sender. A particular noise, of itself, may or may not be wanted. More often it is the unpredictability or lack of control over the source of noise which is the major cause of the frustration.

Temperature

Commonsense would indicate that there is a fairly limited temperature range in which school students might be expected to work at their best. High temperatures will tend to make some students irritable and uncomfortable. In extreme cases students can become lethargic and even nauseated. Then again, cold temperatures seem to bring out aggression and negative behaviour in some students.

Judgments about temperature control in schools are typically made at head office in that decisions about the architectural design of schools and the use of specific building materials are made at this level. The use of particular designs, the siting of buildings and the use of insulating material will clearly affect maximum and minimum temperatures. Within each school, a principal may be able to seek additional equipment to maintain the temperature at moderate levels. For example, oscillating ceiling fans are commonly used now in many schools and the traditional hearth and wood fires have given way to oil and gas-fired heaters. The thoughtful teacher needs to be aware of the possibilities of temperature stress if abnormally high or low temperatures prevail and adjust his/her instructional activities accordingly. Some students are easily prone to discomfort from temperature excesses while others are not unduly affected. Sensitivity to these individual differences is the mark of the flexible and understanding teacher.

Reflections and Issues

1 'Judging from what is said and from what is available as a measuring stick, schools are architecturally and environmentally sterile ... Their structure is insipid, cavernous and regimented. They are only now and then really creature-comfortable. Their designs maximize economy, surveillance, safety and — maybe — efficiency.' (George and McKinley, 1974, p. 141)

'(Open planned classroom environments) are a liberatory measure capable of emancipating children from the authority of teachers.' (Cooper, 1982, p. 268)

Compare and contrast these two statements about schools.

2 'The classroom environment is such a potent determinant of student outcomes that it should not be ignored by those wishing to improve the effectiveness of schools.' (Fraser, 1986, p. 1)

In what ways does the classroom environment determine student outcomes? What can a class teacher do to maximize the positive elements of a classroom environment?

3 According to Evans (1990), a school is both the temple and the exhibition hall of the modern world. Brightly coloured curtains and carpets are part of the intentions to display desired features to the public. But important aspects of teaching and administration remain hidden. In fact, care is often taken to indicate the 'official' way into the school.

Do you agree with this statement? To what extent do the physical forms of schools give out messages to the public?

References

ABBOT-CHAPMAN, J., RADFORD, R. and HUGHES, P. (1993) 'Research project 3 — Teacher competencies — A developmental model', *Unicorn*, **19**, 3, pp. 37–48.

BANGERT, R.L., KULIK, J.A. and KULIK, C.C. (1983) 'Individualized system of instruction in secondary schools', *Review of Educational Research*, **53**, 2, pp. 143–58.

BELL, P.A., FISHER, J.D. and LOOMIS, R.J. (1976) *Environmental Psychology*, Philadelphia, W.B. Saunders.

BENNETT, S.N. (1981) 'Time and space: Curriculum allocation and pupil involvement in British open-space schools', *The Elementary School Journal*, **82**, 1, pp. 18–26.

BROPHY, J. (1981) 'Teacher praise: A functional analysis', *Review of Educational Research*, **51**, 1, pp. 5–32.

COOPER, I. (1982) 'The maintenance of order and use of space in primary school buildings', *British Journal of Sociology of Education*, 3, 3, pp. 45–63.

DEPARTMENT OF EDUCATION AND SCIENCE (1975) *Acoustics in Educational Buildings*, London, HMSO.

ERIKSEN, A. and WINTERMUTE, M. (1983) *Students, Structure, Spaces: Activities in the Built Environment*, Washington DC, ERIC Research in Education, ED233796.

EVANS, K. (1990) 'Messages conveyed by physical forms', in LOFTHOUSE, B. *The Study of Primary Education: A Source Book, Volume 2, The Curriculum*, London, Falmer Press.

FISHER, D.L. and FRASER, B.J. (1981) 'Validity and use of the "My class inventory"', *Science Education*, **65**, pp. 3–11.

FRASER, B.J. (1981) 'Australian research on classroom environment: State of the art', *Australian Journal of Education*, **25**, pp. 31–42.

FRASER, B.J. (1986) *Classroom Environment*, London, Croom Helm.

FRASER, B.J. (1990) *Individualised Classroom Environment Questionnaire*, Melbourne, ACER.

FRASER, B.J. and WALBERG, H.J. (1991) (Eds) *Educational Environments*, London, Pergamon.

FRASER, B.J., SEDDON, T. and EAGLESON, J. (1982) 'Use of student perceptions in facilitating improvement in classroom environment', *Australian Journal of Teacher Education*, 7, pp. 31–42.

GEORGE, C.J. and McKINLEY, D. (1974) *Urban Ecology*, New York, McGraw-Hill.

GLASS, G.V. and SMITH, M.L. (1978) *Meta-analysis of Research on the Relationship of Class Size and Achievement*, San Francisco, Far West Laboratory for Educational Research and Development.

JAVOR, C.M. (1986) *Effects of Classroom Design on Student Achievement*, Washington, DC, ERIC Research in Education, ED278111.

MOOS, R.H. and TRICKETT, E. (1974) *Classroom Environment Scale Manual*, Palo Alto, Consulting Psychologist Press.

MORRISON, K. and RIDLEY, K. (1988) *Curriculum Planning and the Primary School*, London, Paul Chapman.

NIELSEN, H.D. and MOOS, R.H. (1978) *Classroom Environment Scale Manual*, Palo Alto, Consulting Psychologist Press.

PARKER, J.A. (1983) *Impact of the Microcomputer on the Physical Environment for Learning*, Washington DC, ERIC Research in Education, ED250835.

ROSS, R.P. (1982) 'The design of educational environment: An expression of individual differences or evidence of the "press toward synomorphy?"', Paper presented at the Annual Meeting of the American Educational Research Association, New York.

SEBBA, R. (1986) *Architecture as Determining the Child's Place in the School*, Washington DC, ERIC Research in Education, ED284367.

WOODS, P. (1990) *The Happiest Days?*, London, Falmer Press.

4   Hidden Curriculum

Introduction

Phillip Jackson (1968) highlights the term 'hidden curriculum' in his book *Life in Classrooms*, and he is generally cited as the originator of the term. Yet it appears to have been used by William Waller in the early 1930s (Eisner, 1985).

Hidden Curriculum and Related Terms

There are many other terms and expressions which relate closely to the term 'hidden curriculum' including:

- unwritten curriculum;
- null curriculum.

Exponents of 'unwritten curriculum', such as Blumberg and Blumberg (1994), contend that the unwritten curriculum simply exists as a byproduct of educational system and not because anyone has deliberately hidden certain learning experiences. These authors conclude that schools focus on the work of learning and as a consequence can't be involved in nurturing/caring roles.

Eisner (1985) refers to 'null curriculum' as those aspects of curriculum which schools do not teach. He contends that 'subjects that are now taught are part of a tradition, and traditions create expectations, they create predictability, and they sustain stability' (p. 90). Eisner considers that schools ignore or minimize visual, auditory and metaphoric ways of knowing.

Jackson (1968) focuses upon psychological aspects of schooling which socialize students in very powerful ways. He emphasizes three elements of the 'hidden curriculum' as being:

- the crowded nature of the classroom — pupils have to cope with delays, denial of their desires and social distractions;
- contradictory allegiances required to both teachers and peers;
- unequal power relations given to teachers over pupils.

These three elements of 'crowds', 'praise' and 'power' give rise to norms of behaviour in classrooms — 'the sum total of unofficial institutional expectations, values and norms aimed at by educational administrators, and perhaps teachers and to a lesser extent parents, and which are initially completely unknown to the students' (Portelli, 1993, p. 345). Jackson's analysis of hidden curriculum is labelled as a 'functionalist' perspective because it is assumed that schools promote the goals and functions of the wider society. That is, Jackson was intent on explaining how structures within schools operate or function.

There have been many neo-Marxist perspectives about 'hidden curriculum'. For example, Bowles and Gintis (1976) argue that schools function to maintain the capitalist system because of particular social relations which occur in schools, namely:

- the hierarchical division of labour between teachers and pupils;
- the alienated character of pupils' school work;
- the fragmentation in work (and the destructive competition among students).

They argue that a student's social class/race/gender all have significance in determining the social experiences they have at school — that is, there is not a unitary hidden curriculum but 'many'.

Michael Apple (in several major books (1979, 1982, 1986)), argues from a slightly different neo-Marxist stance. Apple (1979) argues in 'Ideology and Curriculum' that there is high-status and low-status curriculum knowledge. The poor and minorities are excluded from the high-status (technical) knowledge and this is used as a device to filter for economic stratification and future career prospects. In 'Education and Power', Apple (1982) argues that schools are producers of culture and its reproduction in schools is presented in forms which is either accepted (by career-oriented bourgeoisie) or contested and resisted (by lower classes). In 'Teachers and Texts', Apple (1986) describes how reproduction occurs through the control of teachers and textbooks in schools. He argues that the variety of textbooks and curriculum packages on the market causes teachers (and especially females as they are in the majority in the teaching profession) to be deskilled.

The Logic of Hidden Curriculum

Portelli (1993) emphasizes that the term is 'hidden' and not 'hiding'. He suggests that there are three possible options in terms of logic:

- X actually hid himself/herself, that is X is responsible for the hiding, X is an agent;
- X was intentionally concealed by someone else (Y);
- X is concealed, X is hidden unintentionally.

Portelli (1993) proceeds to argue that the hidden curriculum is not an agent and so the first option is incorrect. The other two options are possible, especially when it is remembered that a curriculum could be hidden from one person but not another.

Seddon (1983) asserts that there can be degrees of hiddenness. Can the effects of the hidden curriculum be beneficial as well as detrimental? According to Seddon (1983), the hidden curriculum involves the learning of attitudes, norms, beliefs, values and assumptions often expressed as rules, rituals and regulations. They are rarely questioned and are just taken for granted. The judgment about whether a hidden curriculum is positive or negative depends upon the value stance of the person concerned.

Examples of Hidden Curriculum

A very powerful impression of the hidden curriculum at work is contained in Paul Willis (1977) 'Learning to Labour'. He portrays how twelve 'lads', observed at a northern county secondary school, resisted the authority of the school system and developed their own counter culture. The boys were able to penetrate the arbitrariness of the power relationship between teachers and students and in fact developed their own powers within the school environment (Lynch, 1989, p. 17). But in practising their resistance at school they reproduced their male working-class position, which is likely to lead to a subordinate social position in adult life. Willis argues that it is not school structures which are important in understanding the hidden curriculum but pupil resistances.

Connell *et al.* (1982) also provide compelling images in their analysis of working class comprehensive schools and independent schools:

> There is a lot more noise, movement and mess in the working-class comprehensives. The kids rush, slouch, stroll and huddle around, in a mixture of uniform, part-uniform and anti-uniform clothes. At breaks, the grounds give off a tremendous babble punctuated by yells (some from the teachers), with a general air of undisciplined energy. After breaks, there is likely to be a layer of wrappers, paper bags, leaves and other junk left stirring in the breeze.

> By contrast, the impression created by the Independent schools is one of effortless good order. The contrast forces itself on anyone coming from the state school system. The buildings may not be palatial but the grounds are carefully planted and cultivated and punctiliously clean. All the kids wear uniforms and all the uniforms are neat. There are rarely raised voices to be heard and (apart from the junior boys) not much running in the playground at breaks. (Connell *et al.*, p. 79)

The authors argue that a student typically uses three strategies, in different degrees, to cope with the hidden curriculum namely:

- resistance: the school is a focus of struggles with authority;
- compliance: enthusiastic engagement with the school on certain matters;
- pragmatism: a 'fitting in' where there are benefits to be gained.

35

Lynch (1989) argues that inequality is perpetuated via the hidden curriculum because of 'universalistic' and 'particularistic' aspects of schools. Many of the universalistic qualities of schools are highly visible and include such elements of provision as syllabuses, prescribed content, length of school periods and examination procedures. They apply to all students regardless of social class and background. Particularistic aspects of schools apply more to consumption elements such as streaming and grading, timetabling practices and reward systems. These elements are more familiar to some social groups and are used by them to further their own ends. It is the particularistic elements that increase inequalities but they are not widely known or understood and are 'hidden' from many groups.

In her study of 1990 schools in Ireland she discovered that schools which were predominantly middle and upper class maximized the consumption of educational resources among all students (frequent assessments, strong academic climate) whereas in schools with large numbers of working class students, consumption was maximized only for a minority of the higher achieving students. Whitty (1995) suggests that policies included in the Education Reform Act for England and Wales (1988) have produced this differentiation, with LEA schools becoming yet again the paupers compared with the public schools.

'Examinations' seem to carry a hidden curriculum of their own (see also Chapter 7). Although the major purpose of examinations is to assess students' performance they can also have a considerable effect upon:

- methods of teaching;
- students' levels of motivation;
- assignment of senior teachers to particular classes;
- interactions between a teacher and students.

Turner (1983) suggests that for some students the hidden curriculum effects of examinations are to stimulate conformity to teachers' demands. However some students may seek deviant behaviour because it is more attractive to them than passing examinations. Some of the very able students may be very selective and only conform in activities that they perceive are directly related to the passing of examinations.

Reflections and Issues

1   Is the hidden curriculum a process *or* an outcome of learning *or* both? Use examples to illustrate your answer.

2   'To make sense of the hidden curriculum means that schools have to be analysed as agents of legitimation, organized to produce and reproduce the dominant categories, values, and social relationships necessary for the maintenance of the larger society.' (Giroux, 1981, p. 72)

    Provide arguments to support or refute this stance.

3   'The reason why the term "hidden curriculum" has become so accepted is that by definition its mechanisms are so difficult to uncover; cause and effect remain largely at the speculative level and it is a convenient concept to explain the large part of school life rarely open to quantitative research, but full of conjecture.' (Davies, 1990, p. 188)
    Discuss.

4   Whose interests are served by a hidden curriculum? Is it possible to reveal and incorporate a hidden curriculum into a 'taught' curriculum?

5   Consider the matter of school uniform: what rule violations are ignored by teachers? Are the rules more prescriptive for boys or girls? Does the school uniform try to play down sex differences? What are some symbolic meanings of school uniform (for example, hair length)? What aspects of ingenuity by students are tolerated so that students can compete with current fashions?
    Reflect upon these matters and provide answers based upon your teaching experiences and point of view.

6   'Schools uphold certain limited kinds of academic skills — particularly logical mathematical and linguistic intelligences — and demean and marginalise the rest.' (Lynch, 1989)
    Discuss.

7   'The differences in social, racial, ethnic and class backgrounds that students bring to schools are "maintained" or "magnified" as a result of their interaction with its organizational structures.' (Bullivant, 1987, p. 15)
    Discuss.

8   'Individual competition is only fair if one competes in a world with equally privileged peers. In a materially and culturally hierarchical society, competition between equals is impossible without either handicapping the privileged or compensating the relatively disadvantaged.' (Lynch, 1989, pp. 147–8)
    Discuss.

9   Cornbleth (1991) describes the following as examples of hidden curriculum:

    • arrangement of time, facilities, materials and examinations;
    • compartmentalization of school programme into separate subjects;
    • texts treated as the most authoritative sources of knowledge;
    • grading systems;
    • district policies, school rituals.

    Comment upon the extent to which you consider these examples are significant in the light of your teaching experiences.

10 Walker (1990) distinguishes between the teacher in the formal situation where he/she is constantly the centre of attraction and the informal situation when the teacher can be less conspicuous and more personal. Do hidden curriculum elements assume greater importance in formal or informal learning situations? If so, what are the implications for teachers?

11 'It is incumbent on teachers to unveil the hidden curriculum as much as possible because of their moral obligations to students — treating them with respect, being honest with them.' (Portelli, 1993)

Critically analyse this statement. To what extent can a teacher minimize a hidden curriculum? Is it possible for teaching to largely be an intentional and cooperative activity?

12 Student alienation is a highly complex phenomenon (Cumming, 1996), endemic to many schools, and in many ways, a cause and an effect of hidden curriculum.

Explain how student alienation can be both a cause and an effect. To what extent can student alienation issues be addressed through the reform of middle schooling?

References

APPLE, M.W. (1979) *Ideology and Curriculum*, London, Routledge and Kegan Paul.

APPLE, M.W. (1982) *Education and Power*, London, Routledge and Kegan Paul.

APPLE, M.W. (1986) *Teachers and Texts: A Political Economy of Class and Gender Relations in Education*, London, Routledge and Kegan Paul.

BLUMBERG, A. and BLUMBERG, P. (1994) *The Unwritten Curriculum*, Thousand Oaks, CA, Corwin.

BOWLES, S. and GINTIS, H. (1976) *Schooling in Capitalist America*, New York, Basic Books.

BULLIVANT, B.M. (1987) *The Ethnic Encounter in the Secondary School*, London, Falmer Press.

CONNELL, R.W., ASHENDEN, D.J., KESSLER, S. and DOWSETT, G.W. (1982) *Making the Difference*, Sydney, George Allen and Unwin.

CORNBLETH, C. (1991) *Curriculum in Context*, London, Falmer Press.

CUMMING, J. (1996) *From Alienation to Engagement: Opportunities for Reform in the Middle Years of Schooling*, Volume 3, Canberra, ACSA.

DAVIES, L. (1990) *Equity and Efficiency*, London, Falmer Press.

EISNER, E.W. (1985) *The Educational Imagination: On the Design and Evaluation of School Programs*, 2nd edition, New York, Macmillan.

GIROUX, H.A. (1981) *Ideology, Culture and the Process of Schooling*, London, Falmer Press.

JACKSON, P.W. (1968) *Life in Classrooms*, New York, Holt, Rinehart and Winston.

LYNCH, K. (1989) *The Hidden Curriculum*, London, Falmer Press.

PORTELLI, J.P. (1993) 'Exposing the hidden curriculum', *Journal of Curriculum Studies*, **25**, 4, pp. 343–58.

SEDDON, T. (1983) 'The hidden curriculum: An overview', *Curriculum Perspectives*, **3**, 1, pp. 1–6.

TURNER, G. (1983) 'The hidden curriculum of examinations', in HAMMERSLEY, M. and HARGREAVES, A. (Eds) *Curriculum Practice: Some Sociological Case Studies*, London, Falmer Press.

WALKER, D. (1990) *Fundamentals of Curriculum*, New York, Harcourt Brace Jovanovich.

WHITTY, G. (1995) 'School-based management and a National Curriculum: Sensible compromise or dangerous cocktail', Paper presented at the Annual Conference of the American Educational Research Association, San Francisco.

WILLIS, P. (1977) *Learning to Labour*, London, Saxon House.

5   Student Learning Outcomes

Introduction

The term 'outcomes' is clearly a vogue term in the 1990s. Various related terms are used synonymously, such as 'outcome-based education', 'performance assessment' and 'student learning outcomes'.

It is all very confusing because 'outcomes' mean different things to different people. Some critics would argue that (along with competency-based education and training) it is a solution being offered when the problem itself has not been firmly enunciated (Porter *et al.*, 1992), and that it is a way to control the behaviour of practitioners (Grundy, 1992). These are, however, glib reactions to a very serious issue and it is important to analyse the meaning of these terms.

Some Major Terms

The term 'standards' has been advocated especially by training exponents in terms of competency-based standards. For example Jessup (1991) argues for the adoption of general competencies or outcome standards which are created independently of the content of a course or programme. These standards are packaged in the form of training modules.

Education writers use the term 'entitlement' to argue for a student's entitlement which includes 'equality of opportunity, a right of access to the full curriculum, a curriculum which covers broadly all important areas of human experience and endeavour, and a right to have such a curriculum properly resourced' (Barber, 1992, p. 452). Student entitlements were also a document priority in the devising of national curriculum learning areas in Australia in the period 1991–3 (Marsh, 1994).

According to Spady (1993) ' "Outcome-based education" means focusing and organising a school's entire program and instructional efforts around the clearly defined outcomes we want all students to demonstrate when they leave school' (p. ii).

That is, the intended learning results are the start-up points in defining the system (Hansen, 1989). A set of conditions are described that characterize real life and these are used to derive a set of culminatory role performances. Students are required to provide a culminating demonstration — the focus is upon competence as well as content but not on the time needed to reach this standard. Specifically, an outcome is an actual demonstration in an authentic context (Spady, 1993, p. 4).

Spady (1990) differentiates between 'transformational' outcomes-based education (OBE) as a form which might be experienced in a fully operational outcomes-based school from 'transitional' OBE and 'traditional' OBE.

Figure 5.1: A continuum of Outcomes-based Education (OBE) approaches to schooling

OBE Types	Traditional OBE	Transitional OBE	Transformational OBE

Transformational OBE:

- is future oriented;
- is committed to success for all students;
- includes clearly defined and publicly derived 'exit outcomes' that reflect changing societal conditions;
- includes a curriculum framework that derives from the exit outcomes;
- includes a variety of methods that assures students successful demonstration of all outcomes and provides more than one chance for students to be successful;
- incorporates a criterion — referenced and consistently applied system of assessment, performance standards, credentialing and reporting. (Glatthorn, 1993, p. 354)

As might be anticipated, 'traditional' OBE focuses upon existing curricula with outcome principles being derived from these documents, chiefly in terms of skills and competencies. The traditional school day hours are maintained but students are likely to have greater success because the targets (outcomes) are more specific than under current practices. As revealed in Figure 5.1, traditional and transformal OBE would be depicted at opposite ends of the continuum.

'Transitional' OBE lies between these two extremes (see Figure 5.1). According to Spady, transitional OBE extends beyond the traditional OBE in that higher order competencies are emphasized — 'it centres curriculum and assessment design around higher order exit outcomes. Having graduates who are broadly competent persons best reflects its vision' (Spady, 1993, p. 8).

'Mastery learning' places a high priority on the organization of time and resources to ensure that students are able to master particular instructional objectives. According to Bloom (1984) all children can learn when they are provided with conditions that are appropriate for their learning. Yet, the approach draws heavily on behaviourism in terms of reinforcement, feedback and monitoring procedures. OBE incorporates mastery learning as a basic, underlying principle.

In the United Kingdom, the term 'core skills' has been used to refer to generic or general skills where 'learning requirements are stated as outcomes and stated independently of a particular subject, discipline or occupation. Thus the specification of core skills . . . can stand independent of, and outside, any syllabus . . .' (Jessup, 1990, p. 2).

'Attainment targets' were developed for each of the foundation subjects under the National Curriculum, established by Act of Parliament in the UK in 1988. The number and scope of attainment targets has been difficult to establish and to justify.

41

For example, science was established in 1988 with twenty-two attainment targets but by 1991 the number had been reduced to four (Campbell, 1993).

Attainment targets developed in the Netherlands are also geared closely to individual subjects. Their attainment targets, termed core objectives, have been developed for fourteen subjects for 5–16 year olds and are required to provide a balance between elements of the conceptual structure of the discipline, practical skills to be developed in each subject and to reflect the sociocultural context of each subject. That is, these three types of objectives will form a balanced mixture to prepare students for society and for further study or work (Van Sten Brink, 1991).

'Benchmarks', a standards framework for judging student performance, have been developed by the Toronto Board of Education in Canada. Benchmarks, or outcomes, have been developed for specific grade levels (grades 3, 6 and 8) in language and mathematics. The board has developed an elaborate system of benchmarks using print and videotape-based tasks (Rutledge, 1993).

National 'profiles' developed by the Curriculum and Assessment Committee (CURASS) of the Australian Education Council during 1991–3 are another development which are outcomes-based but more directly related to curriculum areas (Marsh, 1994). Although there is correspondence with traditional subjects in some learning areas (English, mathematics, science, languages other than English) the remainder are more broadly based and will require new approaches in terms of assessment, recording and certification. As a consequence they are located at the middle point on the continuum in Figure 5.1. A Profile as defined by CURASS is a statement of student outcomes. It is not a course; it does not set out content or learning methods; is not a form of assessment; is not a report; but is simply a statement of student outcomes (Wilson, 1993, p. 3).

In several states of Australia, education systems are using the nationally developed profiles but are focusing directly on the 'student outcome statements'. Student outcome statements are defined as statements which 'are intended to meet both the curriculum policy and standards framework requirements. They are both objectives and assessment criteria, set at an appropriate level of generality' (Education Department of Western Australia, 1994(a), p. 3).

Some of the purported advantages of using student outcome statements include:

- they reflect the knowledge, skills and processes that the government school system considers to be essential for all students;
- they enable the teacher to identify the achievements of each student and then plan and provide for further student learning;
- they provide the curriculum guidelines necessary for teachers to confidently plan a sequence of learning activities;
- they represent an appropriate framework to give the government and the community confidence that government school education is soundly based;
- they will be a focus for school development planning and will provide a basis for teachers and schools to monitor and account for their performance. (Education Department of Western Australia, 1994(b), p. 5)

As might be expected, the OBE student outcome statements as used in some schools in the USA, are wide-ranging and cover a school's entire programme. Fitzpatrick (1991) lists the following as important exit outcomes for all students:

- ability to communicate (in reading, writing, speaking, listening and numeracy skills);
- facility in social interaction;
- analytic capabilities;
- problem solving skills;
- skill in making value judgments and decisions;
- skill in creative expression and in responding to the creative work of others;
- civic responsibility;
- responsible participation in a global environment;
- skill in developing and maintaining wellness;
- skill in using technology as a tool for learning;
- skill in life and career planning. (Fitzpatrick, 1991, pp. 18–9)

These are an admirable list of student outcome statements but are they really inclusive of the 'worthwhile' aspects of schooling? Some educators such as Eisner (1991) would be likely to question whether they can be pre-specified at all.

In other countries such as the United Kingdom, New Zealand and Australia, outcome statements have been developed within specific subjects or learning areas. For example, 'attainment targets' have been developed for twelve levels in the UK. An example from the technology subject is included below:

Example 1
Identifying needs and opportunities.

Attainment Target 1, 'Through exploration and investigation of a range of contexts (home, school, recreation, community, business and industry) pupils should be able to identify and state clearly needs and opportunities for design and technological activities.' (Ribbins, 1992, p. 42)

An example from the Australian learning area of technology is listed below:

Example 2
Band C Designing, Making and Appraising.

'Students present arguments in a variety of media to promote their work to particular audiences.' (South Australian Education Department, 1995, p. 23)

Some Issues and Problems

Although these subject-specific student outcome statements are being widely used in the UK (and emerging gradually in Australia) there are many critics of the approach:

For example, Collins (1994) and McGaw (1995), with reference to the Australian profiles, question whether the learning outcomes can be represented in developmental sequences from level 1 to 8. Is it plausible that all students go through the same development? Do the levels of outcome statements simply reflect majority cultural patterns? What does this indicate if individual students do not conform to this developmental pattern? Is it knowledge, rather than the student which has built-in step by step layers? (Collins, 1994).

McGaw (1995, p. 73) also cautions whether student outcome statements assumes that 'the full range of educational objectives can be expressed adequately in the language of learning outcomes'. Ribbins (1992) contends that the National Curriculum in the UK has led to a reliance upon narrow indicators.

McKernan (1993) argues that student outcome statements assume that knowledge and curriculum content can be sequentially broken down into 'micro-outcomes' and that this assumption is educationally unsound. Jacob and Cockshutt (1995) assert that the outcome statements are too neatly packaged — 'the notion of a smooth progression along a path of ever increasing difficulty is attractive for its tidiness but may not always be reflected in either subject structures or student behaviour' (p. 62). Criticisms have also been raised that under an outcomes-based approach, content is subservient to the outcome statements. For example, Glatthorn (1993) argues that outcome statements produces a slighting of subject matter knowledge.

Using student outcome statements involves a quantum leap for teachers when compared with traditional methods of planning and instruction (Marsh, 1994). Education systems in Australia have initiated comprehensive trialing approaches and support structures to assist teachers to move to an outcome statements approach which requires heightened levels of professional judgment about students' levels of achievement. Teachers need opportunities to talk out the problems and issues with their colleagues. In many cases, negative attitudes about an outcomes approach have to be addressed (Cox and Sanders, 1994). The approach requires teachers to have 'greater skills and enhanced professional attitudes' (Lawton, 1988, p. 22).

Collins (1994) argues that student outcome statements should not be used for comparing and reporting of any kind because it presupposes 'normal' stages of development of students' learning which cannot be sustained.

Daugherty (1995) criticizes the publication in UK newspapers of performance levels of school and the invidious comparisons between schools given the questions that can be raised about the validity and usefulness of the aggregate data.

From evidence produced to date, student outcome statements are difficult and expensive to assess. Zlatos (1993) notes that many outcome statements are very ambiguous and difficult to measure. Linn *et al.* (1991) argue that assessments may be very expensive per student and may require the use of special equipment. They can also be very time demanding in an already crowded school timetable.

Ensuring that teachers are consistent in making judgments about student outcome statements is a complex one. Methods of moderating teacher judgment must be done in ways that 'do not contradict the basic tenet of the validity of teachers' professional judgment in the first place' (Stehn and Smith, 1995, p. 66).

Reporting of student outcome statements against a common framework is complicated. There are issues of privacy of information on the one hand and freedom of information on the other. Are there particular forms of reporting that are more helpful to parents than others? Do school systems require other forms of reporting? Without doubt, the introduction of outcome statements has increased the reporting work load for teachers even with the advent of numerous electronic recording systems (Hannan, 1995).

Assessment tasks/standard assessment tasks are being used in several countries to assess outcome statements. These assessment tasks can be very comprehensive and can extend over several lessons. They are intended to be part of the regular classroom instruction and therefore represent more 'authentic' assessment. Some of the assessment tasks developed for trialing in the UK have been very creative and effective, while others are far from unimpressive.

Wragg (1991) lampoons the SATs by suggesting the following level 10 SAT for 14-year-olds!

Snow across the Curriculum.
Students are required to:

* build an igloo (technology);
* measure and weigh it (mathematics);
* write a poem about it (English);
* pole vault over it (physical education);
* melt it (science);
* say 'Merde, mon igloo a disparu' (modern languages). (Wragg, 1991, p. 2)

Some Empirical Results from the USA, UK and Australia

A number of states in the USA have undertaken major developments using OBE. Many reports have been published about individual school endeavours and a number of these have been very positive. Yet there are also a number of critical accounts published recently. Brandt (1994) poses the question, is outcome-based education dead? The examples included in Table 5.1 include several positive accounts but also caveats from teachers who have experienced OBE and are now disaffected by it as an educational reform.

Teachers in the UK have now experienced the National Curriculum since 1988 although the attainment targets have been progressively introduced from Key Stage 1. Although it requires tight accountability control it has provided a more coherent framework across elementary/primary and secondary school levels (see Table 5.2).

In Australia the introduction of student outcomes statements is at an exploratory, trialing phase. Some state education systems are moving faster than others but there does seem to be overall support for the new structures (see Table 5.3).

Hannan (1995, p. 2) argues that introducing student outcome statements is powerful in that 'it can guide curriculum, assessment and reporting as well as learning'. He may be right. Outcome statements are corruptible and they are all flawed but perhaps they are a major breakthrough in the 1990s.

Table 5.1: Examples from USA schools practising OBE

- We have restructured the grading procedures at our school — we now have predetermined standards for student achievement of outcomes rather than predetermined distributions of achievement (Fitzpatrick, 1991).
- A report of 300 teachers in Minnesota noted support for OBE principles but results were divided (44 per cent, 56 per cent) about whether teachers could guarantee success for all students (King, Evans and Ding, 1994).
- 'Students remain the most powerless group in OBE reform. They come to school with varying family backgrounds, experiences and interests. Yet, select adults decide what *all* children need to know to become good workers.' (Schwarz and Cavener, 1994, p. 335)
- The Johnson City School District (New York), a lower-middle class community with high levels of poverty has been extremely successful in adopting OBE — students have out-performed other local school districts and Johnson City is now in the top 10 per cent of schools statewide (Evans and King, 1994).
- 'At arts high school in Minnesota we see students who are learning in an atmosphere charged with meaning. Their courses consist of tasks and experiences that their teachers have made pertinent and authentic. They are active in their own assessment and in diagnosing their own learning needs.' (Jasa and Enger, 1994, p. 32)

Table 5.2: Examples from UK schools using attainment targets within the National Curriculum

---

- 'I have felt two conflicting pressures — I have moved toward tighter control over student learning but I have also developed a more responsive and individualised approach.' (Nias, 1993, p. 105)
- 'There has been a move away from thematic/cross-curricula work toward discrete subject teaching.' (Cox and Sanders, 1994, p. 55)
- The planning of attainments (outcomes) is always disrupted by events beyond our control (Campbell, 1993).
- 'It offers continuity and progression and a curricula language which all students and parents can share.' (Ashton, 1993, p. 84)
- There is now far greater time devoted to assessment and record keeping — 'assessment has become more formalised and detailed.' (Cox and Sanders, 1994, p. 45)
- 'It has provided a useful planning framework which still allows us scope for professional initiative.' (Cox and Sanders, 1994, p. 113)
- 'We have produced a good system within our school — the assessment system should remain simple and workable.' (Winfield, 1990)

Reflections and Issues

1   'There is no doubt that skills are developed sequentially. As children grow and learn they are progressively able to handle more complex tasks. The issue is whether this sequential development can be captured in a general curriculum specification that will help teachers and students.' (McGaw, 1995, p. 76)

Critically analyse this statement.

2   'If secondary schools are to be successful in the 1990s there needs to be more evidence — of the sharing out of the attainment targets among subject departments.' (Ribbins, 1992, p. 32)

To what extent can/should attainment targets be assessed across subjects? Does the National Curriculum in the UK allow for integration across subjects?

Table 5.3: Examples from Australian schools using outcome statements

- 'The explicit identification of common agreed and broadly defined outcomes which are open, accessible and used as a basis for improving practice' (Willis, 1995, p. 189), is a major feature of the Australian system and an important social justice consideration.
- 'From the teacher's point of view, the outcomes statements are a constant point of reference in planning programs of work. They provoke the teacher to ask: Why am I getting students to do this? What is the point of it?' (Whiting and McDonald, 1993, p. 45)
- Teachers report that by using student outcomes 'they are gaining new insights into how children think and learn — and appreciate the developmental dimensions and contexts of the vertical maps of progression.' (Jacob and Cockshutt, 1995, p. 61)
- 'It has forced us to examine our assessment and reporting practices in the compulsory years of schooling like no other curriculum initiative.' (Stehn and Smith, 1995, p. 67)
- 'Teachers must be able to make the necessary changes at their own pace ... Working in a team and developing collegiality, an atmosphere of trust and an attitude of "have a go" are also important to successful change.' (Williamson and Cowley, 1995, p. 70)
- 'The trialing process has reinforced the need for time for teachers to become familiar with the student outcome statements. But not just any time and not necessarily additional time. The best time is extended and structured: Extended so that teachers can have a go at ideas and activities and structured so that teachers are talking with their colleagues and actively engaging with the student outcome statements.' (Randall and Kerr, 1995, p. 75)

3 'Teachers are concerned about the sheer number of attainment targets to be covered in the core subjects.' (Cox and Sanders, 1994)

Are there difficulties of achieving depth and quality of students' learning if there are specific outcomes to be covered? Does this require additional class management skills for teachers? Are there benefits which outweigh these problems?

4 'The emphasis on "student outcomes" runs the danger of signalling the return of behaviourism, where the only learning that is valid is that which is expressed in observable student behaviours.' (Reid, 1995, p. 76)

Discuss.

5 'Student outcomes statements enable teachers to share a comprehensive curriculum provision and benefit from a shared language for planning courses and for describing and reporting student achievement.' (McLean and Wilson, 1995, p. 56)

How realistic is this statement? What are potential problems for teachers and how might these be overcome?

6 'Should the school curriculum be thought of as a collection of separate subjects, or should it deal directly with the demands of life outside school?' (Brandt, 1994, p. 5)

Does OBE create a tension between academic subjects and 'real life'? What are some possible resolutions to this problem?

References

ASHTON, M. (1993) 'Influences on curriculum balance at school level: A case study', in CAMPBELL, R.J. (Ed) *Breadth and Balance in the Primary Curriculum*, London, Falmer Press.

BARBER, M. (1992) 'An entitlement curriculum: A strategy for the nineties', *Journal of Curriculum Studies*, **24**, 5, pp. 449–56.

BLOOM, B.S. (1984) 'The search for methods of group instruction as effective as one-to-one tutoring', *Educational Leadership*, **41**, 8, pp. 4–17.

BRANDT, R. (1994) 'Overview: Is outcome-based education dead?', *Educational Leadership*, **51**, 6, p. 5.

CAMPBELL, R.J. (1993) (Ed) *Breadth and Balance in the Primary Curriculum*, London, Falmer Press.

COLLINS, C. (1994) 'Is the National Curriculum profiles brief valid?', *Curriculum Perspectives*, **14**, 1, pp. 34–47.

COX, T. and SANDERS, S. (1994) *The Impact of the National Curriculum on the Teaching of Five Year Olds*, London, Falmer Press.

DAUGHERTY, R. (1995) *National Curriculum Assessment*, London, Falmer Press.

EDUCATION DEPARTMENT OF WA (1994a) 'Using student outcome statements: A working paper', Perth, Education Department of Western Australia.

EDUCATION DEPARTMENT OF WA (1994b) 'Student outcome statements', Working edition, Perth, Education Department of Western Australia.

EISNER, E. (1991) *The Enlightened Eye: Qualitative Inquiry and the Enhancement of Educational Practice*, New York, Macmillan.

EVANS, K.M. and KING, J.A. (1994) 'Research on OBE: What we know and don't know', *Educational Leadership*, **51**, 6, pp. 12–7.

FITZPATRICK, K.A. (1991) 'Restructuring to achieve outcomes of significance for all students', *Educational Leadership*, **48**, 8, pp. 18–22.

GLATTHORN, A. (1993) 'Outcome-based education: Reform and the curriculum process', *Journal of Curriculum and Supervision*, **8**, 4, pp. 354–63.

GRUNDY, S. (1992) 'Beyond guaranteed outcomes: Creating a discourse for educational praxis', *Australian Journal of Education*, **36**, 2, pp. 157–69.

HANNAN, B. (1995) 'Why teach to outcomes?', *IARTV Occasional Paper*, **40**, pp. 1–8.

HANSEN, J.M. (1989) 'Outcome-based education: A smarter way to assess student learning', *Clearing House*, **63**, 4, pp. 172–4.

JACOB, S.E. and COCKSHUTT, N. (1995) 'Mainstreaming profiles in schools', *Curriculum Perspectives*, **15**, 3, pp. 61–2.

JASA, S. and ENGER, L. (1994) 'Applying OBE to arts education', *Educational Leadership*, **51**, 6, pp. 30–2.

JESSUP, G. (1990) *Common Learning Outcomes: Core Skills in A/AS Levels and NVQ's*, Report No. 6, London, NCVQ.

JESSUP, G. (1991) *Outcomes: NVQs and the Emerging Model of Education and Training*, London, Falmer Press.

KING, J.A., EVANS, K.M. and DING, S. (1994) 'An exploratory study of teachers' perceptions of outcome-based education', Paper presented at the Annual Conference of the American Educational Research Association, New Orleans.

LAWTON, D. (1988) 'The international debate on education: Searching for quality', in HUGHES, P. (Ed) *Quality in Education*, Sydney, Ashton Scholastic.

LINN, R.L., BAKER, E.L. and DUNBAR, S.B. (1991) 'Complex, performance-based assessment: Expectations and validation criteria', *Education Research*, **20**, 8, pp. 15–21.

MARSH, C.J. (1994) *Producing a National Curriculum: Plans and Paranoia*, Sydney, Allen and Unwin.

McGAW, B. (1995) 'Outcome specification in curriculum design', in COLLINS, C. (Ed) *Curriculum Stocktake*, Canberra, ACE.

McKERNAN, J. (1993) 'Some limitations of outcome-based education', *Journal of Curriculum and Supervision*, **8**, 4, pp. 343–53.

McLEAN, K. and WILSON, B. (1995) 'The big picture', *Curriculum Perspectives*, **15**, 3, pp. 56–7.

NIAS, J. (1993) 'Balanced thinking?: Curricula tensions in school journey', in CAMPBELL, R.J. (Ed) *Breadth and Balance in the Primary Curriculum*, London, Falmer Press.

PORTER, P., RIZVI, J. and LINGARD, R. (1992) 'Competencies for a clever country: Building on a house of cards?', *Unicorn*, **18**, 3, pp. 50–8.

RANDALL, R. and KERR, D. (1995) 'Trialing student outcome statements', *Curriculum Perspectives*, **15**, 3, pp. 74–5.

REID, A. (1995) 'Profiles: Real problems or real gains: From whose perspective?', *Curriculum Perspectives*, **15**, 3, pp. 76–80.

RIBBINS, P. (1992) (Ed) *Delivering the National Curriculum: Subjects for Secondary Schooling*, Harlow, Longman.

RUTLEDGE, D. (1993) *Benchmarks: A Standards Framework for Judging Student Performance*, Workshop Report No. 7, Canberra, ACSA.

SCHWARZ, G. and CAVENER, L. (1994) 'Outcome-based education and curriculum change: Advocacy, practice and critique', *Journal of Curriculum and Supervision*, **9**, 4, pp. 326–38.

SOUTH AUSTRALIAN EDUCATION DEPARTMENT (1995) *Technology*, Adelaide, DECS.

SPADY, W. (1993) *Outcome-based education*, Workshop Report No. 5, Canberra, ACSA.

STEHN, J. and SMITH, R. (1995) 'Review and reform using profiles', *Curriculum Perspectives*, **15**, 3, pp. 66–8.

VAN STEN BRINK, G. (1991) 'The development of proposals for nationwide attainment targets', Paper presented at the International Association for Education Assessment, 17th International Conference, Nairobi.

WHITING, D. and McDONALD, C. (1993) 'Inputs and outcomes', *EQ Australia*, **2**, pp. 45–8.

WILLIAMSON, J. and COWLEY, T. (1995) 'Case studies about implementing profiles', *Curriculum Perspectives*, **15**, 3, pp. 69–71.

WILLIS, S. (1995) 'Social justice and the mathematics profile', in COLLINS, C. (Ed) *Curriculum Stocktake*, Canberra, ACE.

WILSON, B. (1993) *National Curriculum and National Profiles: Development Implementation and Use*, Seminar Series No. 23, Melbourne, IARTV.

WINFIELD, E. (1990) 'National Curriculum: In the light of experience', *Child Education*, **67**, 5, pp. 16–7.

WRAGG, T. (1991) *Mad Curriculum Disease*, Stoke-on-Trent, Trentham.

ZLATOS, B. (1993) 'Outcomes-based outrage', *The Executive Educator*, **15**, 9, pp. 12–6.

6 Students' Role in Curriculum Decision Making

Introduction

Schools have an obligation to consult with the consumers of their services — the students (and their parents). It is very evident that these consumers are being far more vocal, especially when they are dissatisfied with the services provided, as witnessed by the rapid increase in the number of court cases for legal action. Traditionally, students have not had a major role in curriculum decision making. In this chapter various options are considered ranging from minimal to major involvement by students.

Student Participation: Pros and Cons

Allen (1995) argues that if we are serious about empowerment in education then students 'must be encouraged to voice their concerns, opinions and plans as learners, to discuss decisions, to talk and act like citizens in a democracy' (p. 286).

The legal rights of students are being given increased attention in many countries but especially in the USA. In Australia, the National Children's and Youth Law Centre (NCYLC) was established in 1994 and distributes information widely to schools. In particular, they cite principles from the United Nations convention on the rights of the child:

- children should have a say in decision affecting them, and a right to have their views taken seriously;
- children should not be treated less favourably just because they are young;
- all children have equal rights regardless of race, colour, sex or religious beliefs;
- all children have the right to express their ideas and needs. (NCYLC, 1994, p. 1)

In business dealings clients have certain rights and expectations and a relatively high standing. In terms of schools, students are the recipients — the ultimate audience for certain learning activities.

Students, especially at the secondary school level, are already participating in leadership positions in other spheres such as sporting clubs, leisure groups, religious organizations and clubs. These students have already developed effective leadership and communication skills and therefore have the potential to be effective participants in curriculum-planning activities.

If students are permitted to become active participants in decision-making then more positive collegial relationships will develop between teachers and students. As noted by Fullan (1991), 'we must start treating students as people — we should stop thinking of students just in terms of learning outcomes and start thinking of them as people who are being asked to become involved in new activities' (p. 189).

To summarize, some of the major reasons for promoting student participation include:

- students are not merely passive receivers of a curriculum — they become engaged with it;
- students have legal rights;
- students are the clients and they have rights and expectations;
- some students have already experienced decision-making roles in extra curricular activities;
- students and teachers will work collaboratively in many situations.

Yet, reasons are often cited why student participation in curriculum decision-making should be restricted.

Some writers argue that teachers should be the sole decision-makers because they command a body of specialized knowledge and they have had intensive training in such areas as child development and learning styles, philosophical studies, educational measurement, subject methods. A classroom teacher spends inordinate amounts of time creating a particular classroom climate, producing order and stability out of a sea of faces, a cacophony of requests and comments, and a bewildering array of behaviours. It is an extremely difficult task. The creation and maintenance of a productive working environment requires respect for, and harmonious, interactions between teacher and students.

Providing students with opportunities to participate in decision-making can break down all the established norms and codes of behaviour essential for class discipline and a positive class tone. A teacher must maintain his or her respect from students as the professional decision-maker.

External constraints, such as public examinations, give little scope for teachers to deviate from established and relatively narrow academic syllabuses. There is little point therefore in encouraging student participation in curriculum planning if, in fact, there is no viable alternative to an academic syllabus which is textbook and examination-oriented.

Ainley's (1993) research on Australian students notes that many students expressed concern about the choices of subjects available to them at senior secondary school level — examinations create high status knowledge and limit this to acceptable, traditional subject areas.

Abraham (1995) examined sex-based harassment as a disruptive and increasing element in schools in the UK. It can be argued that any increased participation

Table 6.1:   Student participation continuum at two levels: (a) individual classroom, and (b) school-wide

a Individual classroom level continuum		
Students consulted	Students take an active role in planning	Students share in decision-making for most classroom activities
(e.g., needs analysis)	(e.g., research projects)	(e.g., all subjects require negotiated conditions)

b School-wide level continuum		
Students consulted	Students take an active role	Students share in the decision-making
(e.g., school evaluation)	(e.g., student)	(e.g., school council, representative council)

in decision making by students might accentuate levels of sex-based harassment of females by males.

To summarize, some of the major reasons for limiting student participation include:

- decision-making should be done solely by the professionals — the classroom teachers;
- there is little real opportunity because public examinations constrain alternative curriculum development initiatives;
- it could lead to increased sex-based harassment problems in schools.

It is far from clear whether there is a strong trend toward greater levels of student participation in decision-making in schools. The 'alternative schools' have always had an open decision-making approach involving students, teachers and parents and their numbers are continuing to grow.

For example, Short and Burke (1991) describe learning processes in schools in the USA which emphasize collaborative planning between teachers and students. Wasley (1994) describes decision-making in schools which are member schools of the Coalition of Essential Schools and where there is a major emphasis upon student participation in curriculum decision-making.

However, the opportunities for increased participation in government and high-fee-paying independent schools appears to be far less common. High-fee-paying independent schools, relying upon the patronage of parents tending to be from conservative social classes, are unlikely to progress very far in this direction.

Levels of Student Participation

Student participation can be conceptualized at two different levels, at the 'individual classroom' and the 'total school' levels. At each level it is useful to consider a continuum ranging from minimal to high degrees of student participation (see Table 6.1).

Student Participation at the Individual Classroom Level

Within an individual classroom teachers have the opportunity to encourage student participation in the planning and implementation of particular curricula; or they can restrict it, and perhaps stifle participation opportunities quite deliberately.

At the minimal participation end of the continuum (Table 6.1), students are not given opportunities to participate directly in the planning of their curricula, but teachers may, in various ways, seek out student needs and interests. The type of input from students is largely that of *receiver* to questions asked by a teacher. It could be almost entirely a 'passive role', in that the teacher might make certain planning decisions based upon his or her observations of the class of students in different learning situations (Davies, 1984). A middle position on the 'individual classroom' continuum is where students take an active role in planning 'selected classroom activities'. Although it might be possible to provide some choice to students in lower primary grades it would appear to be more relevant to older students such as upper primary and secondary school students. It is very much a compromise position, with teachers relinquishing a certain degree of control in areas and activities where it is considered that students could become highly self-motivated and innovative in their approaches.

Allen (1995) observes that voting by students was a common way that students made decisions but they were typically about non-curricula issues such as rewards and class rules. Andrade and Hakim (1995) argue that young children should be encouraged to do their own problem-solving in class and to guide the class's direction — 'children learn using their own language, learning styles, and thought processes, and at their own level of development' (p. 22). This type of decision-making (see Table 6.1) refers to students becoming active participants in all subjects at the classroom level.

Authors, such as Griffiths (1986), provide numerous suggestions about how students might become active participants in classroom-decision-making. Suggestions include:

- students negotiate with the teacher about the types of assessment that might be used (including self-assessment procedures);
- students negotiate with the teacher about the teaching methods/organizational procedures that might be used to accommodate a variety of student backgrounds;
- students negotiate with the teacher about how classroom activities will be monitored and evaluated, to inform future decision-making;
- students negotiate with the teacher about contracts (individual or group) for doing certain tasks/activities within subjects. As an example, contracts involving computer-assisted tasks are becoming increasingly popular and it is an area that students have developed considerable expertise.

For example, Burnaford *et al.* (1994) highlight the use of action research with middle school students whereby students are encouraged to be reflective about their work — 'if students become co-researchers with the teacher in classroom study, curriculum planning and the resulting content becomes incontrovertibly transformed' (p. 9).

Tredway (1995) and Splitter and Sharp (1995) advocate that classrooms should operate as communities of inquiry founded on dialogue, trust and respect. Tredway (1995) discusses the use of Socratic seminars whereby they actively and cooperatively develop knowledge, understanding and ethical attitudes and behaviours.

Davidson (1989) gives examples of how students can be involved in decision-making about assessment such as in the planning of assessment tasks. With schools operating under outcomes-based education approaches, it is necessary for students to be very aware of the assessment targets to be used and to be involved in establishing the criteria for judging the assessment tasks. Self assessment and peer assessment elements could be important aspects of many assessment tasks.

Student Participation at the School-wide Level

When we turn to school-wide activities there are several ways in which student input can and should be obtained, as illustrated on the continuum in Table 6.1. Schools are becoming increasingly involved in periodic 'school reviews and evaluations'. In these various school review efforts, the studies typically examine a number of formal and informal school activities, including of course the teaching and learning activities of teachers and students. Many of the evaluation studies seek data from students because it is realized that this is a valid and reliable source of information. A number of recent research studies (for example, Marsh and Overall, 1979; Aleamoni, 1981; Farley, 1981) indicate that:

- students can make consistent judgments;
- students can make reliable descriptions of classroom activities;
- students can make accurate judgments about specific teachers whom they see every day.

And that:

- students do not typically provide inflated or distorted judgments;
- students are usually very candid in their comments, and they can be brutally honest.

The middle and right-hand position on the 'school-wide' continuum (Table 6.1) indicates quite active student participation. Rather than students merely being consulted on matters such as school reviews, this position involves more elaborate efforts to have students participating in school-wide activities.

In many schools in Victoria, Australia, activities have led to the formation of student representative councils (SRCs). These SRCs are very different from the traditional student councils, usually nominated by staff and typically having token responsibilities such as organizing the annual school ball. The SRCs as they are developing are intended to provide truly representative decision-making for students. As a result, students get involved in many activities (for example, student newspapers, lunchtime meetings, weekend seminars).

Holdsworth (1991) argues that this is an ideal form of participation through school and asserts that students can and should participate in three schooling arenas:

- participation on formal decision-making bodies (for example, School Councils/Boards);
- participation in student-owned bodies (for example, Student Representative Councils);
- participation in classroom-based curriculum decision making and implementation (for example, negotiating on specific projects).

Furthermore, he suggests that:

Like any three-legged stool, we need balance and connection between these three arenas if student participation is to be other than a token and constrained facade. For example, the absence of any 'leg' leads to a distorted and manipulated view of participation. Without participation on formal decision-making bodies, students may go 'cap in hand' to decision makers, but lose any ability to share in determining outcomes to their considerations; without participation in student-owned bodies, representatives can speak only for themselves, and have no arena to reflect and plan with other students; without participation in classrooms, student participation in decision making is restricted to those issues of lesser consequence than those central to the purpose of schooling — learning and teaching. (Holdsworth, 1991, p. 64)

Reflections and Issues

1 'Students are the only group who can portray the lived-in quality of schooling.' (Vallance, 1981)

Do we seek information and understandings from students? What might be some gains for curriculum planning?

2 Examine the following list of legal rights of students:

- the right to an effective education, as measured by outcomes of schooling;
- the right to have access to schools that are geared to respond effectively to different needs and cultures;

- the right to be provided with an educational environment that is comfortable and conducive to learning;
- the right to equality of educational opportunity;
- the right of access to and instruction in all things that affect their social development. (Fitzgerald and Pettit, 1978, p. 34; Blakers, 1980, p. 1)

To what extent are these legal rights provided at your school? Have any of these ever been contested in local courts? What were the outcomes?

3   'Pupil protests are a neglected, but significant, part of schooling, in both developing and developed countries, in the past and in the present — it seems most appropriate to view their protests as expressions of the particular values of young people and as attempts by them to challenge and deal with problems of schooling which they encounter.' (Adams, 1991, p. 215)
    Discuss.

4   Do you agree that there tends to be little opportunity for high levels of student participation in curriculum decision-making in government secondary schools and independent (public) schools? Give reasons to support your stand.

5   'It is important that teachers find out the ways which their students receive school subjects, and their reactions to different areas of the curriculum.' (Measor, 1984)
    Do students receive school subjects differently? If so, can this cause problems for the typical classroom teacher?

6   To what extent do you consider that discipline problems in schools and truancy might be alleviated if students had greater opportunities to be involved in planning school activities? Are there additional deep-seated reasons for student opposition to schools?

7   Allen (1995) argues that if schools provide processes for students to make meaningful decisions, they will express a strong sense of responsibility and a high degree of faith that they can 'make a difference' in their schools.
    What evidence is there to support this assertion? Give examples.

8   'The most difficult areas for student participation are in school organization and management and learning to take personal and group initiatives.' (Van Halen, 1991)
    Elaborate upon these two problem areas. What strategies would you adopt to overcome them?

9   'When students achieve the "impossible", let us recognise it, promote it and their achievements and use them as examples for other students to model.

Students must see themselves as competent and valued and, in turn, share with other students their accomplishments and achieved goals. Students and student groups must take every opportunity to promote themselves and their achievements, blow the bugle, and wave the flag.' (Kent, 1991, p. 70)

Is the problem of student participation largely a lack of recognition? Explain why this is a common problem? What solutions can you offer?

References

ABRAHAM, J. (1995) *Divide and School*, London, Falmer Press.

ADAMS, R. (1991) *Protests by Pupils*, London, Falmer Press.

AINLEY, J. (1993) 'Curriculum choice and program specialisation in the senior secondary years', Paper presented at the Biennial Conference of the Australian Curriculum Studies Association, Brisbane.

ALEAMONI, L.M. (1981) 'The Students' Ratings of Teachers', in MILLMAN, J. (Ed) *Handbook of Teacher Evaluation*, Beverly Hills, California, Sage Publications.

ALLEN, J.B. (1995) 'Friends, fairness, fun and the freedom to choose: Hearing student voices', *Journal of Curriculum and Supervision*, **10**, 4, pp. 286–301.

ANDRADE, A.M. and HAKIM, D. (1995) 'Letting children take the lead in class', *Educational Leadership*, **53**, 1, pp. 22–5.

BLAKERS, C. (1980) 'Principals seven', ACSSO Discussion Paper, Canberra.

BURNAFORD, G., BRODHAGEN, B. and BEANE, J. (1994) 'Teacher action research at the middle level: Inside an integrative curriculum', Paper presented at the Annual Conference of the American Educational Research Association, New Orleans.

DAVIDSON, M. (1989) 'Student participation in assessment', *Assessment Matters*, **2**, 2, pp. 5–6.

DAVIES, L. (1984) *Pupil Power: Deviance and Gender in School*, London, Falmer Press.

FARLEY, J.M. (1981) 'Student interviews as an evaluation tool', *Educational Leadership*, **39**, 3, pp. 184–6.

FITZGERALD, R.T. and PETTIT, D.W. (1978) *Schools in the Community: A Growing Relationship*, Canberra, Schools Commission.

FULLAN, M.G. (1991) *The New Meaning of Educational Change*, London, Cassell.

GRIFFITHS, B. (1986) *Negotiating the Curriculum*, Melbourne, Ministry of Education.

HOLDSWORTH, R. (1991) 'Taking student participation into the nineties', *Curriculum Perspectives*, **11**, 2, pp. 61–5.

KENT, G. (1991) 'Student participation after the shouting and tumult has died down', *Curriculum Perspectives*, **11**, 2, pp. 65–72.

MARSH, H.W. and OVERALL, A.U. (1979) 'Long-term stability of students' evaluations', *Research in Higher Education*, **10**.

MEASOR, L. (1984) 'Pupil perceptions of subject status', in GOODSON, I.F. and BALL, S.J. (Eds) *Defining the Curriculum: Histories and Ethnographies*, London, Falmer Press.

NATIONAL CHILDREN'S AND YOUTH LAW CENTRE (1994) *Know Your Rights at School*, Sydney, NCYLC.

SHORT, K.G. and BURKE, C. (1991) *Creating Curriculum*, Portsmouth, NH, Heinemann.

SPLITTER, L.J. and SHARP, A.M. (1995) *Teaching for Better Thinking*, Melbourne, ACER.

TREDWAY, L. (1995) 'Socratic seminars: Engaging students in intellectual discourse', *Educational Leadership*, **53**, 1, pp. 26–9.

VALLANCE, E. (1981) 'Focus on students in curriculum knowledge: A critique of curriculum criticism', Paper presented at the Annual Conference of the American Educational Research Association, Los Angeles.

VAN HALEN, B.J. (1991) 'Student participation in practice: A principal's perspective', *Curriculum Perspectives*, **11**, 2, pp. 74–8.

WASLEY, P.A. (1994) *Stirring the Chalkdust*, New York, Teachers College Press.

7   Examinations and Testing

Introduction

Examinations have always figured prominently in education systems in most countries but criticisms of exams and tests are legend. Cynicism abounds about the value of tests, such as the following remark made to the Cockcroft Committee (1982) — 'no one has ever grown taller as a result of being measured' (p. 123). Yet, testing has a long history. In China they have been in use as early as the Han dynasty (202BC–190AD). At that period formal examinations were introduced to select persons for key posts in the Imperial household.

During the twentieth century anxieties still remain about examinations and tests. One-off final examinations are being increasingly modified and continuous forms of assessment using teacher-developed tests are more widely used. Yet widespread criticism still occurs about the narrow, stultifying effect of examinations.

Types and Variations

Examinations tend to be administered by independent or quasi-independent agencies consisting of assessment specialists, university personnel, teachers. Examination boards, such as the Cambridge Examination Board in the United Kingdom, operate in many overseas countries. In some countries, such as the Peoples' Republic of China, examinations are administered by the central government.

The term 'public' examination is commonly used to describe examinations open to persons of any age and background. Public examinations are used predominantly to select students for entry to tertiary institutions, but in some countries, for selection at various stages at primary and secondary school levels.

Public examinations are of major importance as regulators of selection into tertiary studies. To date no credible alternatives have been accepted and they are still viewed as legitimate gatekeepers for entry into universities (Broadfoot, 1986). According to Apple (1979), public examinations create high status knowledge. As a consequence, university personnel have maintained tight control over this knowledge over the decades but it presupposes a number of assumptions, including:

- that this high status knowledge has an identifiable content;
- that it has a stable structure and is teachable;
- that it is testable across all disciplines.

Public examinations are being used increasingly in western countries as an indicator of school performance. The compulsory publication of school examination results is very newsworthy.

Parents are very interested in the publication of school results and are keen to make comparisons across school. Brooks (1990) refers to them as 'leagues fables'! Administrators are also very interested in school level results and use this data for making recommendations about school effectiveness. There are many problems with the validity and reliability of public examinations and so extreme caution should be used in examining school results. As noted by Torrance (1986) one should question whether the results of school performance are indeed worth publishing.

External and School-based Examinations and Tests

'External' examinations include those examinations where the syllabus and the examination papers are developed and supervised by an external group, typically an examination board. Members of an examination board are largely drawn from universities but an increasing number of senior teachers are being included on these boards.

'School-based' examinations are developed at the school-level by individual teachers or by groups of teachers. A greater variety of examination modes are possible including oral tests, performance tests, projects and assessment tasks.

The advantages and disadvantages of these forms of examination need to be considered, although it should be noted that particular contexts can produce quite different effects. Further, the effects can be quite different for participants, such as teachers, students and employers.

There are several major advantages of external examinations as depicted in Table 7.1 but there are also many disadvantages (Table 7.2). In Table 7.3, a major advantage listed is that school-based examinations enable a teacher to assess skills not easily measured by external examinations. This is indeed a significant point. For example, the skills involved in formulating a topic, collecting information and writing up a research project are considerable and of value for students in later careers — yet they are rarely addressed in typical external examinations.

Another advantage listed in Table 7.3 is that school-based examinations and tests enable data on students' performances to be collected on a regular basis throughout the school year. This practice, of course, encourages students to work consistently at their highest level throughout the year and not to rely upon a final intensive burst at the end of the year. The title used for Table 7.3 indicates that these purported advantages are of value to a number of stakeholders but especially students, teachers, tertiary institution officers and employers. That is, all these participants want to be involved in assessment schemes which are the most comprehensive and valid available and which enable modern, flexible, teaching methods to be used.

There are also some advantages of school-based examinations which are of special interest to teachers and these are listed in Table 7.4. School-based exami-

Table 7.1: Advantages of external examinations

- it can provide an objective assessment of a student's performance;
- it can define common standards of performance required for adequate completion of a syllabus;
- it has status in the wider community.

Table 7.2: Disadvantages of external examinations

- it can only cover a limited part of the course syllabus;
- it can capture only a small sample of a student's performance, even on the topics tested, within the period of time allotted;
- it can be biased against students who do not perform well under examination pressures;
- it may encourage a concentration in teaching on those aspects of a course which are most readily assessed by an external examination;
- it may encourage didactic teaching and rote learning.

Table 7.3: Advantages of school-based examinations: For teachers, students, tertiary institutions and employers

- can enhance the validity of the total assessment because teacher assessments can assess skills or products not easily assessed by external examinations;
- enables students' performances to be repeatedly sampled over the full school year whereas an external examination can only cover a limited part of the syllabus;
- can provide very satisfactory differentiation and discrimination between the achievement levels of individual students;
- does not produce bias against students who do not perform well under the enormous pressures and strain of external examinations;
- enables the teaching to be more wide-ranging and of interest to students with a consequent reduction in the didactic teaching and rote learning associated with teaching for external examinations;
- problems of subjectivity purportedly associated with teacher assessment are no greater than those associated with external examinations.

Source: Kingdon and Stobbart, 1988; Andrich, 1989

Table 7.4: Advantages of school-based examinations: Special advantages for teachers

- enables teachers to be more flexible in the planning, implementation and assessment of their teaching programmes;
- encourages teachers to use new and different forms of student assessment;
- teachers are encouraged to use their professional judgments about students. They have the most detailed information about students and are appropriate persons to do so.

Source: Kingdon and Stobbart, 1988

Table 7.5: Disadvantages of school-based examinations: For students

- teacher assessments in some subjects can be very demanding and collectively can cause heavy workloads for students, especially conscientious students;
- if the amount of assignment work is too heavy on students it can lead to apathy and student absenteeism;
- on some occasions, teachers and parents can manipulate teacher assessment results in a way that is not possible with external examinations;
- in some cases, it can take too much account of early performance in a course and too little of the level a student finally reaches;
- unless appropriate measures are taken, the criteria used for teacher assessment can vary considerably from school to school.

Source: Kingdon and Stobbart, 1988; McGaw, 1984; Andrich, 1989

Table 7.6: Disadvantages of school-based examinations: For teachers

- not all teachers have a sound understanding of assessment and skills in using a variety of assessment techniques;
- teacher assessment can cause professional/moral problems for some teachers in that it can be difficult to make decisions about how much teacher assistance is legitimate and proper to give to students;
- the procedures and structures used to produce greater reliability of teacher assessment can be overdone and can cause in turn reduced commitment and support by teachers.

Source: Kingdon and Stobbart, 1988; Andrich, 1989

nations at their best are a boon to teachers because they give them far greater flexibility over how they plan their units, the learning activities they introduce, and the forms of student assessment they use. Few would deny that teachers are in the best position to know about and to comment upon the relative strengths and weaknesses of their students. Various education writers over recent years have asserted that teachers should be given a more prominent role in assessment activities because they have the professional knowledge and skills [Connelly and Clandinin (1988), Wilson *et al.* (1989), Pennycuick and Murphy (1988) and Kingdon and Stobbart (1988)].

Yet, there are also a number of disadvantages about school-based examinations, as listed in Tables 7.5 and 7.6. An important one which is listed in Table 7.5 revolves around the matter of heavy workloads for students. Enthusiastic teachers, in their endeavours to get students to reach high achievement levels in their particular subjects, can be very demanding in terms of student assignments and projects. This pattern tends to be multiplied five or six times with different teachers over a typical student load. Not surprisingly, some students can suffer from stress or they may decide to opt out of traditional schooling.

As indicated in Table 7.6, there can also be some disadvantages for teachers. For those teachers who did not obtain a background of educational measurement and assessment in their preservice training, school-based examination procedures can be quite bewildering. They require teachers to adopt dual roles of 'judge' and 'teacher' which can be difficult to reconcile.

Recent Developments

As indicated above, stereotypes of 'pure' external and school-based examinations are difficult to find in the 1990s. Some very interesting developments are occurring which involve the creation of hybrid varieties.

Four examples include:

- Standard Assessment Tasks (SATS);
- differentiated examinations;
- profiling/records of achievement;
- cooperative external assessment.

Standard Assessment Tasks (SATs)

Standard Assessment Tasks (SATS) have been developed by educators in the United Kingdom as part of the change to a national curriculum in 1989. SATs are undertaken in classroom settings under the supervision of teachers. Under the National Curriculum structure, all students are required to be tested at the ages of 7, 11, 14, and 16 years. The SATs have been developed and piloted over recent years by research groups.

Some of the characteristics of the SATs materials include:

- each SAT takes two to three weeks to complete;
- they are extended classroom activities based around topics similar to activities teachers themselves would set up;
- teachers receive the SATs in advance;
- much of the recording is done while the teacher works with students in small groups;
- SATs provide a rich learning experience involving oral, written, graphical and practical work.

Results indicate that the SATs do have a lot of potential. It has been suggested by some educators that SATs are revealing that teachers expect too little from their pupils and that they are challenged insufficiently. There are also the detractors who argue that SATs are deskilling teachers.

Differentiated Examinations

According to Kingdon and Stobbart (1988):

a differentiated examination is one in which different components are deliberately set at different levels of difficulty to meet the needs of candidates with different levels of ability. (Kingdon and Stobbart, 1988, p. 40)

There are two main methods of differentiation, namely:

- Differentiation between papers: Common papers plus alternatives, the 3-in-line method, the 4-in-line method (the teacher nominates in advance which papers a student will be enrolled in).
- Differentiation within papers: Structured questions, sections, differentiation by outcome, differentiation by task.

The General Certificate of Secondary Education (GCSE) is a public examination which was introduced in 1988 for fifth formers in the United Kingdom and which uses differentiated examination models.

The 3-in-line method consists of a common paper (paper 2) which is aimed at the middle ability range of students and harder (paper 3) and easier option papers (paper 1). There is some overlap of grades between the three papers. This method is currently used in some GCSE science and mathematics subjects. The 4-in-line method consists of four papers of increasing difficulty and students can take any adjacent pair. The lowest of the papers (paper 1) provides for only basic proficiency whereas the other papers (papers 2–4) enable students to obtain higher grades. This approach is also used in some GCSE science and mathematics subjects.

A major advantage of differentiated examinations is that it allows students of differing abilities to have a greater chance of success. However, there are disadvantages such as the extra workloads for examiners and teachers; the possibility that parents will put pressure on teachers to enrol their children in higher level papers; and that it could encourage teachers to undertake differentiated teaching.

Profiling/Records of Achievement

Records of Achievement (RoAs) have been trialed in the United Kingdom since the mid-1980s. RoAs have a number of positive aspects in that they:

> bring together the wide range of pupils' achievements and progress both within and outside the classroom, including experiences and achievements not tested by examinations. (National Steering Committee, 1989, p. 2)

RoAs are important in themselves in that they provide a very comprehensive record of achievements. In addition, the processes involved by students and teachers in producing the record are also of considerable importance. Students in particular are encouraged to undertake self-appraisals and to become self-motivated.

The RoA schemes currently developed involve:

- pupils contributing statements and details on a regular basis to their teachers;
- pupil–teacher interviews;
- teacher assessments via observations, rating scales and written tests;
- pupil self-assessments.

Teachers involved in RoA schemes have noted the learning gains for students and the opportunity for much greater rapport between teachers and students. Nevertheless, they also point out that the procedures are very time consuming. Furthermore, a difficult task is for each school to develop procedures which are acceptable for validating the accreditation principles.

Cooperative External Assessment

A Canadian School Board has developed an innovative approach to external examinations. The Carleton Board of Education has developed a programme for examining senior students in English involving conference marking and the use of exemplar materials for students. The assumptions of the programme are that:

- teachers are the best assessors of students' work;
- assessment is an open and cooperative process involving students and teachers.

The external English examination is set each year by a team of experienced teachers. Apart from setting the examination, an additional task is to produce exemplar booklets for teachers and students.

These exemplars are very comprehensive and include:

- objectives of the syllabus;
- detailed marking guides used in previous examinations;
- sample examinations and marked examples of student performances showing how the criteria have been applied.

Senior students in this school district all sit for the English examination on the same day. Teachers undertake a preliminary marking of their own students. At a conference marking session held a week later, teachers meet and mark a sample of papers representing grade ranges from A to D. At this stage, marks are finalized for all students.

An evaluation study of the programme has revealed that English teachers have gained considerably from the experience. According to the evaluator, the programme, 'for the first time, has brought teachers together so that they can critically examine their marking techniques and standards and develop their skills in assessment' (Moskos, 1989, p. 2). It has also helped students considerably in their preparation for examinations and has maintained positive relationships between students and their teachers.

There is a tendency for educators to consider assessment in terms of the two stereotypes of external examinations and school-based examinations. They no longer exist in pure forms, if they ever did. Some promising hybrid versions have been developed over recent years which minimize the disadvantages and maximize the advantages of these two basic forms.

Some recent innovatory practices which have been developed in the United Kingdom and in Canada appear to be quite promising. SATs are externally developed examinations but they involve classroom tasks and they are supervised by classroom teachers. Differentiated exams are external exams but they vary in difficulty level to suit the different ability levels of students. Records of achievement emphasize wider aspects of assessment and encourage students to undertake self-assessment and self-managed learning. The Canadian example of cooperative external assessment illustrates how teachers can gain from collaborative marking procedures and students can benefit from studying examination exemplars.

Reflections and Issues

1   'It is important not to overestimate the influence examinations have on teachers ... Teachers are not passive subjects of controlling forces. They may even be able to play some sources of power off against others.' (Horton, 1987)

Give examples of how teachers may be able to use these sources of power to their own advantage.

2   'Over recent years examination structures have changed whereby there is now a greater measure of internal freedom in both syllabus and assessment, while preserving the authority of an external examining agency.' (Kay, 1978)

Has this been the case in your experience? Give reasons.

3   'It is certainly the case that success in competitive examinations is, for most people, an essential prelude to the legitimate exercise of power, responsibility and status throughout modern societies.' (Eggleston, 1984)

Do you agree with this statement in the 1990s? Give reasons for your acceptance or rejection of the statement.

4   'Examinations, perhaps more than any other single factor in the schooling process, are widely regarded as having an educationally undesirable effect on schools and as representing a significant constraint on curriculum innovation.' (Hammersley and Hargreaves, 1983, p. 11)

Can these claims be justified? Is there any empirical evidence? Alternatively, do examinations form a normal and natural part of teaching?

5   Some commonly attributed negative effects of examinations include:

- They are an unreliable measure of learning achievement. (Nuttall, 1986)
- They are strongly correlated with social class and occupational attainment. (Scarth, 1983)
- They play a key role in selective assessment for cultural reproduction. (Broadfoot, 1984)

Critically analyse these statements in the light of your teaching experiences.

6 'Arrangements for assessing the National Curriculum in the United Kingdom include the use of teacher assessments and a variation of public examinations termed standard assessment tasks (criterion-referenced tasks to be undertaken by all students at particular age levels). This assumes an whole-school approach to assessing, recording and reporting achievement.' (Flude and Hammer, 1990)

Is this a feasible assumption to make? What do you envisage as some possible difficulties in UK schools?

7 'Some students do work very hard to pass high-stakes external examinations but many do not acquire lasting competencies.' (Kellaghan and Maudaus, 1993)

What evidence of this do you have in your teaching situation? What are some possible solutions?

8 There is a flurry of excitement when league tables for schools are published in newspapers — somewhat akin to sporting league tables. What do league tables say about the performance of schools for parents? What are some caveats that need to be considered?

9 'Changes in public examinations impact most positively on curriculum when teachers have an active role in the development process.' (Torrance, 1993)
Discuss.

10 'External examinations results, when published, can cause teachers considerable negative emotions.' (Smith, 1991)

What concerns might a teacher have? To what extent can these concerns be alleviated?

References

ANDRICH, D. (1989) *Upper Secondary Certification and Tertiary Entrance*, Perth, Government Printer.
APPLE, M. (1979) *Ideology and Curriculum*, London, Routledge.
BROADFOOT, P. (1984) *Selection, Certification and Control: Social Issues in Educational Assessment*, London, Falmer Press.
BROADFOOT, P.M. (1986) 'Alternatives to public examinations', in NUTTALL, D.L. (Ed) *Assessing Educational Achievement*, London, Falmer Press.
BROOKS, C.S. (1990) 'League tables', *Times Educational Supplement*, 19 January 1990, p. 8.
COCKCROFT, W. (1982) (Chair) *Mathematics Counts*, London, HMSO.
CONNELLY, E.M. and CLANDININ, D.J. (1988) *Teachers as Curriculum Planners*, New York, Teachers College Press.
EGGLESTON, J. (1984) 'School examinations: Some sociological issues', in BROADFOOT, P.M. (Ed) *Selection, Certification and Control*, London, Falmer Press.
FLUDE, M. and HAMMER, M. (Eds) (1990) *The Education Reform Act: 1988*, London, Falmer Press.

GRANT, M. (1989) *GCSE in Practice*, London, NFER-Nelson.

HAMMERSLEY, M. and HARGREAVES, A. (1983) *Curriculum Practice: Some Sociological Case Studies*, London, Falmer Press.

HORTON, T. (1987) *GCSE: Examining the New System*, London, Harper and Row.

KAY, B.W. (1978) 'Monitoring pupils' performance', in HOPKINSON, D. (Ed) *Standards and the School Curriculum*, London, Ward Lock Educational.

KELLAGHAN, T. and MAUDAUS, G. (1993) 'Using public examinations to improve student motivation', Paper presented at the Annual Conference of the American Educational Research Association, Atlanta.

KINGDON, M. and STOBBART, G. (1988) *GCSE Examined*, London, Falmer Press.

McGAW, B. (1984) *Assessment in the Upper Secondary School in Western Australia*, Report of the Ministerial Working Party on School Certification and Tertiary Admissions Procedures, Perth, Government Printer.

MOSKOS, P. (1989) *Report on the OACI English Examination 1987–8*, Nepeen, Ontario, Carleton Board of Examination.

NATIONAL STEERING COMMITTEE (1989) *Records of Achievement*, London, DES.

NUTTALL, D.L. (Ed) (1986) *Assessing Educational Achievement*, London, Falmer Press.

PENNYCUICK, D. and MURPHY, R. (1988) *The Impact of Graded Tests*, Lewes, Falmer Press.

SCARTH, J. (1983) 'Teachers' school-based experiences of examining', in HAMMERSLEY, M. and HARGREAVES, A. (Eds) *Curriculum Practice: Some Sociological Case Studies*, London, Falmer Press.

SMITH, M.L. (1991) 'Put to the test: The effects of external testing on teachers', *Educational Researcher*, **20**, 5, pp. 8–11.

TORRANCE, H. (1986) 'What can examinations contribute to school evaluation?', *Educational Review*, **38**, 1, pp. 31–43.

TORRANCE, H. (1993) 'Using public examinations to improve school curricula and student achievement', Paper presented at the Annual Conference of the American Educational Research Association, Atlanta.

WILSON, J.D., THOMSON, G., MILLWARD, B. and KEENAN, T. (1989) *Assessment for Teacher Development*, London, Falmer Press.

8 Core Skills and Generic Competencies

Introduction

Over the 1980s and 1990s there has been considerable interest in core skills and generic competencies for diverse reasons including:

- more effective learning;
- greater breadth of education and training programmes;
- more flexible, adaptable workers;
- greater levels of monitoring and/or controlling standards.

The focus has been especially on post-compulsory education and training students (the 16–19 year olds in the United Kingdom, the Year 11–12 students in Australia, sophomores and seniors in the USA).

Which Skills and Competencies?

Various countries have produced lists of core skills/generic competencies. In most cases different terms are used because there are different underlying assumptions about what is considered to be essential. Some authors (for example Collins, 1993), point out that other core skills are omitted in many countries because they are not considered to have an essential, employment-related focus, such as critical thinking and caring, and aesthetic sensibility.

The examples that are included below demonstrate the development of core skills and generic competencies in several OECD countries.

United Kingdom

The rhetoric and reality of core skills in the United Kingdom emerged in the mid-1980s. For example, the Secretary of State for Education announced in February 1989:

> We want to equip young people with the knowledge and skills so that they have greater chances. In the changing employment world they will need broadly based qualifications. . . . As I see it, there are a number of skills . . . which young people and adults in future will all need. They could be expressed as a list of core skills . . . (Baker, 1989)

There was a flurry of activity in the 1980s and 1990s to produce 'core skills', 'transferable skills', 'generic skills' and 'common skills' (Ryan, 1991). For example the Manpower Services Commission's Work Based Learning produced 103 core skills in fourteen groups in 1988; the Business and Technician Education Council produced Common Skills (eighteen skills in seven groups) in 1989; the Confederation of British Industry in 1989 identified eight core skills.

Of special interest was a revised list of core skills proposed by the National Curriculum Council (NCC) in March 1990 in response to the Secretary of State for Education's request to ascertain which core skills could be defined and incorporated into the study programmes of 16–19 year olds taking A levels and AS level courses (Werner, 1994).

This list included:

- communication;
- problem solving;
- personal skills;
- numeracy;
- information technology;
- modern language competence.

The National Council of Vocational Qualifications (NCVQ) endorsed this list but only included the first three in all NCVQ units. The latter three were considered to be only relevant to particular NCVQs where they were necessary for occupational competence.

The NCC also identified several cross-curricular themes which they considered to be essential and generic for post-16 education:

- social and economic understanding;
- scientific and technological understanding;
- aesthetic and creative understanding.

In addition, the following themes were required for 5–16 year olds:

- economic and industrial understanding;
- careers education and guidance;
- health education;
- education for citizenship;
- environmental education.

The rhetoric at the time about core skills was extremely positive. For example, the NCVQ stated that fundamental core skills will:

- enhance the transferability of competent performance between different contexts and occupations;
- help employees to respond flexibly to changing skill requirements;
- provide a basis for progression within the NVQ framework.

In addition, given that the core skills are common to NVQs and A/AS examinations, it will:

- facilitate transfer between A/AS examinations and NVQs, thus improving the transition from general to vocational education and training;
- facilitate progression from NVQs to higher education. (NCVQ, 1990, p. 2)

Jessup (1991) was an active exponent of core skills in the early 1990s. He provided an Outcomes Model of the Curriculum involving initial assessment, unit targets and learning units. He envisaged that core skills would be:

- defined as outcomes in the form of elements of competence;
- they will be independent of any qualification and will be able to be delivered within any programme;
- they will be assessed separately;
- where performance criteria are met, credit will be given for their achievement. (Jessup, 1991, p. 82)

As it turned out, the idea of including core skills across A level and A/S level courses did not eventuate (Green, 1995). Further, some specialists were raising caveats about the use of core skills. For example, Wolf (1991) and Oates (1986, 1992) raised concerns about transferability. Oates noted that although there is great enthusiasm for the benefits that core or transferable skills might bring:

- technical rigour has not been applied to examine the extent to which transfer is enhanced;
- the types of skills which are transferable have not been fully identified;
- there is no consensus around a single, robust model of transferable skills, proven in its capacity to enhance skill transfer. (Oates, 1992, pp. 227–8)

Research on core skills has been occurring and is continuing to occur in the UK. Cognitive psychologists have been examining various aspects of transfer (Holyoak, 1991; Salthouse, 1991); and on distinctions between 'near transfer' and 'far transfer' (Fotheringhame, 1989). Longitudinal studies are occurring currently at the Open University (Hodgkinson and Coats, 1994) and a number of studies are occurring at Middlesex University, University of Surrey, Sheffield Hallam University and University of East London on aspects of core skills and literacy, problem solving and empowerment (Oates, 1992).

There has also been increased interest in other European countries to develop core skills. For example, Trier and Peschar (1994) refer to the Cross-Curricular Competencies project which includes participants from Norway, Switzerland and the Netherlands. They are examining cross-curricular competencies of problem solving and critical thinking; communication skills; political, democratic, economic and social values; self perception and self confidence, within a framework of International Indicators of Educational Systems. Studies have also been undertaken on the application of core skills in higher education institutions. For example Otter (1992) undertook research on learning outcomes and credits in higher education and Eraut (1985, 1992) researched the knowledge base of the professions.

There has been and continues to be in the UK, enormous pressure to establish practical programmes, courses and certificates which incorporate core skills.

USA

Similar initiatives occurred in the USA in the 1990s. Most noteworthy was the Secretary's Commission on Achieving Necessary Skill (SCANS), established by President Bush as part of the America 2000 Education Strategy in 1990.

Over a period of twelve months six special panels of experts examined a variety of jobs ranging from hotels and catering to manufacturing, health and finance. Intensive interviews were held with job-holders or their supervisors to identify what knowledge or foundation was needed by young people leaving school to find and hold a good job (SCANS, 1991). The panels identified a set of eight competencies and skills which they labelled as 'workplace know-how' needed for solid job-performance.

Three skills and qualities were perceived to be a foundation and were at the heart of job-performance. These included:

* basic skills: reading, writing, arithmetic and mathematics, speaking and listening;
* thinking skills: thinking creatively, making decisions, solving problems, seeing things in the mind's eye, knowing how to learn and reasoning;
* personal qualities: individual responsibility, self-esteem, sociability, self-management and integrity.

The competencies included:

* resources: allocating time, money, materials, space and staff;
* interpersonal skills: working in teams, teaching others, serving customers, leading, negotiating, and working well with people from culturally diverse backgrounds;
* information: acquiring and evaluating data, organizing and maintaining files, interpreting and communicating, and using computers to process information;
* systems: understanding social, organizational and technological systems, monitoring and correcting performance, and designing or improving systems;
* technology: selecting equipment and tools, applying technology to specific tasks, and maintaining and troubleshooting technologies. (SCANS, 1991)

As noted by Werner (1994) several principles were developed by SCANS pertaining to these eight requirements, namely:

- they were considered to be essential preparation for all students whether they were continuing with their education or going directly into the workforce;
- the eight competencies are highly integrated;
- they need to be incorporated into existing school subjects;
- they are most effectively learnt in context, within a real environment.

This latter principle is especially significant, because it is suggesting, along with current cognitive science literature, that skills are context focused. For example, Chi, Glaser, as cited in Brownell and Scarino (1993, pp. 36–7), conclude from a large number of studies contrasting experts with novices in a wide range of specific domains that:

- experts excel mainly in their own domains. They have a good deal of domain knowledge;
- experts perceive large meaningful patterns in the domain. This reflects an organization of the knowledge base, not simply perceptual ability;
- experts see and represent a problem in their domain at a deeper more principled level than novices; novices tend to represent a problem at a superficial level. Both have and use conceptual categories, but expert categories are semantically or principle-based, whereas categories of novices are syntactically or surface-feature oriented.

Since the publication of the SCANS report (1991) other agencies in the USA have been involved in development and assessment activities, such as the New Standards Project (Tucker, 1994). Standards are being developed at three levels (elementary, middle and high school levels) with a strong emphasis on using student portfolios (Stern *et al.*, 1995).

New Zealand

As part of their National Curriculum, the Ministry of Education in New Zealand produced a list of seven essential skills in 1991, and an additional skill, physical skill, was added in 1993. The skills include:

- communication skills;
- numeracy skills;
- problem solving skills;
- self-management and competitive skills;
- social and cooperative skills;
- work and study skills;
- physical skills.

These essential skills are to be developed through the seven essential learning areas of the National Curriculum and are to be incorporated into the National Qualifications Framework.

The emphasis in New Zealand is on a specific list of useable skills. Knowledge is not emphasized nor is transferability a requirement, simply a desirable outcome.

Australia

The Mayer Committee was established in September 1991 at a time when there was a concerted push for change by the Federal Government and by employers and the unions.

The Federal Minister for Employment, Education and Training, John Dawkins, launched a major skills initiative in 1987 with the publication *Skills for Australia*.

The Business Council of Australia and the National Industry Education Forum (NIEF) were influential in determining educational priorities on the national scene. Various position papers were published by these organizations together with well-crafted media publicity. For example, *A Declaration of Goals for Australian Schools* was published by the NIEF in June 1991. In February 1992 this was followed by a further publication *Improving Australia's Schools*. Follow-up consultations with stakeholders ensured that politicians were aware of their proposals.

The Australian Council of Trade Unions (ACTU) had broad concerns about education in terms of general reforms that they perceived were needed in the labour market. As a result of an ACTU/Trade Development Council visit to western Europe, they published an influential paper entitled *Australia Reconstructed* (1987), in which priority was given to developing skills in communications and numeracy and a common curriculum for all students.

The Australian Education Council (AEC), largely due to the energies of John Dawkins, initiated a curriculum mapping exercise across all states and territories in 1988. The AEC began exploring an outcomes model and the use of national statements and profiles. Concurrently, the AEC established a national review of the future development of post compulsory education and training in Australia in 1990, with the committee to be chaired by Brian Finn, Chief Executive Officer of IBM. The Finn Committee emphasized the growing partnership needed between 'education' and 'training'.

Workers of the future are:

> ultimately more productive because they know and understand their work, their product or their service. They are encouraged to work in teams, to become involved in problem solving, planning and decision making . . . They are also better equipped to participate actively in the range of roles outside employment which are required as members of a complex society. (Finn, 1991, p. 6)

These elements were categorized by the Finn Committee into a set of employment-related key competencies. Building upon general competencies espoused by the Karmel Committee (1985), the Finn Committee outlined the following key areas of competence:

- language and communication;
- mathematics;
- scientific and technological understandings;
- cultural understanding;
- problem solving;
- personal and interpersonal.

The Mayer Committee was established by the AEC in September 1991, under the Chair of Eric Mayer, former Chief Executive of National Mutual and Chair of the Business/Higher Education Round Table, to develop the employment-related key competencies recommended in the Finn Report. Within a very tight time frame the Mayer Committee and the secretariat (seconded personnel from the school sector and the training sector) worked on the development of key areas, strands, and competencies.

The set of strands included:

- collecting, analysing and organizing ideas and information;
- expressing ideas and information;
- planning and organizing activities;
- working with others and in teams;
- using mathematical ideas and techniques;
- solving problems;
- using technology.

The Mayer Committee provided details about how these seven key competency strands were drawn from the key areas of competence recommended in the Finn Report and argued that each strand drew to some extent upon knowledge and skills of all the key areas.

It should be noted that the Committee decided to exclude two of the Finn Committee key areas, cultural understanding (although this was revisited later) and scientific and technological understanding. It was argued that scientific and technological understanding provided a basis for using technology as a key competency strand and hence did not need to be included. Further, it was argued that cultural understanding had been examined carefully but all efforts had been unsuccessful in identifying a strand which met the definition of competence and which did not overlay considerably with other key competency strands.

A difficulty for the Committee was to untangle complexities associated with each key competency — being able to be transferable to new task, situations or environments. That is, a student must be able to transfer knowledge and skills to new environments. The Committee were far from specific about how widely a competency might be transferred — a different example in the same context or domain or another context and domain? Unfortunately, the Mayer Committee did not appear to address this topic adequately. Having opted for key competencies to be used for integrating and applying knowledge and skills (rather than defining them as skills only, as occurred with the New Zealand essential skills), the Committee seemed to assume this aspect was not problematic and proceeded to concentrate upon providing a credible assessment and reporting framework, complete with performance criteria and examples to illustrate the different contexts.

The Mayer Committee established three levels of performance for each key competency strand ranging from Performance Level 1 (lowest), Performance Level 2 and Performance Level 3 (highest). These performance levels were designed to be linked to the Australian Standards Framework.

Since the publication of the Mayer Report (1992), piloting of key competencies in all states and territories has led to some promising developments. The Queensland project team (1994) has given considerable emphasis to teaching approaches which provide 'real life' contextualization of the key competencies. They have encouraged teachers to explore cooperative learning techniques and for students to actively construct meaning of their experiences. A number of teachers have been inserviced on action research methodology and encouraged to use these techniques to reflect upon and resolve particular classroom teaching problems. A number of the project teams have encouraged student initiatives in developing learning activities. The South Australian project team has explored the use of student portfolios whereby students reflect upon their development of key competencies and select portfolio items which they consider illustrate important developments/achievements. Several project teams have highlighted the use of extracurricular/out-of-school activities (for example, sport, debating, drama productions, student councils, part-time work) for developing the key competencies. Extra curricular activities may consist of clubs and organizations completely external to a school or run directly by the school.

Since the release of the Mayer Report (1992) another major review has been undertaken and is likely to have a considerable impact in the 1990s — the Report of The Civics Expert Group (Macintyre, 1994). This report recommends a close linking of the cultural understanding key competency with civic competence. It should be noted that an increasing number of papers are appearing in the literature which provide important insights into conceptualizations of competencies (Hager, 1994; Walker, 1994; Kennedy and Preston, 1994).

Reflections and Issues

1 To what extent can core skills/key competencies be transferred to different contexts? What are the implications for teacher planning and assessment?

2 Are there some teaching methods which are more effective than others in developing core skills/key competencies?

3   To what extent can students be encouraged to reflect upon their development of core skills and key competencies and develop their own portfolios for assessment purposes?

4   If core skills/key competencies are included in the school curriculum how should they be assessed and reported?

5   'An academically and vocationally integrated education blurs the distinction between practical knowledge and theoretical knowledge. Students deserve opportunities to gain practical experience, context-specific understandings and theoretical knowledge in a variety of ways.' (Kincheloe, 1995, p. 146) Discuss.

References

AUSTRALIAN COUNCIL OF TRADE UNIONS (1987) *Australia Reconstructed*, Canberra, ACTU.

BAKER, K. (1989) Secretary of State for Education Speech to ACFHE, London, Department of Education and Science.

BROWNELL, J.A. and SCARINO, A. (1993) *The Theoretical Bases of the Proposed Target-oriented Curriculum Framework for Hong Kong*, Hong Kong, Institute of Language in Education, Hong Kong Education Department.

COLLINS, C. (1993) (Ed) *Competencies*, Canberra, ACE.

EMPLOYMENT AND SKILLS FORMATION COUNCIL (1994) *Raising the Standard*, Canberra, AGPS.

ERAUT, M. (1985) 'Knowledge creation and knowledge use in professional contexts', *Studies in Higher Education*, **10**, 2, pp. 117–33.

ERAUT, M. (1992) 'Developing the knowledge base: A process perspective on professional education', in BARNETT, R. (Ed) *Learning to Effect*, Milton Keynes, Open University Press.

FINN, B. (Chair) (1991) *Report of the Australian Education Council Review Committee, Young People's Participation in Post-compulsory Education and Training*, Melbourne, AEC.

FOTHERINGHAME, J. (1989) Summary of the proceedings of an invitational seminar on transfer, Warwick University.

GREEN, A. (1995) 'Core skills, participation and progression in post-compulsory education and training in England and France', *Comparative Education*, **31**, 1, pp. 49–67.

HAGER, P. (1994) 'Is there a cogent philosophical argument against competency standards?', *Australian Journal of Education*, **38**, 1, pp. 3–18.

HODGKINSON, L. and COATS, M. (1994) 'Core skills in the higher education curriculum: Research and practice', Unpublished paper, Open University, Milton Keynes.

HOLYOAK, K.J. (1991) 'Symbolic connectionism: Toward third-generation theories of expertise', in ERICSSON, K.A. and SMITH, J. (Eds) *Towards a General Theory of Expertise*, Cambridge, Cambridge University Press.

JESSUP, G. (1991) *Outcomes: NVQs and the Emerging Model of Education and Training*, London, Falmer Press.

KARMEL, P. (Chair) (1985) *Quality of Education in Australia*, Report of the Review Committee, Canberra, AGPS.

KENNEDY, K.J. and PRESTON, B. (1994) 'Teacher competencies and teacher education: Progress report on a research project', Paper presented at the Annual Conference of the Australian Association for Research in Education, Newcastle.

KINCHELOE, J.L. (1995) *Toil and Trouble*, New York, Peter Lang.

MACINTYRE, S. (Chair) (1994) *Whereas the People: Civics and Citizenship Education*, Canberra, AGPS.

MAYER, E. (Chair) (1992) *Employment-related Key Competencies for Post-compulsory Education and Training*, Canberra, AGPS.

NATIONAL COUNCIL FOR VOCATIONAL QUALIFICATIONS (1990) *Core Skills in NVQs Response to the Secretary of State for Education*, London, NCVQ.

NATIONAL INDUSTRY EDUCATION FORUM (1991) *A Declaration of Goals for Australian Schools*, Canberra, NIEF.

NATIONAL INDUSTRY EDUCATION FORUM (1992) *Improving Australia's Schools*, Canberra, NIEF.

OATES, T. (1986) 'The RVQ levels: A critical review and recommendations for development strategy', Policy paper for the Training Commission, London.

OATES, T. (1992) 'Core skills and transfer: Aiming high', *Educational and Training Technology International*, **29**, 3, pp. 227–39.

OTTER, S. (1992) *Learning Outcomes in Higher Education*, London, UDACE.

QUEENSLAND DEPARTMENT OF EDUCATION (1994) *Key Competencies Projects: Interim Report*, Brisbane, Department of Education.

RUMSEY, D. (1994) *Key Competencies in Industry Standards*, Canberra, National Training Board.

RYAN, P. (1991) (Ed) *International Comparisons of Vocational Education and Training for Intermediate Skills*, London, Falmer Press.

SALTHOUSE, T.A. (1991) 'Expertise as the circumvention of human processing limitations', in ERICSSON, K.A. and SMITH, J. (Eds) *Towards a General Theory of Expertise*, Cambridge, Cambridge University Press.

SCANS (1991) *What Work Requires of Schools: A SCANS Report for America 2000*, Washington DC, US Department of Labor.

SCHOOLS BOARD OF TASMANIA (1994) *The Key Competencies: Tasmanian Pilot Program: General Information and Teacher Resources*, Hobart, Schools Board.

STERN, D., FINKELSTEIN, N., STONE, J.R., LATTING, J. and DORNSIFE, C. (1995) *School to Work*, London, Falmer Press.

TRIER, U.P. and PESCHAR, J.L. (1994) 'Cross curricular competencies: Rationale and strategy for developing a new indicator', Paper presented at the Annual Conference of the American Educational Research Association, New Orleans.

TUCKER, M. (1994) 'New standards project', Unpublished Paper, University Park, Pennsylvania State University.

WALKER, J. (1994) 'Competency-based teacher education: Implications for quality in higher education', II R Conference, Canberra.

WERNER, M.C. (1994) 'Australian key competencies in an international perspective', Draft Paper.

WOLF, A. (1991) 'Assessing core skills: Wisdom or wild goose chase?', *Cambridge Journal of Education*, **21**, 2, pp. 189–201.

Part III

Teacher Perspectives

9   Teacher Empowerment

Introduction

Teacher empowerment is all about broadening the base of responsibility and accountability at the school level to include teachers as well as school principals. Many of the contemporary reform reports are advocating site-based, participatory and personalized decision-making and the need for teachers to be key players in these activities.

Some Definitions and Examples

The term 'teacher empowerment' has various meanings associated with it in the education literature. Examples include a slogan for class struggle; a term to connote collegial learning with students; and a term for connoting increased expertise due to technological advances.

Empowerment assumes that persons holding power (for example, state or local managers or school principals) give the power to someone else (for example, teachers or students) in the interests of improving schools (Elmore, 1988). However it is not always clear who has the power and how it might be transferred. Then there is the matter of responsibility — if persons are empowered, to whom are they responsible — to parents and students? To the community? To the teaching profession?

'Power' can be defined as control but in terms of educational settings it is more useful to consider power as 'doing or acting'. Opportunities for teachers to try out new approaches, to problem-solve and to inquire, assist them in becoming 'empowered'. Empowerment of teachers (and students) occurs when they have opportunities to create meaning in their respective schools. By contrast, 'disempowered' teachers are those who teach defensively and control knowledge in order to control students (McNeil, 1988). In these situations schooling becomes an empty ritual, unrelated to personal or cultural knowledge.

Hoyle (1980) uses the terms 'restricted' and 'extended' professionals to highlight different levels of commitment to teaching. The restricted professional is intuitive, classroom-focused and works from experience rather than theory and, as a consequence, has little interest in wider professional activities. By contrast, the extended professional takes a broader stance, compares his/her work with others, undertakes self-evaluation, and has a greater interest in theory and its relation with practice.

Teacher empowerment is seen by writers such as Giroux (1992) as a significant concept in understanding the complex relations between schools and the dominant society. He argues that teachers and students need empowerment to resist and to struggle against the domination in society produced by capitalism.

Some writers argue that teachers are becoming steadily disempowered (Apple, 1986; Ozga and Lawn, 1981). For example, Apple (1986) argues that teachers face the prospect of being deskilled because of the encroachment of technical control procedures into the curriculum in schools. He cites as examples behaviourally based curricula, prespecified competencies for teachers and students and testing activities.

Ball (1993, p. 107) refers to the impact of the National Curriculum upon UK teachers and notes that there has been:

- an increase in the technical elements of teachers' work;
- a standardization and testing for normalization;
- increasingly direct attempts to shape the quality, character and content of classroom practice.

Doring (1994) also acknowledges the disempowering of teachers in the UK and a resultant loss of autonomy.

Empowerment of Teachers and Students

Empowerment can also be considered as teacher and student empowerment, 'jointly developed' (see Chapter 6). Giroux and McLaren (1986) argue for teachers to democratize schools and to empower students to become critical, active citizens. Boomer (1982) and Green (1988) argue that students must be given opportunities to contribute to, and modify, the curriculum, so that they will have a real investment both in the learning processes and the outcomes. The negotiation process between a teacher and his/her students empowers both groups as they share commitments and make decisions about class activities. Green (1988) refers to the affective and cognitive tensions in the classrooms as a teacher and his/her students permit and commission various power sanctions. Different learning situations will permit or require certain actions. Actions of power occur with great subtlety and include legal power, informational power, charismatic power, physical power and many other forms exercised by both teachers and students.

Empowerment and School Support

Teachers can also become empowered through increased resources, such as technology. Recently, educators have been proposing that broad-based use of computer technology (for example, word processors, spreadsheets and data bases) can enhance teaching and teachers can match the technology to their own creativity (Valdez, 1986).

Table 9.1: Rewards and costs for teachers in undertaking an innovation

Costs	Rewards
1 Time demands are heavy	1 More stimulating/interesting teaching
2 Need to acquire new skills, acquire new knowledge	2 Improved discipline among pupils
3 Need to prepare new material	3 More time allocated for planning lessons
4 Have to adopt unfamiliar patterns of teaching	4 More resources made available
5 Requires reorganization of administrative structures	5 More status/recognition for 'innovative' teachers
6 Can be a threat to autonomy	6 More active part in decision making
7 Subject expertise can be undermined	7 More money
8 Involves unwanted collaboration with other teachers	8 Promotion
9 Leads to change in power structure among teachers, teacher/pupils	

With computers, teachers and students can learn together — they can be sharing experiences as they try out new programmes — both groups can become empowered as they master additional uses and ends of computer technology. Individuals use computers in different ways and allow the machine to be integrated into their sense of identity — that is the big payoff.

Sizer, in his interview with O'Neil (1995), refers to the satisfactions teachers gain in the coalition of Essential Schools in the USA in being able to exhibit/demonstrate meaningful student work.

Increased resources can also be a powerful reward. This may take the form of increased pay incentives or it might be additional teacher-aide assistance or additional resources such as lap-top computers (Cornett, 1995). Effective reward systems can be used to increase:

- teacher motivation;
- acceptance of personal accountability;
- continuous professional development;
- acceptance of an enlarged definition of teacher work responsibilities.

Reward systems need to be a mixture of intrinsic satisfactions (for example, exciting work, positive working conditions, interesting co-workers) and extrinsic benefits (for example, promotions, public recognition) (Mitchell and Peters, 1988).

There are also penalties, as indicated in Table 9.1. A new task or opportunity very often requires additional — extra labour-intensive activities which some teachers at least will perceive to be a 'punishment'. Furthermore, it may be a threat to the teachers' established procedures or may require a teacher to work closely in collaboration with other teachers. As indicated in Table 9.1 these are just some of the perceived 'costs' of getting involved with new tasks.

Ideally teachers can become increasingly empowered by:

- working together on joint projects;
- talking to one another at a level of detail that is rich and meaningful;
- shared planning or evaluation of topics;
- observing their colleagues in peer observation arrangements;
- training together and training one another (for example, teaching others about new ideas and classroom practices);
- having access to appropriate levels of material and human support/resources.
  (Little, 1990)

School administrators have the resources and the opportunities to empower teachers. They can provide leadership opportunities for outstanding staff members. They can increase opportunities during the school day for teachers to interact on teaching problems (Nias, 1990).

Clark and Meloy (1990) suggest that problems of schools as organizations can be greatly reduced by developing 'democratic' structures, incorporating the following principles:

- designated leaders (for example, the principal) should be chosen by the teachers;
- the school must be built on shared authority and responsibility, not delegation of authority and responsibility;
- all staff should have terms of work as administrators as well as classroom teachers;
- formal rewards to the staff (for example, forms of promotion) should be under the control of the staff;
- the goals of the school must be formulated by, and agreed to through, group consensus.

Problems and Issues

Some writers consider that teachers are not interested in empowerment because of limiting factors in the culture of teaching. For example, Hargreaves (1989) argues that teachers are present-oriented, conservative and individualistic. They tend to avoid long-term planning and collaboration with their colleagues.

A problem for teacher groups becoming empowered is that teachers are trained to survive in the system as individuals. Teachers have few ways of sharing their experience. As noted by Walker and Kusner (1991, p. 194), 'precious time available for staff meetings tends to be gobbled up by scheduling arrangements and by the need to consider closely each individual child's progress'. There is little opportunity for schools to reflect on their practices. This can be a major deficiency because major problems for teachers are problems of organizations.

For many teachers their career future is featureless, lacking in challenges, and just more of the same. Research studies of life histories of teachers (for example, Huberman (1993), Goodson (1992) and Kelchtermans and Vandenberghe (1994)

Table 9.2: Life cycle phases

Career entry (First year of teaching)
• reality shock, trial and error
• discovery: enthusiasm, learning

Stabilization (2–5 years of teaching)
• firming up on teaching as a career
• more instruction: centred
• greater self-confidence
• more flexibility in classroom management
• less discipline problems
• assertions of independence

Diversification and Change (5–15 years of teaching)
• experimentation to increase effectiveness
• quest for new challenges
• willingness to take up new responsibilities

Stocktaking (12–20 years of teaching)
• bored with the routines of teaching
• consideration of career shifts

Serenity (15–30 years of teaching)
• reduced career ambition
• high levels of self-sufficiency and confidence
• increased distance from students

Conservatism (30–40 years of teaching)
• negative attitudes about students
• negative attitudes about fellow teachers and administrators
• cynical about reform efforts

Disengagement (35–45 years of teaching)
• energies channelled to outside pursuits
• preparing for retirement

Source: Schools Council, 1990

indicate that many teachers follow well defined patterns of behaviour — although there is initial excitement and experimentation, this is superseded by boredom and negative attitudes.

The patterns depicted in Table 9.2 are based upon research studies examined by the Schools Council (1990). Although caveats should be noted about the patterns not applying in all cases and the effects of other external factors (for example economic climate, political initiatives) the consistency of their appearance in research studies is very marked.

McCutcheon (1988) takes a more positive stance. She admits that there are teaching situations in a number of countries where the curriculum to be taught by teachers is specified, so that it can be controlled by administrators or national reformers. Examples which are occurring currently are teacher competency tests and student achievement tests. Yet, each classroom teacher can still make important decisions about what he/she will teach. The teacher is the filter through which the mandated curriculum passes (McCutcheon, 1988). Teachers filter the objectives and conceive of ways of enacting them, they make sense of the teaching context and make the necessary adjustments.

Teachers can and do identify problems and seek ways to define them and find resolutions. They are empowered to inquire into matters critically, in order to improve their own practice. The inquiries and reflections can occur in preactive mental planning of lessons, interactively during lessons and in post-lesson reflections. They can also occur individually or collaboratively among a group of teachers.

Reflections and Issues

1 'We must preserve and protect those teachers (and materials) who without fear examine the problems of our society realistically.' (Littleford, 1983)

   Are teachers discouraged from openly discussing societal issues in your experience? Give reasons.

2 'Teachers are thinkers who make many decisions that create the curriculum in classrooms. They have an important function in shaping what students have an opportunity to learn.' (McCutcheon, 1988)

   Are teachers sufficiently empowered to undertake this function?

3 'At the root of many ill-conceived panaceas of the past is that teachers have been taken for granted and have been treated as classroom furniture rather than as thinking human beings.' (Shanker, 1986)

   Discuss.

4 The three major factors that facilitate empowerment include acquisition of support (for example, endorsement by the principal), information (for example, technical data) and resources (for example, human services).

   Do you agree that these are important factors? Give examples to support your answer.

5 'Teachers seeking empowerment have to resolve the common tensions between management and curriculum. Decisions are often made in favour of management which emphasizes the need to survive above the urge to learn and to develop.' (Walker and Kushner, 1991)

   Is this the typical pattern in your experience? How can both groups' ends be served more appropriately?

6 'We are certain of one thing. We will never move within the bureaucratic structure to new schools, to free schools. That structure was invented to assure domination and control. It will never produce freedom and self-actualisation. The bureaucratic structure is failing in a manner so critical that adaptations will not forestall its collapse. It is impractical. It does not fit the psychological and personal needs of the workforce.' (Clark and Meloy, 1990, p. 21)

To what extent do you support this stance? If the bureaucratic structure is failing why has it survived so long? Are there potential pitfalls with a democratic alternative?

7   'As well as influences such as commitment and interests bearing on teachers from within themselves, as it were, there are forces from without, over which the teacher may have little control.' (Woods, 1990, p. 15)

   What are some of these external constraints? How does a teacher typically cope with them? Can this lead to conflicts between personal goals and external constraints?

8   'Teachers are generally isolated from one another and receive little recognition from either colleagues or administrators ... Everybody does their own thing and nobody helps anybody else. As a consequence, the school becomes atomised and the educational enterprise is hopelessly segmented.' (Webb, 1985, p. 84)

   Explain how teacher isolation deprives teachers of power and leads to powerlessness about school-wide decisions.

9   'Bureaucratic rationality dictates that effective and efficient means be found that match predetermined ends. In pursuit of effectiveness and efficiency, the administrators need to influence the motives of their subordinates, and control and direct them in such ways as to produce maximum benefits to the organisation.' (Rizvi, 1989, p. 71)

   Is this an accurate portrayal of what typically occurs in schools with which you are familiar? What strategies can teachers use, if any, to empower themselves within this structure?

10 'The major problem for the teaching profession is the confrontation between an increasingly postindustrial, postmodern world and a modernistic, monolithic school system that continues to pursue deeply anachronistic purposes within opaque and inflexible structures.' (Hargreaves, 1994, p. 3)

   Discuss.

11 'If teachers are to influence students to live as authentic persons ... then they will have to present themselves to students as people who strive to live their own lives this way. This will require many teachers to take the ethical challenges in their lives much more seriously than they do at present.' (Starratt, 1994, p. 130)

   Discuss.

12 To what extent does teacher isolation in separate classrooms deprive teachers of the opportunity of collegial/professional activities?

   Is it the case that most schools are atomized and hopelessly segmented?

References

APPLE, M.W. (1986) *Teachers and Texts*, New York, Routledge and Kegan Paul.

BALL, S.J. (1993) 'Education policy, power relations and teachers' work', *British Journal of Educational Studies*, **41**, 2, pp. 106–21.

BOOMER, G. (Ed) (1982) *Negotiating the Curriculum*, Sydney, Ashton Scholastic.

CLARK, D.L. and MELOY, J.M. (1990) 'Recanting bureaucracy: A democratic structure for leadership in schools', in LIEBERMAN, A. (Ed) *Schools as Collaborative Cultures: Creating the Future Now*, London, Falmer Press.

CORNETT, L.M. (1995) 'Lessons from 10 years of teacher improvement reforms', *Educational Leadership*, **52**, 5, pp. 26–31.

DORING, A. (1994) 'Teacher training in England: Is the profession being undermined?', *Unicorn*, **20**, 3, pp. 46–53.

ELMORE, R.F. (1988) 'Models of restructured schools', Unpublished paper, Michigan State University.

GIROUX, H.A. (1982) 'Power and resistance in the new sociology of education: Beyond theories of social and cultural reproduction', *Curriculum Perspectives*, **2**, 3, pp. 1–14.

GIROUX, H.A. (1992) *Border Crossings: Cultural Workers and the Politics of Education*, New York, Routledge.

GIROUX, H.A. and MCLAREN, P. (1986) 'Teacher education and the politics of engagement: The case for democratic schooling', *Harvard Educational Review*, **56**, 3, pp. 213–38.

GOODSON, I.F. (1992) (Ed) *Studying Teachers' Lives*, Routledge, London.

GREEN, B. (Ed) (1988) *Metaphors and Meanings*, Perth, Australian Association for the Teaching of English.

HARGREAVES, A. (1989) *Curriculum and Assessment Reform*, Milton Keynes, Open University Press.

HARGREAVES, A. (1994) *Changing Teachers, Changing Times*, Cassell, London.

HOYLE, E. (1980) 'Professionalization and deprofessionalization in education', in HOYLE, E. and MEGARRY, G. (Eds) *World Year Book of Education 1980: The Professional Development of Teachers*, London, Kogan Page.

HUBERMAN, M. (1993) *The Lives of Teachers*, Teachers College Press, New York.

KELCHTERMANS, G. and VANDENBERGHE, R. (1994) 'Teachers' professional development: A biographical perspective', *Journal of Curriculum Studies*, **26**, 1, pp. 45–62.

LITTLE, J.W. (1990) 'Teachers as colleagues', in LIEBERMAN, A. (Ed) *Schools as Collaborative Cultures: Creating the Future Now*, London, Falmer Press.

LITTLEFORD, M.S. (1983) 'Censorship, academic freedom and the public school teacher', *Journal of Curriculum Theorizing*, **5**, 3, pp. 98–131.

MCCUTCHEON, G. (1988) 'Curriculum and the work of teachers', in BEYER, L.E. and APPLE, M.W. *The Curriculum*, New York, State University of New York Press.

MCNEIL, L. (1988) 'Contradictions of control, part 2: Teachers, students, and curriculum', *Phi Delta Kappan*, **69**, 10, pp. 729–34.

MITCHELL, D.E. and PETERS, M.J. (1988) 'A strong profession through appropriate teacher incentives', *Educational Leadership*, **46**, 3, pp. 74–8.

NIAS, D.J. (1990) 'A deputy head observed: Findings from an ethnographic study', in SOUTHWORTH, G. *The Study of Primary Education, A Source Book, Volume 3: School Organisation and Management*, London, Falmer Press.

O'NEIL, J. (1995) 'On lasting school reform: A conversation with Ted Sizer', *Educational Leadership*, **52**, 5, pp. 4–9.

OZGA, J. and LAWN, M. (1981) *Teachers' Professionalism and Class*, London, Falmer Press.

RIZVI, F. (1989) 'Bureaucratic rationality and the promise of democratic schooling', in CARR, W. (Ed) *Quality and Teaching*, London, Falmer Press.

SCHOOLS COUNCIL (1990) *Australia's Teacher: An Agenda for the Next Decade*, Canberra, AGPS.

SHANKER, A. (1986) 'Teachers must take charge', *Educational Leadership*, **44**, 1, pp. 12–13.

STARRATT, R.J. (1994) *Building an Ethical School: A Practical Response to the Moral Crisis in Schools*, London, Falmer Press.

VALDEZ, G. (1986) 'Realizing the potential of educational technology', *Educational Leadership*, **43**, 6, pp. 4–6.

WALKER, R. and KUSHNER, S. (1991) 'Theorizing a curriculum', in GOODSON, I.F. and WALKER, R. *Biography, Identity and Schooling: Episodes in Educational Research*, London, Falmer Press.

WEBB, R.B. (1985) 'Teacher status panic: Moving up the down escalator', in BALL, S.J. and GOODSON, I.F. (Eds) *Teachers' Lives and Careers*, London, Falmer Press.

WOODS, P. (1990) *Teacher Skills and Strategies*, London, Falmer Press.

10   Teacher Competencies and Curriculum

Introduction

Competency-based standards for teachers in the 1990s is again evident in many countries, especially as a tool for granting tenure (for example, in the USA) and as a basis for preservice training (for example, trial versions are occurring in Australia). Although competency-based approaches have been tried in the past and largely found wanting (for example, competency-based teacher-education (CBTE) in the USA in the 1970s), the current interest is widely supported by government and industry groups and has the potential to be more successful.

Some Important Terms

The language used by exponents of this approach is specialized and it is important to appreciate the specific meanings given to terms:

- competent professional: possesses a set of relevant attributes (knowledge, abilities, skills attitudes) necessary for job performance to appropriate standards (Gonezi *et al.*, 1990);
- some attributes are readily recognizable but others may be difficult to recognize. The task is to test whether attributes believed to underlie 'competence' are present or not and at an appropriate level;
- 'performance': refers to performance of a role or set of tasks;
- within a profession there are typically a number of 'roles' and roles typically comprise a wide range of 'tasks' and even 'subtasks';
- an alternative to focusing upon performance in tasks is to examine performance within a 'domain' (for example, the instructional domain of teaching);
- 'standards': are usually defined in terms of 'minimum standards' and this involves establishing certain 'criteria'.

Some Merits and Demerits of Competency-based Standards (CBS)

Teachers traditionally receive a credential (degree/diploma) and use references/testimonials to affirm their competence as teachers. Whether this is the best way of demonstrating professional competence in the 1990s is problematic. Burrow (1993) goes further and suggests that the dominant paradigm of teaching is outmoded and needs drastic changes (for example, outmoded practices include streaming, control of the learning process by the teacher; uneven reward structures based on competition; hierarchical school organization). Whether a competency-based standards approach can alleviate all these 'ills' is also problematic!

In general terms, it is argued that the 'advantages' of competency-based standards (CBS) include:

- they are supportive of a worldwide focus on training reform and accountability;
- they assist professionals obtain positions in various locations, nationally and internationally. Information about key professional tasks can be submitted to employers in diverse locations;
- they provide explicit statements of what people need to be able to successfully practice as a professional. Standards can be established at various levels such as entry level (preservice), experienced teacher, senior teacher;
- they provide impartial benchmarks for professional workers arriving from overseas;
- they improve equity provisions by providing due recognition for disadvantaged groups. More equitable methods to obtain appropriate evidence include direct observation of work activities, skills tests, projects, log books/diaries, portfolios;
- they facilitate the designing and assessment of preservice and inservice teacher education programmes;
- they facilitate articulation of pathways into the teaching profession;
- they facilitate linkages between professional practice and the underlying disciplines;
- they are an effective way of demonstrating quality and accountability to the general public;
- they facilitate the development of transferable generic skills.

The emphasis of CBS 'on explicit statements' about standards may in fact be a major step forward for the teaching profession. Burrow (1993) argues that the profession is mature enough to demystify the nature of the work of teachers:

> to define and promote its richness and complexity, and hence to establish the standards by which we can guarantee our student's quality assurance. (Burrow, 1993, p. 111)

Perhaps it is highly desirable for all professions to 'develop' and 'own' their standards.

Heywood *et al.* (1992) assert that each profession should periodically examine its professional values and overall capacities, and in so doing, can assess its position in the community and its relations with other professions. It is quite possible that if the teaching profession developed a CBS approach it would raise its community image. Further, CBS provides a common ground and a common language for providers, for registering authorities and for the profession:

> they enable the relative roles of the providers and profession to become clearer in a mutually cooperative environment. (Heywood *et al.*, 1992, p. 18)

Purported 'disadvantages' of competency-based standards include:

- produces a levelling down to minimum standards;
- devalues the wider goals of teacher education programmes;
- the emphasis upon standardization and uniformity is a threat to the autonomy of teacher education programmes;
- performance-based approaches have been tried in the past (PBTE in the 1960s) and proved to be a failure;
- in teacher education there can be no absolute levels;
- generic competencies are a fallacy;
- it is undesirable to have a total system-wide, national approach based upon competencies across schools, further education and higher education with one orientation and embedded beliefs and practices.

Some educators argue that CBS approaches are undesirable because they prescribe only 'minimum standards' and therefore discourage empathy, initiative and problem solving ability (Masters and McCurry, 1990).

Lally and Myhill (1994) argue that the goals of many professional courses undertaken at universities (including preservice teacher education) involve scholarly work including:

- fostering student development as a whole person;
- teaching an existing body of knowledge but also creating new forms of that knowledge both in product and process;
- developing students as critical thinkers.

That is, they consider there are much 'wider goals' of university programmes beyond what might be developed using a CBS approach.

Educators have also criticized the CBS approach for its emphasis upon 'standardization and uniformity'. Proponents of CBS (for example Heywood *et al.* (1992), and Thompson (1989)) stress that there is a 'basic format' for all occupations, that competencies must be clearly stated and that programmes should be modularized.

Pusey (1991) refers to the 'locust strike of economic rationalism' that has swept Canberra since 1983. Bartlett (1992) considers that the rationalizations are based on a restrictive, technically-oriented, neoclassical view of economics.

Walker (1994) takes a more moderate stance. He reiterates that the competency-based approaches in the 1960s and early 1970s were failures, based upon the psychology of behaviourism and breaking down a teacher's performance into discrete, observable items of behaviour. However, he contends that there are misconceptions about current CBS approaches. They are more holistic and have a broader, professional approach than the earlier PBTE versions.

Competency Standards for Teaching

In Australia, the National Project on the Quality of Teaching and Learning (NPQTL) over the period 1991–3 has been a noteworthy development. NPQTL was a three year tripartite project with membership drawn from government and non-government school authorities, teacher unions, the Commonwealth and the Australian Council of Trade Unions (ACTU). The NPQTL was concerned about barriers and impediments to improving the quality of teaching and it was considered that the development of national competency standards would greatly assist in alleviating these barriers. In particular, it was asserted that national competency standards could:

- assist teachers to improve their work organization and their workplace performance by encouraging them to reflect critically on their own practice, individually and collaboratively;
- inform professional development to support improvements to teaching;
- boost teachers' self-esteem and their commitment to teaching by enhancing their awareness of the nature of their teaching competence;
- underpin a national approach to improving teacher education programmes, including curriculum and pedagogy;
- underpin a national approach to improving induction programmes in schools and systems;
- possibly form the basis for a nationally consistent approach to registration and probation;
- provide a good basis for communication about the nature of teachers' work and the quality of teaching and learning within the education community and among education interest groups. (After Peacock, 1993, p. 8)

In the first instance the NPQTL concentrated upon the production of national competency standards (NCSs) for beginning teachers, based upon an integrated approach which incorporated performance (set of tasks) and attributes (knowledge, skills and attitudes) into a single framework.

Project teams used expert panels of teachers, critical incident workshops and reference groups of teacher educators to produce 'tasks' and 'attributes'. Five areas of competence were decided upon and for each one, elements, case summaries and indicators of effective practice were produced. The five areas of competence include:

- using and developing professional knowledge and values;
- communicating, interacting and working with students and others;

Table 10.1: *A sample area of competence for beginning teachers*

The Beginning Teacher: At Entry		
Areas of Competence	Elements	Performance Criteria
• Attending, understanding and responding to student development, learning and background	• Student development (physically, intellectually/ cognitively, emotionally, morally, relationally, gender implications) • Student learning (individual differences, stages, styles) • Student background (racial, linguistic, socio-economic, religious, cultural) • Connections with teaching and behaviour management decisions • Self reflection	• Establishes clear, challenging and achievable expectations for all students • Adapts content, resources and activities to suit the learning needs of students • Engages with interest and warmth with all students • Acts equitably to all students • Understands the range of learning and behaviour and social problems students might demonstrate and how to seek advice in handling these

Source: Hughes, 1992, p. 5

- planning and managing the teaching and learning process;
- monitoring and assessing student progress and learning outcomes;
- reflecting, evaluating and planning for continuous improvement.

A sample area is depicted in Table 10.1.

Recent Developments

Some pilot studies recently undertaken on teacher competencies in Australia indicate that they have the potential to provide improved linkages between professional practice and the underlying disciplines. The pilot study undertaken by Preston and Kennedy (1994) for the Working Party on Teacher competencies reveals that the NPQTL competencies do have some potential for preservice teacher education, namely:

- as a common framework for collaboration between university staff, school staff and student teachers;
- as a guide for the organization of school experience — to ensure specific activities are built into the practicum;
- as a framework for student teacher reflection, self assessment and planning;
- as a framework for the assessment of student teachers.

Yet, the authors also issue a number of caveats:

- the language used to describe competencies is not inclusive;
- the competencies represent a particular view of teachers' work and the teaching profession and this view is likely to be contested;
- the competencies focus on beginning teachers rather than on the career needs of a professional;
- the competencies don't address how beginning teachers can best be provided with access to the knowledge base of teaching. (Preston and Kennedy, 1994, p. 5)

A number of Australian universities are currently exploring new approaches to preservice teacher education including a school-based focus (as a consortium with local schools); graduate programmes such as problem-based, Master of Teaching programmes; and competency-based Bachelor of Education programmes. These are likely to continue and expand in number during the 1990s.

These developments in Australia are mirroring major developments in the USA to create teacher standards for preparation and certification and which are being used as a basis for awarding tenure. For example, in Kentucky eight standards have been established, each of which contains eight to fifteen performance criteria (see Table 10.2). First year teachers have to be able to demonstrate competence in these nine areas to gain a permanent teaching position. Similar performance-based standards have been introduced in a number of other states in the USA.

Teaching standards are a major focus in a number of countries in the 1990s and are likely to continue beyond this decade. To a certain extent, the emphasis upon teacher standards and competencies in particular, is part of a wider focus upon micro economic reform and new approaches to work organization. Although the role of a teacher is extremely complex, recent undertakings to provide an integrated competency framework for beginning teachers has potential, even though it needs considerably more refinement.

Reflections and Issues

1 To what extent do you consider that a professional course for teachers must include more than performance-based standards?

2 It is argued that the development of a CBS approach will raise the community's image of teachers. Consider the points for and against this contention.

3 Given that a particular framework of teacher competencies is acceptable, who should be involved in collecting the data?

4 Consider the extent to which disadvantaged groups are not duly recognized in current teacher education programmes. Explain how a CBS approach would improve equity provisions at preservice and inservice levels.

Table 10.2: Examples of new teachers standards in Kentucky, USA

Standard 1 Designs/Plans/Instruction
Performance example: Integrates skills, thinking processes and content across disciplines.

Standard 2 Creates/Maintains learning climates
Performance example: Communicates with and challenges students in a positive and supportive manner.

Standard 3 Implements/Manages instruction
Performance example: Uses appropriate questioning strategies to engage students' cognitive processes and stimulate higher-order thinking.

Standard 4 Assesses and communicates learning results
Performance example: Uses multiple assessments and sources of data.

Standard 5 Reflects/Evaluates teaching/learning
Performance example: Accurately assesses, analyses and communicates the effectiveness of instruction and makes appropriate changes to improve student learning.

Standard 6 Collaborates with colleagues/parents/others
Performance example: Identifies or recognizes situations when and where collaboration with others will enhance learning for students.

Standard 7 Engages in professional development
Performance example: Provides evidence of performance levels and articulates strengths and priorities for growth.

Standard 8 Knowledge of content
Performance example: Accurately communicates the skills and core concepts related to academic areas.

Source: Kentucky Council on New Teacher Standards for Preparation and Certification, 1994

References

BARTLETT, L. (1992) 'Vision and revision: A competency-based scheme for the teaching profession', Paper presented at the Australian Teacher Education Conference, Ballina, NSW.

BURROW, S. (1993) 'National competency standards for the teaching profession: A chance to define the future of schooling or a reaffirmation of the past?', in COLLINS, C. (Ed) *Competencies*, Canberra, ACE.

GONEZI, A., HAGER, P. and OLIVER, L. (1990) *Establishing Competency-based Standards in the Professions*, NOOSR Research Paper no. 1, Canberra, AGPS.

HEYWOOD, L., GONCZI, A. and HAGER, P. (1992) *A Guide to Development of Competency Standards for Professions*, NOOSR Research Paper no. 7, Canberra, AGPS.

KENTUCKY COUNCIL ON NEW TEACHER STANDARDS FOR PREPARATION AND CERTIFICATION (1994) *New Teacher Standards for Preparation and Certification*, Frankfort, Kentucky, Department of Education.

LALLY, M. and MYHILL, M. (1994) *Teaching Quality: The Development of Valid Instruments of Assessment*, Canberra, AGPS.

MASTERS, G.N. and McCURRY, D. (1990) *Competency-based Assessment in the Professions*, NOOSR Research Paper no. 2, Canberra, AGPS.

PEACOCK, D. (1993) 'The development of national competency standards for teaching', *Unicorn*, **19**, 3, pp. 7–12.

PRESTON, B. and KENNEDY, K.J. (1994) 'Models of professional standards for beginning practitioners and their application to initial professional education', Paper presented at the Annual Conference of the Australian Association for Research in Education, Newcastle.

PUSEY, M. (1991) *Economic Rationalism in Canberra: A Nation Building State Changes Its Minds*, Cambridge, Cambridge University Press.

THOMPSON, R. (1989) 'Competency-based training: An industry learning experience', *Asia Pacific HRM*, **27**, 3, pp. 86–90.

WALKER, J. (1994) *Competency-based Teacher Education: Implications for Quality in Higher Education*, Canberra, II R Conference.

11   Collaborative Teacher Planning

Introduction

Lieberman and Miller (1990) lament that 'the greatest tragedy of teaching is that
so much is carried on in self-imposed and professionally sanctioned isolation' (p.
160). Nevertheless, there are growing initiatives and developments with collaborative activities between teachers which are gradually breaking down the traditional
culture of individualism.

Some Definitions

Many definitions of 'collaborative teams' and 'collaborative schools' are exhorta-
tive. For example, schools are collaborative and inclusive when they use diverse
perspectives to frame problems and craft workable solutions — they use cooperative rather than controlling power — vision building and action is used to motivate
and energize others (Anderson and Cox, 1988). Heller (1993) defines a collaborative school as a school which values educational improvement — 'teachers are
encouraged and supported, to engage in positive dialogue about teaching as it
relates to current research and practice' (p. 96). There appears to be implicit in
these definitions a common understanding of terms but is this likely to be the case?
For example, what does it mean to say that teachers should 'work together'? Does
it mean informal interactions or delegated meetings?

Weaver *et al.* (1987) provide the caveat that collaborative work isn't just
doing something with friends — 'collaboration in curriculum development involves
working with friends while cavorting with the enemy' (p. 2). In any collaborative
activity differences of perspective can lead to suspicion and disrespect. As Sarason
(1990) notes, as collaboration gets played out, politics, personalities and financial
constraints may dampen the enthusiasm for collaborative projects.

Young (1989) notes that not all teachers find collaborative activities attractive.
For some teachers, opportunities for cooperative decision-making are unwanted and
rejected. Lortie (1975) has written extensively about this — 'teachers prefer classroom tasks over organisational tasks and classroom claims over organisational
initiations' (p. 164).

Collaborative Approaches

One approach is to use the principle of 'zone of acceptance' (Hoy and Tarter,
1993). There are some school decisions that teachers are not concerned about or are

indifferent about. These might include aspects of financial accounting or head office reporting. Then again there are other decisions about which teachers are most concerned and have a personal stake (relevance), and there are other decisions where teachers have specific expertise and experience and can make a valuable contribution (expertise). According to Hoy and Tarter (1993) it is up to the school principal to ensure that collaborative decision-making occurs with issues relating to teacher relevance and expertise but not for other issues — 'always involving subordinates is as shortsighted as never involving them' (p. 4).

A 'quality system' is an approach developed by Snyder *et al.* (1994). They contend that a school team goes through three stages of growth, namely:

- awareness: learning about new collaborative approaches; setting goals for improvement; emphasizing team activities;
- transition: staff begin to appreciate the interdependence of their activities; achieving success with small projects; exploring different ways to achieve ends;
- transformation: a new belief system about work is shared by all staff; emphasis on student and community needs; common agreement about goals, expectations, collaboration and professional development activities.

Snyder *et al.* (1994) contend that the work culture of schools mature over a period of years and that the quality of collaboration and cohesiveness develops in accordance with the stages of growth described above.

Anderson and Cox (1988, pp. 5–6) propose that developing a collaborative climate within schools can be stimulated by a number of actions which they term 'energizers' namely:

Energiser 1: Harnessing self-interest: encourage staff to go beyond self-interest and to look at the needs of the organization as a whole.

Energiser 2: Compacting tasks: to use larger purposes to find linkages and overlaps in existing activities — to pack more than one meaning into a task — to work smarter.

Energiser 3: Acting for cumulative impact: to assess one's actions for their contribution to the overall goal — each task shouldn't be seen as an end in itself.

Energiser 4: Recasting conflict: looking at multiple perspectives rather than only one right way, allows more energy to be concentrated upon the problem and its solution.

Energiser 5: Enabling communication: to optimize meaning we need to be very careful about the messages we send and how the parts fit the whole.

Energiser 6: Fostering coherence by focusing on the larger meaning: encouraging staff to find the larger connections among things.

Energiser 7: Transforming reactivity to proactivity: the use of cooperative power rather than coercive power spreads responsibility and control among the players.

Energiser 8:   Building knowledge and skills to undergird change: to provide the necessary support and assistance for intended changes.

Energiser 9:   Modelling desired behaviours as the quickest way to produce change: if staff experience collaboration in a positive and useful way they will be likely to consider collaboration in other settings.

Energiser 10:   Creating productive collaboration: is very time consuming but is most likely to succeed when:

- there is trust between partners based on interdependence;
- authentic, two-way communication occurs;
- goals are examined from several perspectives;
- power is used with mutual respect.

Mathews and Hudson (1994) have developed a 'collaborative review of teachers planning' model which enables teaches to see themselves and their work in relation to school plans and broader state and national frameworks. The steps involved include:

- teachers themselves identify and describe the various tasks that make up their daily work;
- self review by teachers is necessary — this may require training so that they can analyse their work objectively;
- classroom observation is undertaken, preferably planned by the group as a whole;
- appraisal discussions occur — focus is on constructive suggestions about work practices;
- plans are made collaboratively with others after thoughtful reflection.

Conditions Necessary for Collaboration

Fullan (1991) strongly supports teacher collaboration and advocates it as an alternative to teacher isolation. He describes learning-enriched schools where staff collaboration is at a high level with shared goals, teacher certainty and teacher commitment (see Figure 11.1).

Fullan and Hargreaves (1991) and others advocate a number of conditions necessary for collaboration to be successful in schools. They include:

- collaboration is linked with norms and with opportunities for continuous improvement;
- interaction sessions are provided whereby teachers develop a greater certainty and sense of efficacy about their teaching (Rosenholtz, 1989);
- opportunities must occur for joint work between teachers such as team teaching, planning, observation, peer coaching (Little, 1990);

Figure 11.1:   Learning enriched schools

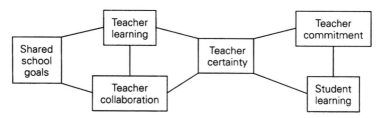

Source: Fullan, 1991, p. 133

- informal, pervasive qualities and attitudes among staff that are based upon support, trust and openness (Nias *et al.*, 1989);
- there is an open and supporting climate to share and discuss failure and uncertainty (Gold and Roth, 1993);
- teachers' purposes are developed and shared with others;
- collaborative cultures respect, celebrate and make allowances for the teacher as a person — the person is not consumed by the group but fulfilled through it (Nias *et al.*, 1989);
- the individual and the group are inherently and simultaneously valued — individuals are valued and so is interdependence;
- the principal plays a major role in enabling and empowering teachers, but not necessarily being the charismatic high flier (Fullan and Hargreaves, 1991);
- many teachers are leaders in fully functioning collaborative schools;
- successful collaborative schools have close working relationships with parents and the wider community.

There are of course 'disadvantages' in developing collaborative arrangements in some schools if they are superficial and likely to fail. Some forms of collaboration which can lead to undesirable outcomes include:

- balkanization: where subcultures develop in a school comprised of competing groups with separate loyalties and identities. This can often occur in high schools between subject departments (Fullan and Hargreaves, 1991);
- superficial collaboration: limited forms of sharing which do not progress beyond advice-giving and material sharing — there are no deeper forms of interaction such as joint planning, observation and experimentation;
- contrived collaboration: can occur when school principals attempt to control or regulate collaboration — although it may be useful as a preliminary phase in establishing more enduring forms of collaboration, there is the danger that they will be perceived by teachers to be additional formal, bureaucratic procedures. Hargreaves and Dawe (1990) contend that these:

collaborative forms of teacher development may in many instances not be empowering teachers towards greater professional independence at all, but incorporating them and their loyalties within processes and structures bureaucratically determined elsewhere. They may be fostering training, not education, instructional closure rather than intellectual openness, dispositional adjustment rather than thoughtful critique. (Hargreaves and Dawe, 1990, pp. 118–9)

Campbell and Southworth (1990) provide additional points about collaborative activities which they perceive to be disadvantages:

- time: teachers in primary schools and principals of small schools have virtually no non-contact time and so collaborative activities can only occur after school;
- reduced roles: some teachers and especially some school principals perceive that collaborative activities reduces their autonomy and reduces their power. Campbell and Southworth (1990) consider that a principal's ego-identification with a school can be greatly affected by collaborative activities and which could in turn produce feelings of losing control, anxiety and conflict for principals. Teachers may also experience anxiety in moving from closed and isolated settings to more open and communal ones;
- capacity of teachers to work in groups: it can be argued that not all teachers accept the assumption that teachers should work together. Further, school structures and policies don't facilitate group activities. Some writers may also be over-optimistic about the extent to which agreement can be reached in collaborative activities (Handy, 1981);
- collaborative activities have been largely recommended by persons outside of schools such as researchers and consultants. There is limited evidence about teachers' views on collaborative activities.

Collaborative Activities and Students

In addition to fostering collaborative activities between teachers there is considerable scope for teachers to embark upon collaborative activities with their respective students. Clark and Moss (1995) highlight some of the contributions that high school students can make in working collaboratively on activities with teachers. Hill and Hill (1990) argue that students should be taught the skills of collaborative learning, group management and organization in primary schools. They contend that there are a number of reasons why collaborative activities are important for students:

- leads to the development of thinking skills and deeper levels of understanding;
- enables students to have more enjoyable experiences, especially in co-operative learning groups;

- provides opportunities for students to develop important leadership and group skills;
- produces more positive attitudes about school, teachers and other students;
- promotes higher levels of self-esteem in students;
- promotes care and respect for others, especially positive peer relationships;
- provides a sense of belonging and identity for students.

Collaborative Activities and Principals

School principals are an important factor in supporting collaborative activities among their staff. Fullan and Hargreaves (1991) counsel principals to resist proprietary claims and attitudes 'which suggest an ownership of the school which is personal rather than collective, imposed rather than earned, and hierarchical rather than democratic' (p. 90). If they are not careful, 'collaboration' among staff becomes 'co-optation'.

Sharing leadership and promoting professional development should be a major target for principals. The effective principal is one who searches out and celebrates examples of teacher leadership. Louis and Miles (1990) suggest the following strategies that a principal can use to foster collaboration among staff:

- power sharing;
- rewards for staff;
- openness, inclusiveness;
- expanding leadership roles;
- patience.

Fullan and Hargreaves (1991) also remind principals that it is perilous to assume that collaboration only takes one form — it can take diverse forms. A fixation on specific kinds of collaboration such as mandatory peer coaching or compulsory team teaching could be counterproductive and disempowering — 'Don't force through one particular approach. Develop awareness of, commitment to, and experience in the general collaborative principle. Commit to the principle, but empower teachers to select from the wide range of practices the ones that suit them best' (p. 94).

Examples

Example 1

The Coalition of Essential Schools is a practical example of collaborative action between teachers, principals and community. The Coalition of Essential Schools was established at Brown University in the USA in 1984 by Theodore Sizer, based

Table 11.1: Coalition of essential schools: Common principles

---

- The school should focus on helping adolescents learn to use their minds well.
- The school's goals should be simple: that each student master a limited number of essential skills and areas of knowledge.
- The school's goals should apply to all students, while the means to these goals will vary as those students themselves vary.
- Teaching and learning should be personalized to the maximum feasible extent. Efforts should be directed toward a goal that no teacher have direct responsibility for more than eighty students.
- The governing practical metaphor of the school should be student-as-worker rather than the more familiar metaphor of teacher-as-deliverer-of-instructional-services.
- Students entering secondary school studies are those who can show competence in language and elementary mathematics. The diploma should be awarded upon a successful final demonstration of mastery for graduation — an 'Exhibition'. As the diploma is awarded when earned, the school's programme proceeds with no strict age grading and with no system of 'credits earned' by 'time spent' in class.
- The tone of the school should explicitly and self-consciously stress values of unanxious expectation of trust, and of decency.
- The principal and teachers should perceive themselves as generalists first and specialists second. Staff should expect multiple obligations and a sense of commitment to the entire school.
- Ultimate administrative and budget targets should include, in addition to total student loads per teacher of eighty or fewer pupils, substantial time for collective planning by teachers, and competitive salaries for staff members.

Source: Sizer, 1984

to a considerable extent upon research into secondary schooling undertaken by Powell, Farrar and Cohen (1985) and Sizer (1984).

A set of Common Principles (see Table 11.1) was the basis for schools joining the coalition. There is no single model. By 1988, fifty schools had joined the Coalition and there are now over 200 schools.

Accounts of Coalition schools (for example, Wasley, 1994) note the need for staff to be committed to the Common Principles — 'the planning for a restructured program takes substantial committing effort and emotional energy. Much planning by a significant number of the staff during summer months and during the academic year are necessary, and both time and arrangements for daily or at least weekly meetings of the key faculty are essential' (Sizer, 1989, p. 4).

Wasley (1994) undertook case studies of Coalition teachers over a four year period during which time she made frequent visits to classrooms and involved teachers in reflecting upon their work. She noted that these collaborating teachers shared some distinct characteristics which were quite different from practitioners working in conventional schools (see Table 11.2).

Example 2

In Australia, the National Schools Network (NSN) emerged as a result of collaborative research undertaken by state education systems, teacher unions and the

Table 11.2: Emerging characteristics of collaborating teachers in Coalition Schools

---

- Students move to the centre of the learning activity.
- Teachers understand that activities, problem solving, and/or projects provide students with worthwhile intellectual work and compelling experiences.
- Teachers are diagnosticians of individual student's intellectual development and skill.
- Teachers select from a wide range of instructional techniques and are constantly expanding their instructional repertoire.
- Teachers accept uncertainty as central to the learning process, both for themselves and for their students.
- Teachers understand the school has to connect the interests of students, teachers, and the local community, and that they are primarily responsible for providing the connections.
- Teachers discover that curriculum, pedagogy, and assessment are planned and reshaped simultaneously.
- Teachers move from a focus on coverage of curriculum to a focus on depth of students' understanding.
- Teachers use student performance as a guide to their own efficacy.
- Teachers are unwilling to work alone because of the personal limitations placed on them.
- Teachers are able to be a critical friend to others and to benefit from the feedback of others.
- Teachers have significant responsibility for making decisions that affect the school and accept that responsibility.
- Teachers have a philosophy and a set of ideas, which they share in common with their colleagues, that guide their work. They know why they are doing what they are doing.
- Teachers accept new responsibilities (new, closer relations with parents) and forfeit old freedoms (the ability to close one's classroom doors).
- Teachers examine school practices and structures *vis-à-vis* their goals for students and change those that aren't synchronized.
- Teachers share responsibility and leadership with their administrators and their teaching colleagues.
- Teachers see change as productive and essential to learning rather than criticism, and seek it out.
- Teachers understand that change for themselves means change for others and work to facilitate that.
- Teachers know their students and their families very well: what they like, what they do in their spare time, what they hope for.

Source: Wasley, 1994, pp. 205–6

Federal government. An overriding focus is for NSN schools to use collaborative approaches to produce work organization reforms (Ladwig *et al.*, 1994). The NSN schools (over 500 in total) have agreed to accept and develop essential principles, which are clearly based upon the Common Principles of the Coalition Schools and these are listed in Table 11.3.

The progress to date for many of these NSN schools has been most encouraging. Groundwater-Smith *et al.* (1994) analysed the committed partnerships undertaken by many teachers, a striving to develop working relationships which permitted risk taking; a tolerance for ambiguity, uncertainty and dilemmas. Wallace and Wildy (1995) have undertaken case studies of NSN schools. They concluded that 'there is little doubt that the NSN has provided a catalyst for school-based thinking, discussion and activities around teaching and learning' (p. 14).

Table 11.3: Principles of the National Schools Network

• Acceptance that the school has the primary responsibility for improving learning outcomes for students.
• A commitment to greater participation of students in the learning process.
• A willingness to examine current work organization in order to identify good practice and impediments to effective teaching.
• A willingness to develop and model participative workplace procedures. This will require:

    * an agreement by the principal and the school community to develop forms of work organization designed to improve student learning outcomes;
    * participation of all staff and the community in the development of objectives of the school and how they are achieved;
    * collaborative problem solving amongst staff; monitoring by staff of progress towards the achievement of objectives, and
    * evaluation of the outcomes as an essential tool for review and redesign.

• An understanding that those in the school will be involved in negotiating goals and objectives, developing strategies to carry out the work, monitoring progress, modifying strategies and evaluating outcomes.
• An understanding and acceptance of the industrial rights and responsibilities of all parties.

Source: Burrow, 1994, p. 7

Reflections and Issues

1 'To work collaboratively and effectively as partners takes both time and commitment. Institutional culture is a powerful agent in keeping teachers apart.' (Groundwater-Smith, 1992)

    Explain why it is that teachers typically operate independently. Give examples of activities which facilitate the process of staff working collaboratively.

2 'Taking small steps, while easier to take in the beginning, are in the long run riskier than bold steps; incremental changes that do not address the fundamental problems get in the way of powerful student learning and simply put off the day of reckoning.' (Sizer, 1989)

    Explain using examples from schools with which you have been associated.

3 'Reculturing the school to create collaborative cultures among teachers and with the wider community is needed. It creates a climate of trust in which teachers can pool resources, deal with complex and unanticipated problems, and celebrate successes. Collaboration also furthers the development of a common professional language, so that teachers can resist the pervasive business vocabulary of quality control and performance targets that is now consuming education.' (Hargreaves, 1995, p. 186)

    Discuss.

4 'It is assumed that improvement in teaching is a collective rather than an individual enterprise, and that analysis, evaluation and experimentation in concert

with colleagues are conditions under which teachers improve.' (Rosenholtz, 1989)

Is this an ideal or actual practice? Take a stance on this assertion, using examples to support your case.

5 Although there are many examples of successful collaborative efforts in schools, many seem to falter after initial enthusiasm.

What are the reasons why some schools cannot maintain their initial momentum? How can these problems be overcome?

6 'Collaborative cultures are highly sophisticated. They cannot be created overnight. Many forms of collegiality are superficial, partial and even counter productive. It is not possible to have strong collaborative cultures without strong individual development. We must avoid crushing individuality in the drive to eliminate individualism.' (Fullan and Hargreaves, 1991, p. 61)

Explain why collaboration and individual development is needed. Describe activities that can be used to foster their development.

7 'Collaborative cultures are difficult to pin down in time and space, living as they do mainly in the interstices of school life. Collaborative cultures are also unpredictable in their consequences.' (Sparkes and Bloomer, 1994, p. 176)

Do you agree? Give examples from schools with which you have been associated.

References

ANDERSON, B.L. and COX, P.L. (1988) *Configuring the Education System for a Shared Future: Collaborative Vision, Action, Reflection,* Andover, MA, Regional Laboratory for Educational Improvement of the Northeast and Islands.

BURROW, S. (1994) 'Research and development as an essential work practice for teachers', *Australian Journal of Teacher Education,* **19**, 1, pp. 4–8.

CAMPBELL, P. and SOUTHWORTH, G. (1990) 'Rethinking collegiality: Teachers' views', Paper presented at the Annual Conference of the American Educational Research Association, Boston.

CLARK, C.T. and MOSS, P.A. (1995) 'Researching with: Ethical and epistemological implications of doing collaborative change-oriented research with teachers and students', Paper presented at the Annual Conference of the American Educational Research Association, San Francisco.

FULLAN, M.G. (1991) *The New Meaning of Educational Change,* London, Cassell.

FULLAN, M.G. and HARGREAVES, A. (1991) *Working Together for Your School,* Melbourne, ACEA.

GOLD, Y. and ROTH, R.A. (1993) *Teachers Managing Stress and Preventing Burnout,* London, Falmer Press.

GROUNDWATER-SMITH, S. (1992) 'Partnership in the professional development of teachers: Towards intercultural understanding', Paper presented at the Annual Conference of the Australian Association for Research in Education, Geelong.

GROUNDWATER-SMITH, S., PARKER, J. and ARTHUR, M. (1994) 'Partnership: Beyond consultation', *Australian Journal of Teacher Education*, **19**, 1, pp. 9–14.

HANDY, C. (1981) *Understanding Organisations*, London, Penguin.

HARGREAVES, A. (1995) *Changing Teachers, Changing Times*, London, Cassell.

HARGREAVES, A. and DAWE, R. (1990) 'Paths of professional development: Contrived collegiality, collaborative culture and the case of peer coaching', *Teaching and Teacher Education*, **6**, 3, pp. 227–41.

HELLER, G.S. (1993) 'Teacher empowerment, sharing the challenge: A guide for implementation and success', *NASSP Bulletin*, **77**, 550, pp. 94–1034.

HILL, S. and HILL, T. (1990) *The Collaborative Classroom*, Melbourne, Eleanor Curtain.

HOY, W.K. and TARTER, C.J. (1993) 'A normative theory of participative decision making in schools', *Journal of Educational Administration*, **31**, 3, pp. 4–19.

LADWIG, J.G., CURRIE, J. and CHADBOURNE, R. (1994) *Toward Rethinking Australian Schools*, Sydney, National Schools Network.

LIEBERMAN, A. and MILLER, L. (1990) 'The social realities of teaching', in LIEBERMAN, A. (Ed) *Schools as Collaborative cultures: Creating the Future Now*, London, Falmer Press.

LITTLE, J.W. (1990) 'The persistence of privacy: Autonomy and initiative in teachers' professional relations', *Teachers College Record*, **91**, 4, pp. 509–36.

LORTIE, D.C. (1975) *Schoolteacher: A Sociological Study*, Chicago, University of Chicago Press.

LOUIS, K. and MILES, M.B. (1990) *Improving the Urban High School: What Works and Why*, New York, Teachers College Press.

MATHEWS, C. and HUDSON, M. (1994) 'Teachers' own learning', *EQ Australia*, **1**, Autumn, pp. 22–4.

NIAS, J., SOUTHWORTH, G. and YEOMANS, R. (1989) *Staff Relationships in the Primary School*, London, Cassell.

POWELL, A., FARRAR, E. and COHEN, D. (1985) *The Shopping Mall High School*, Boston, Houghton Mifflin.

ROSENHOLTZ, S. (1989) *Teachers' Workplace: The Social Organisation of Schools*, New York, Longman.

SARASON, S.B. (1990) *The Predictable Failure of Educational Reform*, San Francisco, Jossey Bass.

SIZER, T. (1984) *Horace's Compromise: The Dilemma of the American High School*, Boston, Houghton Mifflin.

SIZER, T. (1989) 'Diverse practice, shared ideas: The essential school', in WALBERG, H. and LANE, J.J. (Eds) *Organising for Learning: Toward the 21st Century*, Reston, VA, National Association of Secondary School Principals.

SNYDER, K.J., ACKER-HOCEVAR, M. and SNYDER, K.M. (1994) 'Organisational development in transition: The schooling perspective', Paper presented at the Annual Conference of the American Educational Research Association, New Orleans.

SPARKES, A.C. and BLOOMER, M. (1994) 'Teaching cultures and school-based management: Towards a collaborative reconstruction', in SMYTH, J. (Ed) *A Socially Critical View of the Self-Managing School*, London, Falmer Press.

WALLACE, J. and WILDY, H. (1995) 'Shifting into top gear: Restructuring classrooms over the long haul', Paper presented at the Annual Conference of the American Educational Research Association, San Francisco.

WASLEY, P.A. (1994) *Stirring the Chalkdust*, New York, Teachers College Press.

WEAVER, R.A., KOESTER, R.J. and MCINTOSH, D. (1987) 'Collaboration in curriculum development: A case study', Paper presented at the Annual Conference of the American Educational Research Association, Washington, DC.

YOUNG, J.H. (1989) 'Teacher interest in curriculum committees', *Journal of Curriculum Studies*, **21**, 4, pp. 363–76.

12   Teacher Appraisal

Introduction

'Appraisal' is part of the everyday life of a school. Teachers appraise students for a number of reasons and do so informally through observations and conversations, and formally by the use of various written tests. Teachers form views about each other, based largely upon informal happenings. 'Teacher appraisal' is more formalized and systematic and, in fact, it is often defined as 'a systematic and overt appraisal of the work of teachers' (Thomas, 1988, p. 21).

Meanings of the Term

How persons define teacher appraisal will depend on their attitudes and values. Parents at local social events often swap war stories about 'good' and 'bad' teachers.

In private industry and increasingly in the public service, 'performance appraisal' activities are commonly undertaken (see also Chapter 10). These involve managers and staff in planning particular targets. Criteria are used to judge levels of performance of staff in achieving, or working toward these targets. In these situations the targets are clearly defined and so the measurement of achievement or not is usually easily prescribed. Wragg (1987) argues that an interpolation of 'performance appraisal' to teaching is very problematic because do we really know what effective teaching is and can we recognize it when we see it?

Bell (1988) argues that teachers attach different meanings to staff appraisal, namely:

- to identify incompetent teachers;
- to improve pay and promotion;
- to provide external accountability;
- to improve teacher performance;
- to provide effective management of teachers;
- to provide professional development.

The weeding out of incompetent teachers is of course a less than helpful reason for implementing teacher appraisals but it is cited regularly in education documents, and given great prominence in the media. A more positive meaning is to link appraisal to improving pay and promotion. This approach to appraisal is promoted by Ingvarson and Chadbourne (1994) in terms of a career development model.

Teacher appraisal is frequently cited as a requirement to provide accountability to a range of external parties, especially parents and employers. This point of view seems to indicate that there is considerable room for improvement within the teaching profession — there are deficits to be overcome. School councils could be appropriate groups to initiate these accountability measures. It is also argued that teacher appraisal schemes are a powerful way of motivating teachers to perform better. Again this appears to be based on a deficit model that teachers need assistance in refining their strengths and overcoming their weaknesses. Another view is that teacher appraisal is needed because management in schools by principals, deputy-principals and senior teachers relies on effective deployment of staff — they need to know more about the skills and competencies and individual teachers. A less threatening view of teacher appraisal is to perceive it as a basis for professional development. Systematic assessment of each teacher's performance provides the information needed for designing appropriate staff development activities. It provides for professional enhancement because it pinpoints areas where a teacher can obtain specific inservice or related assistance. Some would argue that this is *the* major meaning that should be attributable to teacher appraisal — it would increase job satisfaction and benefit the school as a whole.

This preliminary analysis of meanings of teacher appraisal reveals that it is a very slippery term! Depending upon how the term is interpreted there is likely to be opposition and rejection or support. The degree of support or opposition is also dependent upon the historical contexts and these matters are explored in the next section.

Teacher Appraisal Developments

United Kingdom

In the UK, the Education Act of 1986 enabled local education authorities to consider teacher appraisal schemes for their respective schools. In due course, various pilot schemes were introduced during the period 1987–9, centred upon six LEAs.

According to Bennett (1992) the pilot schemes were influenced by two conflicting models — a control model and a staff development model. The control model had its antecedents in the 'Great Debate' era of the 1970s with the emphasis upon efficient and effective use of resources and parent-power, governor-power and national intervention. The staff development model can be traced to the James Report (James, 1972) and its emphasis upon the inservice needs of teachers, the prioritizing of these needs and the provision of appropriate resources to service them.

The directors of the pilot schemes, coordinated under the School Teacher Appraisal Pilot Study, eventually accepted the staff development model as the basis for their activities, after some initial disagreements. Each of the pilot schemes trialed procedures involving teacher self-appraisals and designed targets to improve performance. Subsequently the Education Regulations for School Teacher Appraisal were passed by parliament in mid-1991 and by 1995 the phased in requirement applied to all teachers.

The Education Regulations unfortunately contain regulations that could be used as threats against teachers. As a consequence, they have distorted any professional growth process which could have been possible under a truly staff development model. Bennett's (1992) reminder is timely.

> Appraisal systems which seek to control the professional will fail to do so in exactly the same way. We all know the teachers who can do the job, but who have lost the commitment. Will control by appraisal work for them? . . . Should we, therefore sacrifice the potential for staff development in an appraisal scheme to try to bring these teachers into line? (Bennett, 1992, p. 5)

USA

In the USA there was a rapid move toward teacher appraisal (termed teacher evaluation) in the 1980s, largely as a result of a National Commission on Excellence in Education. Most states took urgent action to implement schemes to evaluate teachers' basic educational competencies and pedagogical performance (Wells, 1989).

In keeping with USA educators' penchant for testing, it is not surprising that the schemes have largely depended upon assessment instruments to measure teacher performance. Most states have introduced legislation requiring assessment of all beginning teachers and in some cases for principals, superintendents and continuing teachers. The assessment instruments tend to be standardized tests which either are low inference (relatively objective counts of behaviours) such as direct instruction behaviours or are high inference (more subjective, professional judgments) ones dealing with descriptions of classroom behaviour. For example, the Georgia Teacher Performance Assessment Instrument requires an assessor to visit a classroom and to make yes–no decisions on a range of areas. Six assessments are made on each teacher (two assessments each from an external assessor, a peer and an administrator) and the results are pooled. To get a pass, a teacher must obtain a score of at least 75 on each competency (Tobin, 1989).

In some states in the USA students' results on standardized tests have been used to evaluate teaching and to cause some merit pay arrangements to be made (mainly in wealthy districts which can afford to pay merit increments above and beyond the salary schedule). In other states, career ladders were initiated in the 1980s. This involves breaking up the different 'jobs' of teaching, ranking them and paying teachers based upon the proportion of complex jobs they do. Supposedly this enables a relatively objective assessment of teaching and a teacher is paid more if he/she undertakes tasks more complex or important than others (Conley, 1994). Yet, it might be argued that it places considerable restrictions on what teachers do and generally deprofessionalizes teaching.

In Australia, teacher appraisal is evolving on a number of fronts but is still embryonic in terms of major developments. During the 1980s and 1990s the major players have been very concerned with reforming education in terms of economic needs. In terms of teacher appraisal, award restructuring initiatives in education led to the widespread adoption of the Advanced Skills Teacher (AST) classification as a new career path for teachers but it became yet another automatic layer in most states with little change to career opportunities.

Apart from position papers on teacher quality developed by national agencies such as the National Board of Employment, Education and Training's (NBEET) Schools Council (1989) a major initiative was the establishing of the National Project on the Quality of Teaching and Learning (NPQTL) in 1990, involving representatives of Federal and State Governments, employers and teacher unions. As one of its tasks, NPQTL focused upon standards of teacher education and entry to the professional, especially the potential of using a competency-based framework for teachers (see also Chapter 10). Meanwhile at state and territory education system levels a variety of teacher appraisal schemes are occurring, mainly focused upon assessing newly appointed teachers after their probationary period, appraising of school principals as part of fixed term contracts in some states, and numerous school-initiated appraisal schemes.

As noted by McRae (1994) teacher appraisal is developing on many fronts in Australia and is very much on the agenda of education groups. A number of local experiments and trials are occurring but as yet, there are no major pushes from national or state entities.

To answer the question why do teacher appraisals, the ultimate answer is of course to improve the education of all students but to get to this end, it is important to note that groups have very different priorities about why teacher appraisals are necessary. As depicted in Table 12.1, the basic questions asked will depend upon how close the person is to the classroom and the extent to which they are accountable to external groups. For example, the classroom teacher will want feedback about his/her efficacy with a group of students. The information needed will be specific, highly localized and to be used by the teacher for modifying future classroom actions.

By contrast the questions asked by the school principal and the school council chairperson relate to the overall school policies, who is contributing and to what extent, and who needs assistance and why (see Table 12.1). Senior officials of the education system have wider accountability priorities and are concerned especially about the documentation and distribution of plans to all the stakeholders (especially parents) and especially the extent to which school programmes reflect government policies. However, despite the different priorities between groups it would appear that there is considerable consensus over some of the key reasons for undertaking teacher appraisal. These can be summarized below.

Table 12.1: *Three perspectives on teacher appraisal*

Questions for the individual teacher	Questions for the school principal or council	Questions for the education system
1 What should I be doing?	1 Are teaching tasks being carried out? How well? What needs changing?	1 Are schools reviewing their policies and curriculum to ensure they are relevant?
2 How am I doing?	2 Which teachers are performing well? Who needs additional support? Who needs professional development? Who should be rewarded? Who is incompetent? What solutions are possible?	2 Are specific details of school plans made available to parents and the community?
3 What am I doing well?	3 Are school's policies being implemented? How are they delegated, coordinated?	3 Do school programmes reflect government priorities?
4 What can I do better?		4 Are teachers effective in undertaking their duties?
5 Who do I go to for assistance?		
6 How can the school support what I am trying to do?		

Why Do Teacher Appraisals?

- knowing ourselves: teachers need to obtain feedback about what they are actually doing compared with what they think they are doing;
- curriculum planning: part of the curriculum planning cycle must include evaluation and appraisal. The appraisal component provides a powerful incentive to undertake thorough planning;
- general school planning: for schools to be involved in sound decision-making they need to have in-school appraisal schemes to decide which policies and activities are worthwhile;
- professional development: appraisal provides a teacher with feedback so that he/she can develop professionally — adjusting, improving, keeping abreast of new ideas. It can help to identify specific in-service needs;
- claim for resources: to justify claims we might make for resources, administrators almost invariably require appraisals of how teachers use the resources;

- accountability: the community and parents in particular want more details and evidence that schools and teachers are accomplishing what they profess they are doing. This can also involve removing incompetent teachers.

What Should Be Appraised?

Teacher appraisals typically focus upon:

- behaviour of the teacher: detailed observations of what a teacher does in the classroom and in related settings;
- behaviour of the teacher working with colleagues and in teams: observing the context of the school and how the procedures enhance or limit a teacher's actions;
- behaviours and experiences of students: the activities they are engaged in, their interactions with each other and with the teacher;
- outcomes of students: details obtained from informal (for example, observations) and formal (for example, written tests) techniques.

Who Should Appraise?

- peer appraisal: for example by pairs of teachers of equal rank or seniority;
- superior–subordinate appraisal: typically by principals/heads appraising their teachers;
- outsider appraisal: for example, by teachers or principals from another school, or by specialist evaluators;
- appraisal by lay people: for example, by school council members or governors;
- self-appraisal: this can be undertaken by the use of checklists and self reports.

There is also the matter of deciding whether appraisals should be 'closed' (people being appraised do not see any written report or grade) or 'open' (people being appraised do see any reports) (Wragg, 1987).

Criteria Used in an Appraisal

- methods for appraising teachers have to be based upon specific criteria or qualities. There is no unequivocal research evidence on what 'effective teaching' really means;
- it is possible to list important qualities of effective teachers such as subject knowledge, empathy, communication skills, but it is not possible to produce a definitive list of priorities which should apply to all teachers;

- 'job descriptions' for teachers working in particular schools are an important first step for appraisers and appraisees. They provide the criteria for any subsequent appraisals and can be readily understood by all parties. As a minimum, each job description should include components relating to 'planning, interactive' and 'review' phases of teaching.

Methods of Appraisal

Dependent upon the appraisal approach and the particular priorities, a number of methods can be of value. However many involve considerable resources in terms of time and money and therefore decisions about appropriate methodology need to be weighed up very carefully.

- classroom observation: using open-ended descriptions or checklists;
- sitting in: observing other activities such as interviewing parents, task force meetings;
- interviews: open-ended or structured; two-way to allow interviewee to ask questions;
- analysis of work-samples: viewing notebooks, records of work;
- self-appraisal forms: structured or open-ended;
- assessment of students: analyse student results in key subjects;
- questionnaire completed by the person being appraised;
- student feedback: using total class discussions, small groups, or questionnaire;
- teacher portfolios.

Self-appraisal

- ideally, all teachers should be committed to self-monitoring their teaching and the consequences of their actions;
- various checklists are available which serve as a framework for reflection (see Figure 12.1);
- self-appraisal reflections need to be carried out regularly and systematically if they are to be of any value. Teachers must be committed to act upon deficiencies they discover from such reflections;
- self-appraisal enables teachers to become empowered, to develop their self-motivation and creativity and yet to maintain their trust and dignity (see Chapter 9).

Aftercare

- if appraisal is to be credible then a carefully planned series of events must occur after appraisals have been undertaken and processed;

Figure 12.1: An example of a self-appraisal checklist

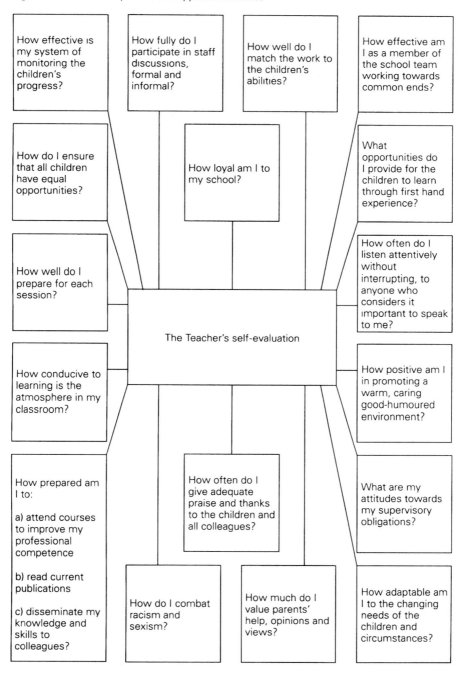

How effective is my system of monitoring the children's progress?

How fully do I participate in staff discussions, formal and informal?

How well do I match the work to the children's abilities?

How effective am I as a member of the school team working towards common ends?

How do I ensure that all children have equal opportunities?

How loyal am I to my school?

What opportunities do I provide for the children to learn through first hand experience?

How well do I prepare for each session?

How often do I listen attentively without interrupting, to anyone who considers it important to speak to me?

The Teacher's self-evaluation

How conducive to learning is the atmosphere in my classroom?

How positive am I in promoting a warm, caring good-humoured environment?

How prepared am I to:

a) attend courses to improve my professional competence

b) read current publications

c) disseminate my knowledge and skills to colleagues?

How often do I give adequate praise and thanks to the children and all colleagues?

What are my attitudes towards my supervisory obligations?

How do I combat racism and sexism?

How much do I value parents' help, opinions and views?

How adaptable am I to the changing needs of the children and circumstances?

Source: Whitaker and Wren, 1987

- teacher appraisals should be able to pinpoint teachers in need of professional development. Carefully planned professional development activities (for example, workshops, seminars) need to be scheduled;
- there may be a need for follow-up support for individual teachers in the form of regular visits, informal or formal discussions;
- considerable resources may be needed to provide the level of support required.

Reflections and Issues

1 'It must be recognized that the process of appraisal will involve a shift in perceptions, roles and activities. It will mean that private assumptions and practices must be shared with, and opened up for questioning by, others . . . Thus the process of appraisal is unlikely to be comfortable — even where extensive negotiations have taken place, contracts have been made and forms of confidentiality ensured.' (Day, Whitaker and Wren, 1987, p. 19)

   What are the benefits of doing appraisals if the problems loom so large? Can any of the problems be minimized?

2 If properly conducted, teacher-appraisal procedures can be in the interests of many individual teachers, students, parents and education authorities.

   In your experience can there be positive effects of teacher appraisals?

3 'An appraisal procedure will have value only if it appraises aspects of the teacher's performance and competence which there is reason to believe tend to result in favourable pupil outcomes of a specified kind.' (Byrne, 1987, p. 40)

   Can we make sound judgments about what is valid data? If not, what are some alternative solutions?

4 'Schemes for teacher appraisal, written in the language of business (for example, performance indicators), implemented in traditionally hierarchical contexts, without the necessary accompaniment of experienced process facilitators, stand little chance of succeeding.' (Hall, 1990, p. 66)

   Does this quotation mirror your experiences with teacher appraisal schemes? Are there any advantages in having such unilateral initiatives? How feasible is it to introduce a scheme using process facilitators?

5 'Opposition from teachers and unions about systems of teacher appraisal in the UK are fundamental issues about power.' (Elliott, 1989)

   Is it of concern about how the central government is legitimating teacher appraisal? Is it a wider concern about power at work in educational systems? What can teachers do to ensure that the positive elements of appraisal can be retained without accepting the coercive, standardizing elements?

6 'The teaching profession is more than most professions subject to the control and powers of intervention exercised by others.' (Adams and Tulasiewicz, 1995, p. 63)

To what extent is this due to appraisal schemes established by outsiders and superordinates.

7 'Although teacher appraisal panels espouse preferences for collaborative leadership styles they tend, in practice, to prefer forthright, aggressive leadership styles.' (Milligan, 1994)

Do you have evidence to support or refute this claim? Are there significant complications for the female teachers?

8 'Teacher portfolios are becoming an important source for appraising teachers but if they are to be used they must have a standard, the contents need to be clearly identified, the scoring criteria need to be specified in detail, and all who work with the portfolio need to understand the nature of the portfolio.' (Scriven, 1995, p. 17)

References

ADAMS, A. and TULASIEWICZ, W. (1995) *The Crisis in Teacher Education: A European Concern?*, London, Falmer Press.

BELL, L. (1988) (Ed) *Appraising Teachers in Schools*, London, Routledge.

BENNETT, H. (1992) *Teacher Appraisal: Survival and Beyond*, London, Longman.

BYRNE, C. (1987) 'Can teachers be validly appraised?', in BUNNELL, S. (Ed) *Teacher Appraisal in Practice*, London, Heinemann Educational.

CONLEY, S. (1994) 'Teacher pay systems', in INGVARSON, L. and CHADBOURNE, R. (Eds) *Valuing Teachers' Work: New Directions in Teacher Appraisal*, Melbourne, ACER.

DAY, C., WHITAKER, P. and WREN, D. (1987) *Appraisal and Professional Development in the Primary School*, Milton Keynes, Open University Press.

ELLIOTT, J. (1989) 'Knowledge, power and teacher appraisal', in CARR, W. (Ed) *Quality and Teaching*, London, Falmer Press.

HALL, S.H. (1990) 'Accounting for teachers' work: The need for a multifaceted approach', *Curriculum Perspectives*, **10**, 4, pp. 63–8.

INGVARSON, L. and CHADBOURNE, R. (1994) (Eds) *Valuing Teachers' Work: New Directions in Teacher Appraisal*, Melbourne, ACER.

JAMES, E.J.F. (Chairperson) (1972) *Teacher Education and Training*, London, HMSO.

McRAE, D. (1994) 'The place of appraisal in education reform', in INGVARSON, L. and CHADBOURNE, R. (Eds) *Valuing Teachers' Work: New Directions in Teacher Appraisal*, Melbourne, ACER.

MILLIGAN, S. (1994) *Women in the Teaching Profession*, Canberra, NBEET.

SCRIVEN, M. (1995) 'Fundamental problems with personnel evaluation in the professions', Paper presented at the Annual Conference of the American Educational Research Association, San Francisco.

THOMAS, N. (1988) 'The appraisal of teachers', in BELL, L. (Ed) *Appraising Teachers in Schools*, London, Routledge, Chapman and Hall.

TOBIN, K. (1989) 'Teacher assessment systems: A personal view', in LOKAN, J. and McKENZIE, P. (Eds) *Teacher Appraisal: Issues and Approaches,* Melbourne, ACER.

WELLS, P. (1989) 'Policy developments in the United States of America', in LOKAN, J. and McKENZIE, P. (Eds) *Teacher Appraisal: Issues and Approaches*, Melbourne, ACER.

WRAGG, E.C. (1987) *Teacher Appraisal: A Practical Guide*, London, Macmillan Education.

13 Multicultural Education and Inclusive Curriculum

Introduction

Over the centuries an accepted policy was that people coming to a new country would, after an initial adjustment period, become assimilated or integrated with the local population. A more realistic policy is multiculturalism whereby diversity of cultural groups coexist and have a shared commitment to a country.

There are important implications for a school curriculum if it is to reflect multicultural practices. These curricula need to establish wider goals and pursue knowledge, skills and attitudes which are relevant to diverse cultural groups.

Some Definitions

A 'multicultural society' is one in which a variety of different cultural groups co-exist harmoniously, free to maintain their distinctive religious, linguistic or social customs, equal as individuals in their access to resources and services appropriate to them and their needs, to civil and political rights, and sharing with the rest of society particular concerns and values (National Advisory and Coordinating Committee on Multicultural Education, 1987). That is, some of the major elements include:

- existence of diversity;
- valuing of cultural diversity;
- a sharing and interaction with other groups;
- equality of access to resources;
- shared commitment to the nation.

Preston (1991) makes the distinction between education *in* a multicultural society/education which empowers children from a non-English speaking background and which gives due recognition to their cultural identity/and education *for* a multicultural society (education which develops intercultural understanding in all children and combats negative attitudes in the form of racism and group prejudice).

Bullard (1992) asserts that there is plenty of rhetoric about multicultural education but plenty of disagreement about the goals. She cites the following examples and asks whether it should be:

- to promote understanding of and sensitivity to other cultures;
- to advance academic achievement of minorities;
- to model a multicultural society where every group shares equal power;
- to offer a radical critique of western culture;
- to provide intensive studies of single ethnic groups;
- to train students in social action skills.

'Culture' consists of shared meanings: a frame of reference for action. It can be described as:

- a system of rules of action or statements which indicate the range of behaviour that is considered acceptable (Preston, 1991);
- a social construction;
- a situation where participants are nurtured and develop;
- providing a means of communication.

'Ethnicity' is a feeling of identification or belonging to a particular culture. In particular:

- it indicates a sense of peoplehood or group identity;
- it is reinforced and strengthened by association with others sharing the same background (Preston, 1991);
- members of an ethnic group share a common historical heritage. (Anderson and Cushner, 1994)

An 'inclusive curriculum' is one which enables all students to participate equally. Some characteristics include:

- interdependence is valued as well as dependence;
- underlying values are acceptance, belonging and community (Pearpoint and Forrest, 1992);
- there is a focusing on the special gifts and needs of each and every student in the school community to feel welcomed and secure and to become successful. (Villa and Thousand, 1995)

In the USA the term 'inclusive classrooms' refers especially to classrooms where all students (including those with disabilities) participate and interact — students with disabilities are integrated into mainstream classes.

Classroom Approaches

Multicultural education is important for all students and not just for those schools where there are students from various ethnic backgrounds. Typically, units of study are organized as:

- units within courses;
- separate courses;
- integrated courses.

Specific units are highly focused on multicultural education issues such as 'migration patterns'. Separate courses on multicultural education are sometimes included in a programme by groups of enthusiastic teachers but they are difficult to justify with all the other pressures on the school timetable. Integrated courses are those where a multicultural perspective is incorporated across most subject areas such as maths, science, art, music and literature.

It is also possible to categorize approaches in terms of a major focus, such as:

- cultural understanding;
- ethnic studies;
- a multicultural perspective;
- anti-racist teaching;
- intercultural studies.

A common approach is to focus upon 'cultural understanding'. The purpose of this approach is for teachers to acquaint students with an understanding of culture and to value cultural difference. However this can be very difficult in practice when students and teachers have very different cultural codes. As noted by Eckermann (1994), in the case of the minority child there is often conflict between home and school values. Teachers often have been socialized into stereotyping students and these attitudes are difficult to change.

When the focus is upon 'ethnic studies' attention is paid to a particular culture, examining such aspects as language and literature, history and geography. It can be a very effective approach when there is a high proportion of students from the one culture in the classroom or within the school community.

A 'multicultural' focus is to ensure that existing topics do not have an ethnocentric bias. This can often require protracted sessions by the teacher to talk through opinions and views that are clearly ethnocentric but may not be recognized as such.

'Anti-racist' teaching requires in-depth analyses of inequalities which exist in society and the levels of discrimination that can occur. Brandt (1986) refers to the power structures in society that can promote racism, in terms of political, social and cultural values and how difficult these are for teachers to counteract in their teaching.

'Intercultural' teaching involves focusing upon the feelings and experiences of diverse cultural groups. Within the classroom inclusive activities are initiated by the teacher to achieve a sense of belonging and to enable students to accept and integrate various cultures, languages and experiences.

Teaching Strategies

Clearly cognitive and affective strategies are useful in multicultural education. Preston (1991) argues that cognitive skills are important in terms of:

- identifying similarities and differences;
- predicting;
- distinguishing facts from opinions;
- formulating questions and assessing authenticity, accuracy and worth of knowledge;
- evaluating and testing opinions.

Affective strategies are also very important, especially experience-centred teaching materials which lead students to reflect and think and feel about issues. Simulations are an extremely powerful tool for providing students with experiences similar to those encountered when a person moves into another culture (for example, Bafa-Bafa) or to explore interactions and confrontations associated with power and differences in socio-economic status (for example, Starpower). In the case of Bafa-Bafa, participants struggle to develop skills in verbal and non-verbal communication and experience the alienation and discomfort of culture shock. In Starpower, participants engage in trading experiences but soon find that power produces abuses of power.

Cooperative group learning activities are also an important tool because they promote:

- positive goal interdependence: members of the group are accountable to one another;
- face-to-face interaction: students interact with one another as they attempt to complete a given task;
- individual accountability: each student must achieve the objectives of specific lessons;
- development of social skills: students have to learn to work together;
- group processing: each member is aware of the extent to which his/her actions contribute or detract from the group activities.

A number of books (fiction and nonfiction) can be used to illustrate major concepts and issues relating to a multicultural approach. They are often very stimulating for students and can provide an important link between subject areas. For example, *Animal Farm* is useful for presenting concepts about prejudice, stereotyping, individual identity, and group conformity.

Books, documents and curriculum sets are widely available on a range of topics. However, it is important to note that most have various biases. Teachers and students need to be able to recognize stereotypes; they need to be watchful for highly loaded words; it is necessary to distinguish between verifiable and unverifiable data. The set of questions included in Table 13.1 can provide a useful guide in selecting appropriate materials.

Potential Problems for Teachers

Teachers are expected to cope with the educational and emotional needs of children from many diverse cultural backgrounds with minimal background or support.

Table 13.1: *Questions to use as a guide in selecting material*

- Are different ethnic groups included and are they shown as diversified and heterogeneous?
- Are demeaning adjectives used (for example, 'primitive')?
- Are opportunities provided for students to examine in depth the values, beliefs, points of view and/or experiences of other ethnic groups?
- Does the material contain expressions of the opinions of members of the different ethnic groups?
- Is the group's cultural heritage represented only in terms of a few 'typical' examples that emphasize the different and the exotic?
- Are some facts ignored or others over-emphasized?
- Are interrelationships and the interdependence of different groups demonstrated?
- Does the material recognize both differences and similarities between cultures?
- Are cultures judged from a western standard or described in terms of deficits, based on some assumed standard — usually our own?
- Is there an assumption of 'social Darwinism', with development equated with economic growth and material possessions?
- Are minority groups treated as social problems?
- If inequities are portrayed, are the causes of these clearly presented?
- Are issues placed in context and related to social, cultural and political context at regional, national and global level?
- Does the material foster appreciation of ethnic and cultural diversity as a positive value?
- Would the treatment of the group assist children from that background to develop a positive self-image?

Source: Preston, 1991, p. 309

There are numerous potential difficulties lurking and some of these are listed below:

- stereotypes are reinforced if the focus is upon artefacts and facts about the past rather than the present — often described as the 'museum mentality'. A classic example of this in many Australian schools is when teachers teach about Aboriginal society in simplistic terms (hunting and gathering activities and related tools) and focus on their lifestyles prior to the arrival of white settlers — it stereotypes Aborigines as 'clever savages' and does not tap the complexity and diversity of Aboriginal society (Folds, 1991);
- there is a tendency for teachers to emphasize the Anglo roots of our culture together with an unquestioning use of this as a frame of reference (Preston, 1991);
- there is a tendency to concentrate upon differences to the exclusion of also recognizing similarities. For example, a concentration upon different food traditions and forms of dress can subtly reinforce ethnocentric attitudes;
- teachers tend to present other cultures as homogeneous groups. They fail to recognize the dynamic nature of culture and the ongoing changes and differences within a culture;
- it is inadvisable to take a stance in favour of cultural relativism — that is, if a behaviour is valid in one culture and since all cultures are equally valid, all behaviours must be equally good. Bullard (1992) contends that

cultural relativism cannot be condoned — the context of a nations' laws must be given primacy. She cites the dilemma:

> What should a teacher do if he or she comes across a Turkish boy giving his sister a severe beating outside the school gates because he saw her talking to boys during the morning recess . . . If a child is being beaten, someone should try and stop it. There's no multicultural issue at work here. Our cultural differences must take their expression within the context of a nation with laws. (Bullard, 1992, p. 6)

- there can be a tendency for teachers to take an emotionally detached view of issues. This is more likely to occur if the resources available on a cultural group are lacking in multimedia examples or if there is little first-hand experience about a group from students in the class. It is certainly undesirable to minimize the 'real life' issues affecting the culture being studied;
- there is no guarantee that more informed student knowledge about a culture will lead to more positive attitudes;
- the assumption is often made that because more informed understanding has been achieved, that social equity will follow. This of course, underestimates the impact of social structures within the host society.

Examples from Research

Kalantzis *et al.* (1990) provide six case studies of schools in Australia where the vast majority of students are of non-English speaking background. The populations served by the schools are extremely transient and the schools serve lower socioeconomic status or working class communities.

In terms of teaching practices, Kalantzis *et al.* (1990) highlight some common features for the six case study schools:

- students' cultural and linguistic diversity has been incorporated into the curriculum rather than excluded as academically and socially inappropriate;
- strong attempts to involve the community in the running of the school and their children's education;
- classroom pedagogy is experiential and involves students in the active making of their own knowledge;
- assessment is based on individual development in relation to tasks;
- collaborative decision making is practised. (p. 217)

As an example, teachers at Brunswick East High School (Kalantzis *et al.* 1990), in an inner city Melbourne suburb, have been working on a multicultural education programme for over twenty years. The Brunswick community is ethnically very diverse and as a result it has been essential that the curriculum reflects the ethos of multiculturalism. Teachers testified that the school has changed their lives in a profound sense — 'It's a really exciting and important place and we should be revelling in it. We have this wonderful opportunity. It's like New York at the turn of the century. It's vibrant and exciting, and rather than putting a brake on this, schools should be making the most of it.' (p. 75)

Burwood Girls' High School, in an inner city Sydney suburb, developed an Interpreting, Translating and Multicultural Studies course which was student-centred. Not only did the course develop important vocational skills in interpreting, but students developed heightened feelings of self-worth and began to 'recognise and value the wealth of their cultural and linguistic backgrounds' (Kalantzis *et al.*, 1990, p. 111).

Griffiths and Troyna's (1995) book brings together a collection of perspectives on the issues of anti-racism, culture and social justice in the UK. For example, in this volume Connolly (1995) describes a local primary school which draws on a diverse catchment area 'where roughly half its children are white, a quarter are Asian and a quarter are black' (p. 135). Connolly notes that school decisions destined to assist one group can have detrimental effects on others. He describes how the senior management of the school tried to engage black boys through the promotion of football and this increased the popularity of football generally but Asian boys were excluded and/or subjected to racist abuse — 'a multicultural/anti-racist strategy targeted at black boys, inadvertently had the adverse effect of increasing the exclusion and racist abuse experienced by Asian boys and fostering a masculine and sexist culture' (Connolly, 1995, p. 147).

Research on multicultural education is steadily increasing and the results to date indicate the complexities and problems for teachers, parents and students in achieving desired results. In referring to the US scene, Bullard (1992) is more pragmatic about ongoing research on multicultural education which she concludes is divergent and confused. Bullard states that teachers can't wait for these research studies and their related debates — 'teachers have to make their own honest efforts to build diverse communities in the classroom, using the research that makes sense and their own best instincts' (p. 7).

Reflections and Issues

1   Ravitch (1992) argues that 'priority must be given in US schools to teaching about the history and culture of the United States. American history and literature should explain who the American people are and where we came from. What were the turning points, the crises, that shaped and changed our nation? Who are our heroes? What are our ideals? Which poems, novels, essays, orations, and songs best typify the American spirit? What ideas, institutions, and values have held this polyglot people together as a nation for more than 200 years?' (p. 8)

Does this disparage the role and contributions of minor groups? Alternatively if the separate identities of ethnic cultures are given priority will this encourage ethnic separatism and cause intergroup tension?

2   'There's very little evidence that some children need segregated settings in which to be educated. At another level, we know that the world is an inclusive community. There are lots of people in it who vary, not only in terms of disabilities, but in race, class, gender, and religious background. It's very important for children to have the opportunity to learn and grow within communities that represent the kind of world they'll live in when they finish school.' (O'Neil, 1995, p. 7)

Take a stand for inclusion or exclusion in schools? Use examples to support your stance.

3   Singh (1995) contends that curriculum representations of Asia will be distinctive imprints of the host country and respond to the cultural, social and economic requirements of that country. If this is the case, teachers need to carefully analyse the efficacy and veracity of what is included in the curriculum and what has been excluded and displaced.

Elaborate upon this issue.

4   To 'culture switch', to know what behaviour is appropriate in different social situations, in different environments, is probably much more difficult than bilingual switches.

'Is it in fact possible to encourage children to become "bicultural", to culture switch as effectively as they code switch to become bilingual, within a curriculum which is predominantly monocultural, delivered by predominantly monocultural authority figures?' (Eckermann, 1994)

5   'Trying to force everybody into the inclusion mould promises to be just as coercive as trying to force everybody into the mould of special class or institution. There are wide differences in children's needs and the kinds of environments that can address those differences.' (O'Neil, 1995, p. 8)

Present a case for or against this statement using examples that you have experienced or are aware of in school settings.

6   'Since Australia has no shared international boundaries we need to ensure that we do not create outsiders within our society. Within a culturally diverse nation there is an ever present potential for misunderstanding and conflict, arising out of the different value and belief systems, means of communication, patterns of interaction and modes of thinking which characterise this very cultural diversity.' (Clyne, 1994, p. 5)

Discuss these implications for a multicultural curriculum in Australian schools.

7   'The "colonization" strategy (Woods, 1980) for many minority groups at school in a basically foreign territory, is to establish their own cultural and territorial base from which they could deal with the natives-teachers.' (Walker, 1993)

Use examples from your teaching experiences or from the literature to explain how minority groups adjust to, and/or exploit the school culture.

8 'The organizational norms of schools can augment or depress the educational progress of minority ethnic groups.' (Troyna, 1992)

Use examples to support or refute this statement.

9 'Legislation will not change the attitudes which lie at the heart of racism. This will only occur through a continuing and extended education programme' (National Multicultural Advisory Council, 1995, p. 20)

What role do schools have to play? What are some of the possible achievements and problems in changing attitudes?

10 'Though the school is a distinct institution, with walls and doors of its own, education is never a closed system. Schools are interwoven with their milieux. Both their design and functioning presuppose relationships with families, workplaces, labour markets and neighbourhoods.' (Connell, 1995, p. 9)

Discuss how these external factors can affect multicultural education initiatives and programmes.

References

ANDERSON, R and CUSHNER, K. (1994) 'Multicultural and intercultural studies', in MARSH, C. (Ed) *Teaching Studies of Society and Environment*, Sydney, Prentice Hall.

BRANDT, G.L. (1986) *The Realisation of Anti-Racist Teaching*, London, Falmer Press.

BULLARD, S. (1992) 'Sorting through the multicultural rhetoria', *Educational Leadership*, **49**, 4, pp. 4–7.

CLYNE, I.D. (1994) 'Developing cross-cultural literacy in teachers', Paper presented at the Annual Conference of the International Association for Inter-Cultural Education, Adelaide.

CONNELL, B. (1995) 'Social justice in education', in KALANTZIS, M. (Ed) *A Fair Go in Education*, Canberra, ACSA.

CONNOLLY, P. (1995) 'Reconsidering multicultural/anti-racist strategies in education: Articulations of "race" and gender in a primary school', in GRIFFITHS, M. and TROYNA, B. (Eds) *Anti-racism, Culture and Social Justice in Education*, Stoke-on Trent, Trentham.

ECKERMANN, A.K. (1994) *One Classroom, Many Cultures*, Sydney, Allen and Unwin.

FOLDS, R. (1991) 'Aboriginal studies', in MARSH, C. (Ed) *Teaching Social Studies*, 2nd edition, Sydney, Prentice Hall.

GRIFFITHS, M. and TROYNA, B. (1995) *Anti-racism, Culture and Social Justice in Education*, Stoke-on Trent, Trentham.

KALANTZIS, M., COPE, B., NOBLE, G. and POYNTING, S. (1990), *Cultures of Schooling*, London, Falmer Press.

NATIONAL ADVISORY AND COORDINATING COMMITTEE ON MULTICULTURAL EDUCATION (1987) *Education in and for a Multicultural Society, Issues and Strategies for Policy Making*, Canberra, AGPS.

NATIONAL MULTICULTURAL ADVISORY COUNCIL (1995) *Multicultural Australia, The Next Steps: Towards and Beyond 2000*, Volume 1, Canberra, AGPS.

O'NEIL, J. (1995) 'Can inclusion work?: A conversation with Jim Kauffman and Mara Sapon-Shevin', *Educational Leadership*, **52**, 4, pp. 7–11.

PEARPOINT, J. and FORREST, M. (1992) 'Foreword', in STAINBACK, S. and STAINBACK, W. (Eds) *Curriculum Considerations in Inclusive Classrooms: Facilitating Learning for all Students*, Baltimore, Paul H. Brookes.

PRESTON, B. (1991) 'Multicultural studies', in MARSH, C. (Ed) *Teaching Social Studies*, 2nd edition, Sydney, Prentice Hall.

RAVITCH, D. (1992) 'A culture in common', *Educational Leadership*, **49**, 4, pp. 8–11.

SINGH, M.H. (1995) 'Edward Said's critique of orientalism and Australia's "Asia Literacy" curriculum', *Journal of Curriculum Studies*, **27**, 6, pp. 599–620.

TROYNA, B. (1992) 'Ethnicity and the organisation of learning groups: A case study', *Educational Research*, **34**, 1, pp. 45–55.

VILLA, R.A. and THOUSAND, J.S. (1995) *Creating an Inclusive School*, Alexandria, Virginia, ASCD.

WALKER, J. (1993) 'Cultural perspectives on work and schoolwork in an Australia inner-city boys' high school', in ANGUS, L. (Ed) *Education Inequality and Social Identity*, London, Falmer Press.

WOODS, P. (1980) *Sociology and the School: An Interactionist Viewpoint*, London, Routledge and Kegan Paul.

Part IV

Collaborative Involvement in Curriculum

14 Decision-makers, Stakeholders and Influences

Introduction

Schooling occurs as a result of decisions made by various individuals and groups, both professional and lay-persons. To complicate matters, actions occur at different levels, especially national, state and local. It is of considerable value to analyse and understand the contributions of the various players.

Some Definitions

A classroom teacher's work is affected by many individuals and groups. Although various myths abound about the freedom of a teacher to do whatever he/she wishes in the privacy of 'behind the classroom door' this is not true in the 1990s, if in fact, it ever was the case.

'Decision makers' are those individuals or groups who, because of their professional status or position, are able to make specific decisions about what is to be taught, when, how and to whom. Obvious examples of decision-makers include state education systems and their senior officers and school principals and senior teachers. But there are many others, including textbook writers, testing agencies, accreditation and certification agencies.

'Stakeholders' are individuals or groups of persons who have a right to comment on, and have input into, school programmes (Connelly and Clandinin, 1988). In many cases they may have the authority to ensure that their inputs/directives are implemented, such as head office education directors or regional directors. Then again, they may have no official powers but rely upon their modes of persuasion, such as parent groups or newspaper editors.

'Influences' are individuals or groups that hold common interests and endeavour to persuade/convince authorities that certain changes should occur. They may be content to push a certain slogan/ideal or they may focus upon specific activities or processes that should occur in schools. Examples of such influences include various local interest/lobby groups representing environmental issues or specific religious beliefs.

There is obviously no clear demarcation lines between some forms of decision-makers, stakeholders and influence groups as their degree of authority/control depends upon the eye of the beholder. Yet for the purpose of analysis it is useful to produce a tentative list of groups that might be considered under each of these headings.

Table 14.1:   Decision-makers/stakeholders

	Title and Focus	Impact on Schools
Politicians	Ministers of Education/Secretary of State; State/National	High
Superintendents	Superintendents, Chief education officers, Directors general region/state	High
State departments	State/LEAs	High
Assessment boards	State/National	High
Teacher unions	State/National	Medium/High
Parents and school councils/boards	School-focused	Medium/High
Principals/Headmasters Teachers	School-focused School-focused	Medium/High
Students	School-focused	Low
Academics	Universities, TAFE, Further education State/National	Medium/High
Employers	State/National	Medium

A Classification

The detailing of decision-makers/stakeholders in Table 14.1 and influences in Table 14.2 represent a list of individuals and groups who can be involved. Any attempt to designate their respective spheres of influence must be deemed to be tentative and as contexts vary so do their relative impact over different periods of time.

A number of the players operate predominantly at the school level. Whether these individuals/groups are involved in 'actual' decision making is a moot point — rather it may be that they are only 'near' to the decision making. At the state level there are a number of key players participating in decision-making and various interest groups attempting to influence the key players. Interest groups may try to influence these officials by informal personal contacts or by their representation on accreditation and similar formal examination committees. Successes range from new electives being introduced; to the removal of objectionable textbooks from subject examination lists; to the introduction of sports clinics; to photographers being permitted entry into schools to take class photographs.

The rates and levels of activity by players wax and wane over time and in different contexts. Political bargaining has no sacrosanct rules. The categories listed

Table 14.2:   Influences

	Examples	Impact on Schools
Professional associations	National Association for the Teaching of English (UK)	Medium (at secondary school level)
Textbook writers	Authors of major texts for primary/elementary and secondary students	Medium
National agencies	Office of Education (USA)	Low
Media	Editorials and feature articles in major daily newspapers; daily television news	Medium/High
Educational consultants	Specialists in reading instruction	High in individual schools
Lobby groups	Environmental groups	Low
The courts	Mandating instruction in a school district	High
Research and testing organizations	Literacy tests	Medium
Commercial sponsorship/contracting out	Sponsorship for a computer laboratory	Medium/High

in Tables 14.1 and 14.2 will be examined more closely to provide further insights into the actions and impact of some of these players.

Decision-makers/Stakeholders

Politicians

Ministers of Education/Secretaries of State at national and state levels, have had, and continue to have, an enormous influence on curriculum, especially during the 1980s and 1990s. In many cases, individual ministers have initiated major curriculum reforms single handedly, as a result of their position and extremely strong personalities — for example John Dawkins in Australia (Marsh, 1994), Kenneth Baker in the UK (Graham, 1993; Taylor, 1995).

For example, Marsh (1994) analyses Dawkins' efforts as Minister for Education in Australia in the 1980s — 'by using "crisis rhetoric" he steered state ministers into collaborative efforts to produce national statements and profiles in eight learning areas. His statements were largely economics-driven, coupled with assertions that education had failed' (p. 44).

Taylor (1995) provides a penetrating account of Baker's activities in the UK — 'because Baker was so personally ambitious and at the same time so personally involved in education issues he was able to exhibit such tenacity in the face of the Prime Minister's hostility to his schemes — his struggle was unusually successful. Normally, with Thatcher firmly in control of all Cabinet Committees and unassailable in Cabinet itself, Baker might have expected to give way to Prime Ministerial authority, but during the period when the details of legislation were being hammered out, an ebullient Baker was placed in the adventitious position of facing Thatcher at a low point in her political life just when Baker had reached what eventually proved to be the zenith of his own career (p. 19)'.

It might be argued that the education budget is so large in most countries that it is only politicians who can provide direct levels of accountability to the general public to justify the expenditure. It is certainly the case that politicians have excluded the traditional senior educators and made many changes to the secret garden of curriculum (Lawton, 1980).

Superintendents/Chief Education Officers/Directors General

Senior officers in charge of education systems have different titles in the USA, UK and Australia but they are typically responsible for a wide range of educational decisions, even though they delegate the authority in various ways and degrees. Their personalities, modes of public relations and establishment of priorities are highly significant for the achievements of the education system.

From time to time a number of these senior officers have shown a major interest in curriculum and have been driving forces in establishing innovatory practices. For example, Bill Honig in California in the 1980s was instrumental in changing the nature of teaching and learning in that state by initiating frameworks and by aligning state-adopted textbooks and state tests to the frameworks (Ball *et al.*, 1994). In the UK William Stubbs was an active exponent of LEA responsibilities during his time as Director of the Inner London Education Authority (Stubbs, 1981).

State Departments/Local Education Authorities

Especially over the last two decades in the USA, state departments have greatly increased their influence over schooling. Mazzoni (1994) refers to the waves of reform initiated by states including the mandating of rigorous standards for students and teachers, school restructuring and systemic redesign of K-12 curriculum. In particular, the federal government under Reagan left the territory open to the states and they claimed the territory.

Many states in the USA are now centralizing their education policy and this trend appears to be increasing steadily, to the detriment of local school districts. According to Madsen (1994) 'there has been a shift from local control to the empowerment of state departments of education in regulating educational policy. The "excellence" movement of the mid-1980s has tended to centralise curricula mandates, state-administered testing programs, increased graduation requirements and teacher certification requirements' (p. 2).

In the UK the implementation of the National Curriculum has brought about a diminution of power and responsibilities of the Local Education Authorities (LEAs). The largest LEA, the Inner London Education Authority, was quickly dismantled by the Conservative Government. The provision for schools to opt out of their respective LEA and to operate as grant maintained schools with direct funding from the central government, has further weakened many LEAs (Whitty, 1995).

In Australia, state education systems, protected under the constitution to be solely responsible for the delivery of education, have maintained their responsibilities and influence over recent decades, but major budgetary problems have forced them into collaborative projects with the federal government of which the most recent and important was the national collaborative curriculum project in 1980–93 (Marsh, 1994).

Assessment Boards

Senior Secondary (Year 12) Examination Boards have a long tradition in the UK and Australia. They are responsible for developing examinations for matriculation entry into universities, and as a consequence, greatly influence the curriculum taught at senior secondary school levels. In Australia, such boards as the Board of Studies in NSW, controls the curriculum for all schooling levels K-12 but has a major impact on teaching in Years 11 and 12. In the UK, examination boards such as the Cambridge Examination Board produce syllabuses and examinations for a variety of subjects at GCSE and GCE (A levels).

Examination Boards have traditionally been the preserve of university academics but over recent decades there have been a considerable number of places allocated to senior secondary school teachers and, more recently, to vocational/ further education personnel. As with other major stakeholders, examination boards are now forming alliances with other groups such as universities, research institutes and industry groups, in their endeavours to seek tenders for curriculum development projects, such as those associated with Standard Assessment Tasks (SATs) in the UK and national profile development in Australia.

Teacher Unions

In the United Kingdom and Australia, in particular, teacher unions have been a significant influence upon curriculum. Not unexpectedly, in times of rapid expansion of education, or periods of crisis of funding, teacher unions are especially active.

Teacher unions typically focus upon industrial matters relating to salaries and working conditions but increasingly they have become more involved in curriculum matters. For example, teacher unionists were strongly represented on the Schools Council in the UK, a factor which may have hastened its demise in the 1970s. In Australia, major curriculum papers have been produced by unionists through their union journals (for example Ashenden *et al.*, 1984) and through their nomination to influential state and federal committees.

Their level of influence is heavily dependent upon the political parties in government at a particular time. The dissolutionment of the Inner London Education Authority and pressures on other education authorities deemed to be Labour party strongholds, was very evident in the UK during the 1980s. By contrast, the continuance of the Labour Party in government in Australia over much of the 1980s and 1990s enabled union educationalists to have considerable influence. For example, the Australian Education Union was a very influential player in the National Project on the Quality of Teaching and Learning (NPQTL) which examined new approaches to teaching and learning. The project was innovatory in that the existing regulatory framework and award conditions for teachers in pilot schools were varied to enable different educational programmes to be implemented.

Parents and School Councils/Boards

Parent influence on curriculum issues occurs most frequently through involvement on school boards/councils. In fact, school boards can be an ideal vehicle for parents and teachers to work together on curriculum decision-making. Yet, school councils can never be the sole or even the most important facet of parent participation. They are just one means of trying to provide teacher–parent–student interaction in decision-making. In the everyday life of a school it is important that there are numerous opportunities for this joint decision-making to occur and not to be restricted to the relatively few, formal meetings of a school council (Pettit, 1984).

Parents can also have influence via their participation on textbook selection committees and various community and business organizations. As noted by Beare (1987) to resist parent participation on matters of curriculum is not only anachronistic but also anti-educational. Responsibility for curriculum decision-making has to be shared with parents (McGilp and Michael, 1994). Various parent action groups in many countries are working actively to achieve this end (Morris, 1992; Brown and Reeve, 1993).

School Principals/Headmasters

McNeil (1985) argues that although principals are often described in formal job descriptions to be curriculum leaders they tend to be little more than a middle person between central office, parents and teachers. Their role can vary, dependent upon their interests and personality. In some cases they do initiate curriculum change but more frequently, their major priority is to implement curriculum decisions made by others.

Recent policy moves in some education systems to decentralize and devolve decision-making to schools has given more power to school principals. In a number of cases, innovative schools have emerged (Harris and Hirst, 1995; O'Neil, 1995) but in other situations principals lack the curriculum expertise and technical skills to provide effective curriculum leadership (see also Chapter 35).

Teachers

Teachers are involved in all the complexities associated with daily teaching and are of course responsible for a myriad of classroom decisions. They try to create order and stability in potentially chaotic surroundings. Their decision-making is typically confined to the classes they teach and don't affect their fellow-teachers. However, if decision-making occurs across grades then a number of teachers become involved and time is required to develop collaborative procedures. The rewards have to be substantial for teachers to commit the necessary energy and extra time, and a diversion from their major focus of teaching their allotted class(es).

Various policy discussions are made by other officers without input necessarily from teachers. For example, subject heads at secondary school level may require subject department priorities (Siskin, 1994). Head office personnel may require certain curriculum planning or assessment procedures. As noted above, at the senior secondary school level there are a number of restrictions on teachers imposed by external examination boards.

Teachers have influence in that they are the final link in the chain which affects students and many would argue the most important link. The psychic rewards (Lortie, 1975) that teachers can get from teaching often drives them into fostering remarkable student outcomes. Yet, it is also the case that many teachers struggle with the problems and anxieties of routines, cellular organization of schools and a loss of morale (Fullan, 1991).

Students

Students are an important element in the learning environment and are the ultimate consumers. In some classes teachers may seek out students' views on teaching content and methods, as might be expected in a democratic learning environment (see Chapter 6).

Of course students affect curriculum policy by mediating it — they come to classrooms with different backgrounds and as a result transform the taught curriculum in various ways (Schubert, 1986). Students can provide vision and be constructive participants in curriculum planning, so long as trusting and supportive environments are developed by teachers and administrators (Holdsworth, 1993).

Academics

The influence of university academics has ebbed and flowed over the decades. In the USA in the late 1950s, major curriculum projects were initiated as a reaction to America's apparent decline in technology and science, as revealed by Russia's lead in space endeavours and the launching of Sputnik I. These projects were headed by leading subject area academics (for example, J. Zacharias) and psychologists (for example, J. Bruner). In the UK in the 1960s academics such as L. Stenhouse and A. Blyth were to the fore in similar national curriculum projects.

In subsequent decades, academics have been far less conspicuous, and bureaucratic and political initiatives have been the order of the day. Although key academics were consulted for specific tasks relating to national curriculum initiatives (for example P. Black on assessment in the UK and P. Fensham on science education in Australia), academics in general have largely been bypassed in the 1980s and 1990s. Their influence, limited as it has been, has occurred via *post-hoc* criticisms, such as Australian academics criticizing the Mathematics National Profile (Guttman, 1993; Ellerton and Clements, 1994) — 'the idea of wresting the control of school curricula from vested interests in universities, has been one of the underlying but relatively silent forces in the national curriculum movement' (p. 314). Academics still maintain some influence on matriculation examination boards in most countries, but their influence is declining from major player to a shared role with technical training officers, employers and senior teachers.

Employers

Employer groups have been relatively new but an increasingly powerful player in the education stakes. In many countries, award restructuring, skills training standards and economic instrumentalism ideology have led many employer groups to agitate for a greater voice in the curriculum of schools. Various vocational programmes, generic and core skills orientations and vocational awards have been implemented as a result of initiatives by these groups.

Economic arguments and rationalities are being used to justify changes to the secondary school curriculum (Poole, 1992). In the USA, Apple (1988) notes that 'schools must be brought more closely into line with policies that will "reindustrialise" and "rearm" America so that we will be more economically competitive' (p. 273).

Various writers support the emphasis upon vocation education and the need for schools to prepare students for the working world. Teachers do not have all the knowledge or the skills to prepare students effectively for the world of work (Price, 1991). It is likely that employer groups will continue to have a significant influence on curriculum, especially at the senior secondary school level.

Influences

Professional Associations

Professional associations exercise their influence at national, state and local levels but especially at national levels. Their activities can include lobbying for or against political actions; publishing curriculum guidelines and producing scope and sequence charts; and by establishing networks, workshops and conferences (Glatthorn, 1987).

In the USA various professional associations are currently playing a major role in the development of national standards such as the National Council of Teachers of Mathematics and the National Council for the Social Studies. Professional associations have had mixed fortunes in the UK and Australia over recent decades. In the 1970s in the UK, professional associations such as the National Association for the Teaching of English (NATE) were very influential (Stenhouse, 1980) but their influence waned with the implementation of the National Curriculum. In Australia, professional associations were largely ignored in the development of national statements and profiles (Marsh, 1994) but subsequent intensive lobbying has now enabled national associations to play a role in developing teacher development materials for their respective learning area profiles (Ellerton and Clements, 1994).

Textbook Writers

Textbooks are a major learning source for many students. They can provide a core of important learning; up-to-date information; instruction on basic skills; and an introduction or overview of particular topics. Good textbooks are often very popular with teachers because they bring together a massive amount of important material in one volume, thus saving the busy teacher considerable time.

Writers of popular textbooks can be extremely influential about what is taught and how it is taught. If teachers rely very heavily upon a textbook they are likely to accept the content structure and associated pedagogy put forward by a textbook author.

In countries where textbooks are selected by central committees or state committees, a selected few can dominate the market. In several states of the USA, such as Texas and California, state textbook adoptions are a major activity and wield a significant influence on school education. It is interesting to note that alignment policies, especially in California, have required textbook publishers to ensure that their publications are congruent with state curriculum frameworks and state tests.

Some writers, such as Apple (1993) and Pinar *et al.* (1995) are concerned about the influence of textbooks — 'they are at once the results of political, economic and cultural activities, battles and compromises. They are conceived, designed and authored by real people with real interests. They are published with the political and economic constraints of markets, resources and power. And what texts mean and how they are used are fought over by communities with distinctly different commitments and by teachers and students as well' (Apple, 1993, p. 46).

National/Federal Agencies

In a number of countries national departments of education can have a major influence upon curriculum but there can be peaks and troughs. For example, in the USA, the National Institute of Education/Department of Education oscillated between major and minor involvement in curriculum matters during the 1980s and 1990s due to different political priorities. Boyd (1988) refers to minimal federal expenditure provided by the Department of Education during President Reagan's term of office.

In the UK the Department of Education and Science was moderately influential during the 1960s but became heavily involved during the 1970s with the production of numerous papers on comprehensive curriculum, standards, curricula balance, core curriculum via Her Majesty's Inspectors (HMIs). The development of the National Curriculum in the 1980s led to greatly increased powers for the DES.

The creation of the super-ministry Department of Employment, Education and Training (DEET) in Australia in 1987 produced a major 'implementation arm' for Federal Ministers. Under the incumbent Minister's direction, DEET established priorities for projects, consonant with political priorities and, in many cases, was able to provide substantial funding to ensure that tangible and visible outcomes were achieved. The current funding for national profiles and key competencies is a prime example (Grundy, 1994).

Media

The media through newspapers and television have become increasingly influential over the last decade due in no small measure because the topic of education is very newsworthy. Some daily newspapers provide regular education supplements while all newspapers from time to time, run major feature articles on specific issues. On occasions it would seem that newspaper editors and television reporters deliberately seek out controversial elements to a topic.

Drake (1991) is critical of the reporting of the news media in the USA — 'Do all our schools need reforming and restructuring, or are a few particularly poor schools continually publicised by the media, thereby distorting our overall judgment of the quality of education in America?' (p. 57).

Gill (1992) refers to how the print media in Victoria, Australia, mounted a ferocious attack on a new post compulsory curriculum structure, the Victorian Certificate of Education. This appears to be reminiscent of attacks of the 'New Right' in the UK (Ball, 1990) and in the USA (Apple, 1991). Gill describes the media accounts as 'a representation of a drama of dissonant and often acrimonious voices, of contestation, disruption and anxiety — the educational work of schools and their communities ... was trivialised or ignored' (p. 19).

Educational Consultants

Educational consultants are specialists who are involved in discussing current or potential problems of a class, department or school. In some cases they may be seconded teachers, located in regional or head offices of systems and available at call to assist classroom teachers. Other consultants may include university lecturers and management personnel, external to the system. Consultants have the potential to be very influential for individual teachers or groups of teachers at particular schools because they can pass on a variety of professional skills relating to such areas as curriculum development, management, pastoral care.

Unlike other roles within the field of education, the consultant role within a system is one that is subject to continual pressures and changing priorities. A generous staffing of consultants in one period to assist with the implementation of a new programme is often followed by a period of massive cutbacks. In some situations, subject-area consultants are given top priority, while on another occasion the emphasis might be for process consultants. Typically, consultants work individually, but from time to time teams of consultants (panels) are appointed to work collaboratively on major tasks.

External consultants (change agents) are typically involved on short-term contracts with major projects. In the USA they are frequently involved with projects sponsored by the regional educational laboratories and centres (Fullan, 1991).

Lobby Groups

Lobby groups are always present in society but become very active and conspicuous when controversy arises over particular topics or policies. The media is always eager to publicize the actions of lobby groups because of their newsworthy nature. Kirst and Walker (1971) contend that there are two kinds of policy making processes undertaken by lobby groups, normal policy making and crisis policy making. The day-to-day activities of lobby groups do not gain media attention but the crisis activities certainly do. Lobby groups can be very influential on school curriculum matters. An intensive effort in Queensland, Australia, by six lobby groups attained considerable success which led to the banning of a social studies curriculum Man: A Course of Study (MACOS) on religious grounds.

As described in Marsh and Stafford (1988), two of the most influential of the six lobby groups were the Society to Outlaw Pornography (STOP) and the Committee Against Regressive Education (CARE). Under the leadership of Mrs Rona Joyner, the message of STOP/CARE was designed to appeal to parents by playing on their emotions about what was 'good' and 'evil' for their children as future citizens. Reference was constantly made to two areas which were undermining Queensland society, namely sexual permissiveness and political conspiracy, and these evils, according to STOP/CARE, could only be countered by rigorous censorship (Scott and Scott, 1980, p. 35). In true propagandist style, this message was repeated constantly via the various media outlets.

The Courts

In a number of countries, but especially in the USA, court cases involving teachers, students and parents, are becoming very common (Fischer *et al.*, 1995). In the USA court judges have made decisions about curriculum such as the mandating of specific tests, methods and materials that schools must use (McNeil, 1985).

The number of school law cases in Australia have been relatively low to date due largely to the comparative ignorance of participants about their legal rights and the absence of entrenched rights for Australian citizens in national or state constitutions (Birch and Richter, 1990). However the number of cases are increasing including those about religious teaching, teacher negligence and corporal punishment.

Research and Testing Organizations

Large research and testing organizations who are involved in developing and responsible for major educational tests have a major influence on curriculum. In the USA testing agencies such as the Educational Testing Service (ETS) have largely produced a 'national' curriculum (McNeil, 1985). Standardized tests for college admission have a major influence on what teachers present to students at the senior secondary school level. National standardized reading and mathematics tests greatly influence the content of the elementary (primary) school curriculum.

In the United Kingdom, the National Foundation for Educational Research (NFER) has played a similar role in the provision of testing and its association with the monitoring of student performance through the Assessment of Performance Unit (APU), set up in 1974. Yet, because standardized testing is far less an educational preoccupation in the UK, the NFER has had less influence on schools than the ETS.

Nevertheless the NFER has played a significant role in the National Curriculum, chiefly in undertaking research to develop appropriate assessment materials for the Standard Assessment Tests (SATs). Similar roles have been undertaken by research organization counterparts in Australia and New Zealand — the Australian Council for Educational Research (ACER) (established by a Carnegie (USA) grant in 1930) and the New Zealand Council for Educational Research (NZCER).

The ACER in Australia has developed into a major influence upon curriculum through its research projects on schooling (for example McGaw *et al.*, 1992); its single-handed validation of national profiles in the eight learning areas (Marsh, 1994); its subsequent development of computer-aided teacher development packages for using the national profiles; and its leadership in sponsoring major curriculum seminars and conferences.

In addition, in many countries there are numerous research organizations which undertake public opinion surveys on educational topics (for example Gallop polls in the USA (Drake, 1991)) and are successful in tendering for major government-sponsored contracts on specific educational issues (for example, the Institute of Public Affairs (Nahan and Rutherford, 1993)).

Commercial Sponsorship/Contracting Out

In a period of privatization and corporate sponsorship, schools are becoming increasingly involved in sponsorship arrangements with private industry. To a certain extent schools have always been involved in seeking sponsorship support from the local community — for example local firms advertising in the school magazine or paying for the printing of a programme for a school sporting event.

In the 1990s the opportunities and necessity for sponsorship has widened considerably. It is no longer a matter of gaining sponsorship to acquire resources or to supplement ongoing minor expenditure. For some schools it is rapidly becoming their life-blood. It is very evident that sponsors have the potential to greatly influence the curriculum of a school. Long-term sponsorships could be very helpful and produce a positive commitment from the staff and local community, so long as the integrity of the school and its goals are not compromised (Harty, 1990).

Other Categorizations

The above listing of decision-makers, stakeholders and influences is derived from the assumption that spheres of influence are greatest at the school level or state level. This is, of course, a highly simplified account of what really happens.

Saylor (1982) provides a more elaborate categorization as depicted in Figure 14.1. His model incorporates internal and external agencies and persons to the school. In addition, he suggests that the ideas of the external agencies provides a curriculum reservoir of ideas/concepts which are filtered and monitored at federal and state levels before being implemented at the school level.

Walker (1990) contends that a better understanding of stakeholders is obtained if consideration is given to the 'needs' and their potential areas of 'control'. For example, school principals need support from teachers and resources; their controls include subject offerings, school timetable, access to parents and community. A Secretary of Education (Federal Minister for Education) needs political support, compliance from states and districts and expertise; controls include federal budget, federal grants, authority of position.

The interactions among the many groups and individuals, arenas and decisions can become quite complex and produce unexpected results. New coalitions of groups are occurring in the 1990s. Success factors in one period and a particular context do not necessarily provide success at other times and other contexts.

Reflections and Issues

1 Within your situation which agencies/groups appear to have the greatest influence on the school curriculum?

Give reasons for your answer.

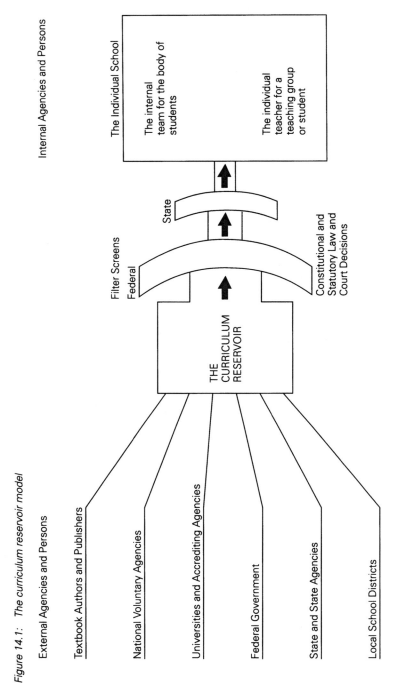

Figure 14.1: The curriculum reservoir model

Source: Saylor, 1982

2   Consider the impact of national/federal versus state initiatives in curriculum. Which have been the most significant for you in your situation? Explain.

3   Describe a recent alliance by two or more stakeholders associated with an innovatory curriculum or curriculum policy. Why do you think the alliance occurred? How successful has it been? Give reasons.

4   How influential are local boards/councils? Give examples of recent curriculum decisions made by a school board in your community.

5   The powerful interests constantly seeking to influence school curricula do not respect local district boundaries. They resort to direct action. Is this an accurate assessment? Give examples to illustrate your stance on this matter.

6   'School children are for sale to the highest bidder . . . Today's corporations are slicker, more sophisticated in their marketing strategies than they were a decade ago. Intrusions into the classroom by business interests continue unabated.' (Harty, 1990, p. 77) Are schools being exploited by these initiatives? Give examples that have occurred in your community. What checks and balances would you advocate?

7   How might greater harmony be developed between competing stakeholders on matters of curriculum? Choose two or more stakeholders and give examples to illustrate your argument.

8   'Much of the information the media offer about education comes from single, troubled schools in large cities.' (Drake, 1991) Does the media provide a balanced picture of schooling? If they are not, what steps might be taken to provide a more balanced coverage?

9   In the USA each side plays to its constituents and struggles for a political victory that will implement its values and priorities. Explain in terms of specific stakeholders and influences operating in your country.

References

APPLE, M.W. (1988) 'What reform talk does: Creating new inequalities in education', *Education Administration Quarterly*, **24**, 3, pp. 272–81.

APPLE, M.W. (1991) 'Is participation enough?: Gender, teaching and technology in the classroom', *Curriculum Perspectives*, **11**, 2, pp. 1–14.

APPLE, M.W. (1993) *Official Knowledge*, New York, Routledge.

ASHENDEN, D., BLACKBURN, J., HANNAN, B. and WHITE, D. (1984) 'Manifesto for a democratic curriculum', *The Australian Teacher*, **7**, pp. 13–20.

BALL, D.L., COHEN, D.K., PETERSON, P.L. and WILSON, S.M. (1994) 'Understanding state efforts to reform teaching and learning: Learning from teachers about learning to teach', Paper presented at the Annual Conference of the American Educational Research Association, New Orleans.

BALL, S.J. (1990) *Politics and Policy Making in Education: Explorations in Policy Sociology*, London, Routledge.

BEARE, H. (1987) 'Parent participation in Victorian schools', *The Education Magazine*, **3**, pp. 7–12.

BIRCH, J.K. and RICHTER, I. (Eds) (1990) *Comparative School Law*, London, Pergamon Press.

BOYD, W.L. (1988) 'How to reform schools without half trying: Secrets of the Reagan Administration', *Educational Administration Quarterly*, **24**, 3, pp. 299–309.

BROWN, J. and REEVE, P. (1993) 'Parent participation, equality and democracy', in SMITH, D.L. (Ed) *Australian Curriculum Reform: Action and Reaction*, Canberra, ACSA.

CONNELLY, E.M. and CLANDININ, D.J. (1988) *Teachers as Curriculum Planners*, NY, Teachers College Press.

DRAKE, N.M. (1991) 'What is needed most: School reform or media reform?', *Phi Delta Kappan*, **73**, 1, p. 57.

ELLERTON, N.F. and CLEMENTS, M.A. (1994) *The National Curriculum Debacle*, Perth, Meridian Press.

FISCHER, L., SCHIMMEL, D. and KELLY, C. (1995) *Teachers and the Law*, 4th edition, New York, Longman.

FULLAN, M.G. (1991) *The New Meaning of Educational Change*, London, Cassell.

GILL, M. (1992) 'A Study in the politics of curriculum change: VCE and the press', Unpublished paper, Monash University.

GLATTHORN, A.A. (1987) *Curriculum Leadership*, Glenview, Scott, Foresman and Company.

GLEICK, E. (1995) 'Privatized lives', *Time*, 20 November, p. 76.

GRAHAM, D. (1993) *A Lesson for Us All*, London, Routledge.

GRUNDY, S. (1994) 'The National Curriculum debate in Australia: Discordant discourses', *South Australian Educational Leader*, **5**, 3, pp. 1–7.

GUTTMAN, T. (1993) 'Petition to the Victorian Minister for Education regarding the mathematics national profile', Melbourne.

HARRIS, N. and HIRST, P. (1995) 'Outcome-based education and change management in four related schools', Paper presented at the Biennial Conference of the Australian Curriculum Studies Association, Melbourne.

HARTY, S. (1990) 'US corporations: Still pitching after all these years', *Educational Leadership*, **47**, 4, pp. 77–8.

HOLDSWORTH, R. (1993) 'Student participation: A decade of unfinished business', in SMITH, D. (Ed) *Australian Curriculum Reform: Action and Reaction*, Canberra, ACSA.

KIRST, M.W. and WALKER, D.F. (1971) 'An analysis of curriculum policy making', *Review of Educational Research*, **41**, 5, pp. 486–95.

LAWTON, D. (1980) *The Politics of The School Curriculum*, London, Routledge and Kegan Paul.

LORTIE, D.C. (1975) *School Teacher*, Chicago, University of Chicago Press.

MADSEN, J. (1994) *Education Reform at the State Level*, London, Falmer Press.

MARSH, C.J. (1994) *Producing a National Curriculum: Plans and Paranoia*, Sydney, Allen and Unwin.

MARSH, C.J. and STAFFORD, K. (1988) *Curriculum: Practices and Issues*, 2nd edition, Sydney, McGraw Hill.

MAZZONI, T.L. (1994) 'State policy making and school reform: Influences and influentials', in SCRIBNER, J.D. and LAYTON, D.H. (Eds) *The Study of Educational Politics*, London, Falmer Press.

MCGAW, B., PIPER, K., BANKS, D. and EVANS, B. (1992) *Making Schools More Effective*, Melbourne, ACER.

MCGILP, J. and MICHAEL, M. (1994) *The Home–School Connection*, Armidale, Eleanor Curtain.

MCNEIL, J.D. (1985) *Curriculum: A Comprehensive Introduction*, 3rd edition, Boston, Little Brown and Company.

MORRIS, W. (1992) 'Parents and school governance', Paper presented at the Annual Conference of the Western Australian Primary Principals' Association, Perth.

NAHAN, M. and RUTHERFORD, T. (1993) *Reform and Recovery*, Perth, Institute of Public Affairs.

O'NEIL, J. (1995) 'On lasting school reform: A conversation with Ted Sizer', *Educational Leadership*, 52, 5, pp. 4–9.

PETTIT, D. (1984) 'Governing in an equal partnership: The move to school councils', *Education News*, 18, 8, pp. 75–88.

PINAR, W.F., REYNOLDS, W.M., SLATTERY, P. and TAUBMAN, P.M. (1995) *Understanding Curriculum*, New York, Peter Lang.

POOLE, M. (1992) (Ed) *Education and Work*, Melbourne, ACER.

PRICE, B. (1991) *School Industry Links*, Melbourne, ACER.

SAYLOR, J.G. (1982) *Who Planned the Curriculum?*, West Lafayette, Kappa Delta Pi.

SCHUBERT, W.H. (1986) *Curriculum: Perspective, Paradigm and Possibility*, New York, Macmillan.

SCOTT, A. and SCOTT, R. (1980) *The Paradox of Reform and Reaction in the 'Deep North': Education and Policy Making in Queensland*, University of Melbourne Press.

SISKIN, L.S. (1994) *Realms of Knowledge: Academic Departments in Secondary Schools*, London, Falmer Press.

STENHOUSE, L. (1980) (Ed) *Curriculum Research and Development*, London, Heinemann.

STUBBS, B. (1981) 'Pressures on the school curriculum', *Curriculum*, 2, 1, pp. 15–20.

TAYLOR, T. (1995) 'Personality, policy and the process of curriculum change: The United Kingdom 1902–1988', Paper presented at the Biennial Conference of the Australian Curriculum Studies Association, Melbourne.

WALKER, D. (1990) *Fundamentals of Curriculum*, New York, Harcourt Brace Jovanovich.

WHITTY, G. (1995) 'School-based management and a National Curriculum: Sensible compromise or dangerous cocktail?', Paper presented at the Annual Conference of the American Educational Research Association, San Francisco.

15 Parent Collaboration

Introduction

Although there is considerable support in principle for parents to have a major decision-making role about schooling, in practice it is very difficult to achieve. However, there are some promising developments and opportunities for involving parents more effectively in schools as a result of devolution.

Some Major Terms

The ways that parents work with schools can vary enormously. For many parents their role is of limited involvement via:

- attendance at parent–teacher nights;
- school sports days;
- fetes;
- tuck shops;
- working bees;
- parents and citizens/parents and friends meetings;
- school council meetings.

As noted by Vick (1994) parents are usually on the sidelines when it comes to their children's education. 'Involvement' means very limited opportunities whereby parents undertake activities that have been designed and initiated by the school principal and staff. 'Participation' is to do with sharing or influencing decisions on policy matters and includes an active decision-making role in such areas as school policy, staffing and professional development of staff, budget, grounds and buildings, management of resources and the school curriculum. Participation can involve students too, especially at the secondary school.

Claims and Counterclaims About Parent Participation

A major reason for parent participation in schools is a powerful pedagogical one, 'the closer the parent is to the education of the child, the greater the impact on child development and education achievement' (Fullan, 1991, p. 227).

Table 15.1: Claims in favour of parent participation

- Parent participation will generally lead to improved student learning, intellectually, socially and emotionally.
- Parent participation increases richness and variety of the school learning environment because of a wide range of skills that can be provided by parents.
- It increases the sense of identity for the local school community.
- It enables parents to understand education processes more fully and to support the goals of schooling.
- By increasing the number of interest groups involved in education there is greater likelihood that the interests of all students will be taken into account.
- Parents and other citizens have the right in democratic countries to participate in school decision-making.

- Parents are also teachers and can and should support the teaching which goes on in classrooms. Parents have their own curriculum and teaching styles which are used in out-of-school learning situations (and in increasing numbers they are choosing home schooling (Jeub, 1994)). Hence the need for close collaboration between parents and teachers if children are to gain the full potential from their in-school and out-of-school learning experiences.
- Parents possess a variety of skills, talents and interests that can enrich the curriculum in so many ways beyond the capabilities of any one classroom teacher, no matter how talented he or she happens to be (Bryk *et al.*, 1990). Having a number of parents as active participants in a school will create a multiplier effect because of the energies, enthusiasm and motivation generated by these additional adults (West, 1993).
- If parents become involved in schools they begin to understand the complexities of the teaching roles and structures. Too often parents are swayed by media accounts which often present derogatory accounts about schools, teachers and students. If parents can experience at first-hand the complicated issues that can arise in the school environment they are less likely to be influenced by superficial media accounts (see Table 15.1). As a specific example, research studies have demonstrated that when parents are employed as paid teacher-aides in a school, they have more positive attitudes about schooling and their children attending the same school develop better attitudes toward their work (Melaragno, Lyons and Sparks, 1981).
- Parents have a democratic right and responsibility to further their children's education in whatever ways they can (Allen, 1990). Other writers argue that democratic decision making rarely operates in other institutions and agencies so why should it apply to schools? (Lareau, 1986).
- Parent participation on school councils and in the general governance of a school contributes to student learning at that school. Research evidence undertaken in the US (Bowles, 1980) and in the UK (Mortimer *et al.*, 1988) did not find any empirical support for this contention. Fantini (1980) noted that the participating adults on councils benefited from their experiences but there was no evidence to confirm or reject any impact on student learning.

Table 15.2: Claims against parent participation

- Many parents do not have the necessary problem-solving and communication skills to be effective participants.
- Many parents make conscious decisions not to participate and as a result a small number of articulate parents can monopolize the decision making.
- School staff are sometimes reluctant or opposed to parent participation activities.
- Governments have not devolved professional authority to parents and community — the rhetoric is stronger than the reality.
- Parents are being encouraged to be individual consumer-citizens and to see schooling as another product in the market place.

There are also a number of *counterclaims* about why parents should not participate actively in school decision-making (see Table 15.2).

- Schools are dominated by middle class norms. In schools where there is active participation by parents, they tend to include articulate, well-educated parents. Parents who cannot speak English, who have difficulty communicating well in groups, or who are poorly educated, are usually not represented (Jackson and Cooper, 1989). That is, a significant number of parents are poorly equipped to be active participants in school decision-making.
- It places additional burdens of time on the teachers. There is more likelihood that parents will be contacting teachers during out-of-school hours — they could be constantly on call to various demands, both trivial and important, and teacher exhaustion and 'burnout' is a very real problem. Small wonder that research studies indicate that only a minority of teachers in schools have goals and programmes for parent participation. For example, Rosenholtz's (1989) study showed that the majority of teachers were in 'stuck' schools rather than 'moving' schools. Teachers from 'stuck' schools held no goals for parent participation while teachers in 'moving' schools 'focussed their efforts on involving parents with academic content, thereby bridging the learning chasm between home and school' (p. 152). In another study Becker (1981) surveyed 3,700 primary school teachers and 600 principals and concluded that 'very few appear to devote any systematic effort to making sure that parental involvement at home accomplishes particular learning goals in a particular way' (p. 22).
- Parents and community members should not be active participants because it leads to a reduction in professional responsibilities of teachers . . .

> No teacher's school or work should be in any way controlled by the decisions of any non-professional or unpaid body or person, except with the teacher's concurrence. (NSW Teachers Federation, 1976, as reported in Hunt, 1981, p. 4)

A recent Australian Council of Educational Research (ACER) survey of over 7,000 school stakeholders which culminated in the report 'Making Schools more

Effective' (McGaw *et al.*, 1992) revealed some opposition by respondents to parent participation, namely: 'The principal concern was that inappropriate roles for lay people were being envisaged and pressed on schools and that this development undervalued the professional role and contribution of teachers' (p. 94).

- Parents are being increasingly perceived by governments to be 'consumer-citizens' (Woods, 1988). That is, parents operate largely as individual consumers in making decisions about schooling and schooling practices for their children. They rarely share school-related interests with other parents or lack the opportunity to do so:

> They do not constitute a monolithic group. Individualism and difference (in priorities, preference, philosophy) characterises the consumer-citizenry. (Woods, 1988, p. 328)

A Continuum of Parent Participation

Various accounts in the educational literature refer to 'tapping parent power' and 'effective parent participation in schooling'. A number have been written by individual enthusiasts or vested interest groups and so their laudatory comments are not surprising (for example, Morris, 1992; Gamage, 1992; Meadows, 1993; Allen, 1990). To provide a balanced picture it is useful to distinguish between the different activities/roles that might be undertaken by parents and depict them on a continuum (see Figure 15.1). The activities range from 'one-way information giving' to 'interactive partnerships' and there are a myriad of possible positions in between these two extremes of passive and active.

The examples listed in the first column of the continuum (Figure 15.1) are simply 'reporting progress' to parents. Variations of this category can include parent–teacher conferences. These face-to-face meetings can be most satisfying to the parent and to the teacher, but few parents tend to take advantage of this opportunity because of their busy daily schedule or their reticence about appearing personally at the school.

Special events for parents are depicted in the second column of Figure 15.1. These can take various forms including parent evenings, open days, concerts and plays. Such events enable teachers to demonstrate certain special student skills (for example: dance routines, art work, but they also provide an opportunity for teachers and parents to interact socially. Special occasions like these can enable a positive rapport to be developed between individual parents and a teacher. Sharing of ideas, as indicated in the third column in Figure 15.1 typically takes the form of informal discussions and special seminars and workshops. The seminars in particular, if held on the weekends or in the evenings, can be valuable occasions for parents and school staff to share ideas about school goals, values analysis, sex education/AIDS, mathematics skills.

Figure 15.1: Continuum of parent participation

One-way information giving	Reporting progress	Special events	Sharing of ideas	Parent assistance at school in non-instruction	Parent assistance at school in instruction	Governance	Interaction partnerships
	• Home–school notebooks • Call-in times • Newsletters • Telephone calls	• Picnics • Art shows • Concerts • Open days • Tuckshops • Working bees	• Seminars • Classroom observation days • Informal discussions	• Playground • Assistance on excursions • Liaison with local business • Organizing sports days • Preparing art material	• Guest speakers • Leaders on school camps • Teaching various skills	• Chairing subcommittees • Members of school council	

Parents can be involved in assisting school staff with a number of non-instructional activities. At the primary school level in particular, parents are in considerable demand to assist as additional supervisors for excursions and visits. If handled sensitively by the school principals, developing a group of volunteer parents for these activities can establish strong links between them and their school. More and more, parents are being sought after to assist school staff with a number of instructional activities (see Figure 15.1). To a certain extent, changes in employment patterns in the 1990s and resultant early retirement and redundancy packages have enabled parents to become available and willing to take on some of these tasks (Halstead, 1994).

In the junior primary school, parents are often sought after to assist with reading and miming stories to small groups of children and also to assist with various art and craft activities. Parents possess a wide range of specialist skills that can be a welcome and varied addition to the school curriculum. For example, Love (1986) lists the activities provided by eighteen parents who provide specialist teaching at his secondary school for periods of half a day per week: maths; art; library; knitting and crocheting; job interviews; tennis; social studies; choir; and fitting and turning (metalwork) (p. 4).

Governance activities by parents is in the final column in Figure 15.1. Many school councils/boards make major decisions about staffing, school building, resources and curriculum for their school.

No outstandingly successful prototype for school councils has yet been found. Various combinations of membership, functions and legal status have been initiated, but these initial versions are often found to be unsuitable and different versions have replaced them.

Intended Practices and Actual Outcomes

To date there have been few accounts in the literature about how parents operate within school communities. It is therefore not known the percentage of parent communities operating at different points on the continuum depicted in Figure 15.1. For example, there have been some accounts of successful governance by school councils (Gamage, 1993; Knight, 1995) but they are relatively few in number. It may be that only small numbers of parents are involved in the other categories listed in Figure 15.1.

It is true that there are difficulties for parents, many of whom venture into the school environment with various anxieties, are considerably overwhelmed and are often poorly informed about typical school activities. McTaggart (1984) notes that:

> parents' knowledge of what goes on in schools tends to be restricted to the treatment of educational problems given by the media . . . The images are both incomplete and confrontationist. (McTaggart, 1984, p. 12)

For parents of lower socio-economic backgrounds, the problem is especially severe. They often perceive the school council to be an appendage of the principal, espousing traditional middle class values. They often consider that the problems of their immediate neighbourhood are not translated into programmes at the school.

These parents need special encouragement and support before they will become regular participants in the school community. Andrews (1985) maintains that the typical response from such parents tends to be:

> Every other time I've complained or spoken out too much, my kid has been picked on.

or

> It doesn't affect my kid, she/he is doing OK. (Andrews, 1985, p. 30)

Teachers' language to the lay person can be almost incomprehensible. Not surprisingly, teachers receive new training in the academic disciplines and theory-building of various kinds and as a result of interaction with their peers establish their education jargon. This is particularly evident when teachers are asked to explain to parents why a child isn't coping with a subject. In many cases, teachers use technical terms that lay persons simply cannot understand.

Perhaps all stakeholder groups are to blame for building up their unique set of language modes, norms and expectations. Parents can certainly build up their barriers around their family life, interests and ambitions (Kenway *et al.*, 1987). These barriers take a considerable amount of time and good-will to break down. Boomer (1986) refers to this as a kind of:

> educational apartheid . . . they develop their own special forms of protection; an array of the equivalent of moats, barricades, deflection and passwords. (Boomer, 1986, p. 1)

In the final analysis it is likely that all stakeholders need skills training if they are to communicate effectively with each other. This is especially the case for parents and teachers.

Training Needs

Parents

Although some parents, as a result of their schooling and professional activities are highly articulate and very capable of participating in school decision-making, there are many who are not. The majority of parents do need assistance in such matters as knowledge of the educational system and interpersonal and communication skills.

Many parents do not have a clear idea of the education system in which their local school operates. They need information about the various levels of the hierarchy and the respective powers and functions of head office, regions and individual school principals. In particular, parents need to know the kinds of activities that a principal and his/her staff can initiate and maintain at a local school level, and an awareness of the constraints and monitoring procedures used by head office officials.

Training needs for many parents are most evident in the areas of interpersonal and communication skills. Experienced parent participants need to be able to break down the apathy of other parents and seek out their support by informal home visits, telephone calls and parent meetings. They have to be able to develop and demonstrate empathy for the needs of the apathetic or uninvolved parent and be able to devise ways of gradually wearing down that person's resistance.

Parent 'drop-in centres' are becoming more widespread in schools as principals realize that the provision of a meeting place for parents is a valuable strategy for getting them more involved in school activities. A drop-in centre can enable parents to interact socially and discuss various matters relating to their school community. In so doing, it may enable many parents to increase their level of confidence and skills in communicating with other adults.

Special provisions need to be made to assist parents with language difficulties. Those staff with second-language expertise can be used on home visits to encourage these parents to support school affairs. Community liaison officers can also be used with good effect to maintain regular home visits to parents. Migrant adviser services are sometimes available to offer assistance. Information booklets about the school, printed in several languages, can also be a useful measure to attract the interest of parents of migrant families.

The building up of positive attitudes about school participation among parents is a time-consuming process and requires the concentrated efforts of many participants, including teachers, liaison officers from various departments, and experienced, supportive parents/friends.

Teachers

The focus of training for many teachers revolves around learning about and demonstrating competence in planning and executing student lessons. Few preservice courses focus upon the role of parents in the school community, especially in terms of techniques for communicating effectively with parents. As a result, some teachers tend to make minimal use of parent assistance or, in some instances, actively resist communicating with parents (Fullan, 1991).

The extent to which teachers communicate regularly with teachers can vary considerably between rural and urban centres. Teachers posted to rural schools have little choice but to be closely involved in the local community and to be in regular contact with parents in various social, cultural and sporting activities. In urban schools there are less opportunities for interaction and there may be difficulties for some teachers in understanding and empathizing with the priorities and values of parents representing low socio-economic levels.

Pettit (1985) raises some interesting questions in Table 15.3 which could be

Table 15.3: Parent participation: Issues for teachers to reflect upon

1   Am I, as a teacher, prepared to consider or reconsider the idea of parents participating with me and the possible benefits that may accrue? If I don't, does that mean that I consider parents have no rights or, if they have, that I'm not prepared to acknowledge them?
2   Am I self-sufficient as a teacher or would I be more effective if I used the skills that other parents and people have and arranged my time to make this possible?
3   How accessible am I to parents?
4   Do I and can I create the best conditions for talking to parents?
5   Do I find reporting to parents useful to me? Do I ever wonder how useful it is to them?
6   If parents don't respond to personal invitations do I follow it up with further invitations?
7   Do I try to explain to parents what I am trying to achieve and to ask for their help?
8   If the help of parents and others is not accepted or acknowledged at my school do I try to do anything about changing this situation?

Source: Pettit, 1985

useful for teachers to reflect upon. It is important for all teachers to consider how accessible they are to parents and to revise, if necessary, the strategies they do use or should use, to increase their level of rapport with parents. The principal can play a major role in a school in encouraging his/her teachers to seek out parental help in their classrooms. The principal may need to use the example of several outstanding teachers on the staff to show how parents can become involved in various ways in providing clerical support staff and teaching help in individual classrooms. Once a few teachers get involved in this way it is likely that others on the staff will follow. One of the purposes of this involvement with parents is, of course, to give teachers the opportunity to work alongside them and gain a better understanding of parents' interests and motivations.

School Councils

School councils/boards are an important element of schooling. Although the composition and powers of school councils vary across the states, the membership typically consists of the principal and representatives of the staff, parents, the community and students (in the case of secondary schools).

In some cases school councils can be radically powerful and can bring about rapid change (Fullan, 1991). Gamage's (1993) studies revealed that 'councils have become effective and efficient organisations, while the principals are highly satisfied and totally committed to the collaborative form of governance adopted in terms of the school council system' (p. 102).

La Rocque and Coleman's (1989) study of school councils in British Colombia conclude that school councils can make a difference. School council members can develop a clear sense of what they want to accomplish and engage in activities to bring about these ends. However, as noted by Fullan (1991), how to increase/improve the effectiveness of school councils is an unstudied problem. There are still many unanswered issues and problems, and some of these are listed in Table 15.4.

Table 15.4: Problems and issues for school councils

1 Do councils have real power if their control over finances is limited?
2 Are school councils really able to practise democratic decision-making?
3 Is an adequate supply of dedicated and well-informed parents and community members available to fill school council positions?
4 Does the size of a school influence the effectiveness of school councils?
5 How can school council members understand and represent all sections of a local community if they tend to be better educated and more affluent than the majority of local citizens?
6 Will school councils ever be able to represent effectively such disadvantaged groups as migrants, the unskilled, the unemployed and low income earners?
7 Do school councils really provide a structure for school principal, teachers and parents to co-exist harmoniously?
8 Do school councils in the Australian context ever get complete control over decision-making?

Lutz (1980) questions whether school councils really practise democratic decision-making. He argues that school council participation of parents from a local school community is very limited and sporadic; that few council members are closely involved in decision-making; and that few issues are ever made public and widely debated. It is certainly evident that for large schools it is extremely difficult for school board members to represent more than a few of the community interests. Many of the disadvantaged community groups are never represented. Yet it might be argued that democracy means the freedom to participate or not to participate and that if individuals and groups feel strongly enough about an issue then they will participate vigorously.

Questions might also be raised whether school councils actually reduce conflicts between various interest groups or heighten the conflicts still more (Table 15.4). For example Knight (1995) highlights some of the conflicts between teacher and parent members. Is it possible that parent priorities (for example, school discipline, and literacy and numeracy) are likely to be different from the priorities expressed by teachers (for example, providing a caring atmosphere and building student self-esteem)?

Finally, questions might also be raised about whether school councils operating an education system can ever anticipate becoming fully independent from head office policies and requirements. Recent accountability measures introduced into a number of education systems would seem to indicate that centralist requirements are increasing rather than decreasing.

Reflections and Issues

1 'It is an open question how far and in what ways it will be legitimate to involve parents in the many different functions of schools.' (Golby, 1989, p. 134)

What functions are legitimate in your opinion? Give examples from your teaching experiences or readings.

2 What role should parents and community members play in school decision-making? For example, discuss your attitude about the following:

   • parent governors being members of a staff selection committee;
   • parent governors discussing a pupil suspension.

3 'Parents and community members could rapidly constitute a large, powerful force in education. They have the potential influence to bring about change in schools; to cause changes in attitudes from politicians, administrators and teachers, and in the long term, changes in policy.' (Beattie, 1985)

   Is this an over-optimistic stance? Consider some possible impediments to this occurring.

4 'It is important that parent governors should be the choice of parents, people that parents feel they can approach with trust and confidence.' (Edwards and Redfern, 1988, p. 109)

   Are there difficulties in getting representative governors? What are some possible solutions?

5 'The parent–teacher partnership is fundamental to effective learning in class-rooms — teachers' professional training, knowledge and experience are complementary to those of parents.' (Allen, 1989, p. 14)

   Discuss.

6 'Parents are the school's best resource, its "social capital" for making education possible. To take advantage of this resource, however, a reconceptualization of the family as part of the school community is needed.' (Jackson and Cooper, 1989, p. 284)

   What changes of attitude are needed — for example, by administrators and teachers? How else might parents be encouraged to become active decision-makers?

7 Some school council members complain that they suffer from a lack of direction, the feeling of being a rubber stamp, and parent and staff apathy.

   How might some of these problems be resolved?

8 'Many parents and teachers are overloaded with their own work-related and personal concerns. They also may feel discomfort in each other's presence due to lack of mutual familiarity and to the absence of a mechanism for solving the problems that arise.' (Fullan, 1991, pp. 249–50)

   Discuss this statement? What are some practical solutions to the problem?

9 'In some schools, principals reveal a degree of reluctance over divulging information and allowing the council to become involved and active.' (Gamage, 1992, p. 28)

   Why is this likely to occur? What steps might be taken to resolve it?

10 'Parents enter the contested public sphere of education typically with neither resources nor power. They are usually not welcomed by schools . . . and they typically represent a small percent of local taxpayers.' (Fine, 1993, p. 683) Do you accept this statement? Give examples to support your response.

11 Some UK writers (for example, Deem, 1990; Sallis, 1990) consider that parents have lost power over curriculum decision-making by the introduction of a National Curriculum which has been designed and will be assessed centrally. Do you agree? Provide reasons for your response.

References

ALLEN, S. (1989) 'Parent participation: Productive partnerships', *The Australian Teacher*, **24**.

ALLEN, S. (1990) 'The parent–teacher partnership in schooling', *Education Australia*, **8**, pp. 5–6.

ANDREWS, G. (1985) *The Parent Action Manual*, Schools Community, Melbourne, Interaction Trust.

BEATTIE, N. (1985) *Professional Parents*, London, Falmer Press.

BECKER, H. (1981) 'Teacher practices of parent involvement at home: A statewide survey', Paper presented at the Annual Meeting of the American Educational Research Association, Chicago.

BOOMER, G. (1982) (Ed) *Negotiating the Curriculum*, Sydney, Ashton Scholastic.

BOOMER, G. (1986) 'Long division: A consideration of participation, equality and brainpower in Australian education', Paper presented at the ACSSO Annual Conference, Launceston.

BOWLES, D. (1980) 'School Community relations, community support, and student achievement: A summary of findings', Madison, University of Wisconsin.

BRYK, A., LEE, V. and SMITH, J. (1990) 'High school organisation and its effects on teachers and students', in CLOUNE, W.Y. and WHITE, J.F. (Eds) *Choice and Control in American Education Volume 1: The Theory of Choice and Control in Education*, London, Falmer Press.

DEEM, R. (1990) 'The reform of school-governing bodies: The power of the consumer over the producer', in FLUDE, M. and HAMMER, M. (Eds) *The Education Reform Act: 1988*, London, Falmer Press.

EDWARDS, V. and REDFERN, A. (1988) *At Home and School: Parent Participation in Primary Education*, London, Routledge.

FANTINI, M. (1980) 'Community participation: Alternative patterns and their consequence on educational achievement', Paper presented at the Annual Meeting of the American Educational Research Association, San Francisco.

FINE, M. (1993) '(Ap)parent Involvement: Reflections on parents, power and urban public schools', *Teachers College Record*, **94**, 4, pp. 682–710.

FULLAN, M.G. (1991) *The New Meaning of Educational Change*, London, Cassell.

FULLAN, M.G. and HARGREAVES, A. (1991) *Working Together for Your School*, Melbourne, ACEA.

GAMAGE, D. (1992) 'Challenges facing school councils', *Education Monitor*, **3**, 3, pp. 23–8.

GAMAGE, D.T. (1992) 'School-centred educational reforms of the 1990s: An Australian case study', *Educational Management and Administration*, **20**, 1, pp. 5–14.

GAMAGE, D.T. (1993) 'A review of community participation in school governance: An emerging culture in Australian Education', *British Journal of Educational Studies*, **41**, 2, pp. 134–63.

GOLBY, M. (1989) 'Parent governorship in the new order', in MACLEOD, F. (Ed) *Parents and Schools: The Contemporary Challenge*, London, Falmer Press.

HALSTEAD, J.M. (1994) (Ed) *Parental Choice and Education*, London, Kogan Page.

HUNT, G. (1981) *The Curriculum and the Community*, Canberra, Curriculum Development Centre, Occasional Paper No. 5.

HUNT, M.P. and METCALF, L.E. (1968) *Teaching High School Social Studies*, New York, Harper and Row.

JACKSON, B.L. and COOPER, B.S. (1989) 'Parent choice and empowerment: New roles for parents', *Urban Education*, **24**, 3, pp. 263–86.

JEUB, C. (1994) 'Why parents choose home schooling', *Educational Leadership*, **52**, 1, pp. 50–2.

KENWAY, J., ALDERSON, A. and GRUNDY, S. (1987) *A Process Approach to Community Participation in Schooling: The Hamilton Project*, Perth, Murdoch University.

KNIGHT, T. (1995) 'Parents, the community and school governance', in EVERS, C. and CHAPMAN, J. (Eds) *Educational Administration: An Australian Perspective*, Sydney, Allen and Unwin.

LA ROCQUE, L. and COLEMAN, P. (1989) 'Quality control: School accountability and district ethos', in HOLMES, M., LEITHWOOD, K. and MUSELLA, D. (Eds) *Educational Policy for Effective Schools*, Toronto, OISE Press.

LAREAU, A.P. (1986) 'Perspectives on parents: A view from the classroom', Paper presented at the Annual Meeting of the Annual Conference of the American Educational Research Association, San Francisco.

LOVE, D. (1986) 'Community involvement', *West Australian High School Principals Association Newsletter*, **10**, 1, 9.

LUTZ, F.W. (1980) 'Local school board decision-making: A political-anthropological analysis', *Education and Urban Society*, **12**, 4, pp. 17–29.

MCGAW, B., PIPER, K., BANKS, D. and EVANS, B. (1992) *Making Schools More Effective*, Melbourne, ACER.

MCTAGGART, R. (1984) 'Action research and parent participation: Contradictions, concerns and consequences', *Curriculum Perspectives*, **4**, 2, pp. 7–14.

MARSH, C.J. (1994) *Producing a National Curriculum: Plans and Paranoia*, Sydney, Allen and Unwin.

MEADOWS, B.J. (1993) 'Through the eyes of parents', *Educational Leadership*, **51**, 2, pp. 31–4.

MELARAGNO, R., LYONS, M. and SPARKS, M. (1981) 'Parents and federal education programs', Vol. 6, *Parental involvement in Title 1 Projects, Systems Development Corporation*, Santa Monica.

MORRIS, W. (1992) 'Parents and school governance', Paper presented at the Annual Conference of the Western Australian Primary Principals' Association, Perth.

MORTIMER, P., SAMMONS, P., STOLL, L., LEWIS, D. and ECOB, R. (1988) *School Matters: The Junior Years*, London, Open Books.

PETTIT, D. (1985) 'Too many cooks or not enough broths?', *School and Community News*, **9**, 1, pp. 17–23.

ROSENHOLTZ, S. (1989) *Teachers' Workplace: The Social Organisation of Schools*, New York, Longman.

SALLIS, J. (1990) 'Governors and parents', in SOUTHWORTH, G. and LOFTHOUSE, B. *The Study of Primary Education, A Source Book, Vol. 3, School Organisation and Management*, London, Falmer Press.

VICK, M. (1994) 'Parents, schools and democracy', *Education Australia*, **28**, pp. 11–13.

WEST, S. (1993) *Educational Values for School Leadership*, London, Kogan Page.

WITHERS, G. and McCURRY, D. (1990) 'Student participation in assessment in a cooperative climate', in Low, B. and WITHERS, G. (Eds) *Developments in School and Public Assessment*, Melbourne, ACER.

WOODS, P. (1988) 'A strategic view of parent participation', *Journal of Education Policy*, 3, 4, pp. 323–34.

16   Teachers as Researchers/Action Research

Introduction

Over the decades various writers have argued that teachers should do their own classroom research. Various terms have been used such as 'teachers as researchers' and 'action research'. Advocates of these approaches suggest that teachers must use the results of their own inquiries to change and improve their practices.

Some Definitions

'Action research' can be defined as 'a way of thinking and systematically assessing what is happening in a classroom or school, implementing action to improve or change a situation or behaviour, monitoring and evaluating the effects of the action with a view to continuing improvement' (Thomson, 1988, p. 3).

Kemmis and McTaggart (1984, p. 6) describe action research 'as a method for practitioners to live with the complexity of real experience, while at the same time, striving for concrete improvement'.

Interest in action research has become very marked over several periods in the twentieth century but especially during the 1940s due to the work of Kurt Lewin (1948) with his social science research in the USA; Stenhouse's (1975) emphasis upon the teacher as researcher in his humanities project in the UK; Elliott and Adelman's (1976) Ford Teaching Project in the UK in the 1970s and 1980s whereby teachers developed inquiry skills; and Kemmis and McTaggart's (1984, 1988), Kemmis (1991) and colleagues ongoing research at Deakin University in Australia.

Making a Start with Action Research

Kemmis and McTaggart (1984, pp. 18–19) suggest that participants in action research should commence by 'addressing questions' such as:

- What is happening now?
- In what sense is this problematic?
- What can I do about it?

and then go on to consider:

- How important is the issue to me?
- How important is it to my students?
- What opportunities are there to explore the area?
- What are the constraints of my situation?

Action research can be conducted entirely by individual teachers but it is more usual for small groups of teachers to do it. Frequently, an 'external facilitator' is invited to enhance the processes. There is some evidence that without ongoing support from facilitators, teachers find it difficult to sustain their action research (Ebbutt and Partington, 1982). The external facilitator can act as a 'sounding board', as a 'critical friend'. He/she can be of considerable value in:

- providing a wider perspective;
- asking participants to clarify ideas;
- giving individuals support when needed.

Nevertheless, the vital aspect is that teachers within the group take responsibility for researching solutions to their problems.

To do action research, according to Kemmis and McTaggart (1988), a person must undertake four fundamental processes or 'moments':

(a) to develop a 'plan' of action to improve what is already happening:
  - it must be forward looking;
  - it must be strategic in that risks have to be taken.
(b) to 'act' to implement the plan:
  - it is deliberate and controlled;
  - it takes place in real time and encounters real constraints;
  - it may involve some negotiations and compromises.
(c) to 'observe' the effects of action in the context in which it occurs:
  - it is planned;
  - it provides the basis for critical self-reflection;
  - it must be open-minded.
(d) to 'reflect' on these effects as a basis for further planning and a succession of cycles:
  - it recalls action;
  - it comprehends the issues and circumstances;
  - it judges whether the effects were desirable.

Figure 16.1 illustrates these processes whereby participants undertake a field of action, develop a specific plan, implement it and reflect upon it.

Although these fundamental processes are useful in describing likely phases of action, McKernan (1991) argues that teachers need additional assistance in selecting

Figure 16.1:   *The action research spiral*

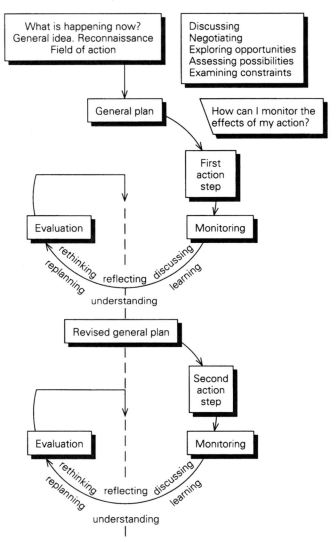

Source: Kemmis, 1982

Table 16.1: Techniques available to teachers

Observational
- unstructured observation in a classroom by a teacher-colleague;
- participant observation;
- structured observation using checklists or rating scales by the teacher or a teacher-colleague;
- anecdotal records completed by the teacher or a teacher-colleague;
- short case study accounts of a project or an event;
- keeping a diary or journal;
- photographs, video tape-recording, audio recording.

Non-observational
- attitude scales completed by students;
- questionnaires completed by students;
- interviews of selected students;
- document analysis.

Technical Action/Research
- directed by a person or persons with special expertise;
- the aim is to obtain more efficient practices as perceived by the directors;
- the activities are product-centred;
- operates within existing values and constraints.

Practical/Collaborative Action Research
- directed by the group;
- the aim is to develop new practices;
- the activities are process-oriented;
- personal wisdom is used to guide action.

techniques for collecting data. His listing in Table 16.1 provides a comprehensive range of techniques which satisfy criteria for rigorous and systematic data collection.

Modes of Action Research

Writers have indicated that 'action research' is an umbrella term for a number of approaches. Some Australian proponents suggest that there are three major subtypes of action research; namely technical, practical and emancipatory (Grundy, 1982; McTaggart and Garbutcheon Singh, 1986; Kemmis, 1991). McKernan (1993) uses the terms scientific, practical-collaborative and critical. McKernan's (1993) survey of action research project leaders in USA, UK and Ireland revealed that the majority of action research projects in the USA and the UK were of the practical/collaborative categories. In Ireland there was an increasing trend toward an emancipatory mode. A brief description of the three modes follows:

Emancipatory Action Research

- directed by the group;
- the aim is to develop new practices and/or change the constraints;
- involves a shared radical consciousness.

Tripp (1987) suggests that emancipatory action research is very rare because it can only occur in circumstances where a critical mass of radical participants can work together over a considerable period of time.

Technical Action/Research

- directed by a person or persons with special expertise;
- the aim is to obtain more efficient practices as perceived by the directors;
- the activities are product-centred;
- operates within existing values and constraints.

Practical/Collaborative Action Research

- directed by the group;
- the aim is to develop new practices;
- the activities are process-oriented;
- personal wisdom is used to guide action.

Constraints

Carr and Kemmis (1986) identify a number of constraints especially autonomy and emancipation. McKernan's (1993) survey of action research project leaders, as described above, revealed the following constraints:

Major constraints:

- lack of time to do action research;
- lack of resources;
- school organization (for example, problems of timetable);
- lack of research skills and knowledge.

Moderate constraints:

- obtaining consent to do action research;
- the language of educational research;
- student examinations;
- disapproval of school principal.

Minor constraints:

- disapproval of fellow teachers;
- personal beliefs about the role of the teacher;
- professional factors (for example, union contracts);
- disapproval of students.

Impact of Action Research upon Schools

Positive:

* increased self-confidence for teachers;
* feelings of empowerment;
* greater school-staff collegiality;
* greater willingness to experiment;
* improved teaching practice and performance;
* increased understanding of research processes;
* increased practical knowledge;
* increased understanding and reflection;
* increased teacher autonomy. (Cochran-Smith and Lytle, 1993; Burnaford *et al.*, 1994)

McKernan (1991) emphasizes that the major positive aspect of action research is that it enables teachers 'to solve their own problems and to improve practice — it is a growing form of professional development for the reflective practitioner — and it is necessarily collaborative' (p. ix).

Negative:

* limited impact on school staff not directly involved;
* limited impact because teachers are not allocated time or resources to engage in action research;
* teachers are not free to make changes that they might feel are educationally worthwhile;
* teachers are not skilled in examining and reflecting upon what is actually happening in classrooms — it takes considerable time to develop these skills;
* difficulties can arise about areas of confidentiality such as who has control of materials gathered and who has access to them. (Beattie, 1989; Bell, 1988; Day *et al.*, 1990)

Anning (1986) contends that the action research movement has to question whether this professional personal development really brings about changes in teaching practice and whether the formulation of a pedagogic language fosters meaningful discussions about the processes of teaching and learning.

Reflections and Issues

1   To what extent do you consider that school-based curriculum development has encouraged action research initiatives?
    If appropriate, describe your experiences in this regard.

2   'Action research provides a way of working which links theory and practice
    into the one whole: ideas-in-action.' (Kemmis and McTaggart, 1984, p. 5)
    From your experience does this happen? Give details.

3   Action research involves values and norms of behaviour. What are the rights
    and responsibilities of participants in action research? Can this cause unreal-
    istic demands or expectations on the part of participants/administrators?

4   'Emancipatory action research is essentially a political act — to change the
    consciousness of and constraints for those other than the immediate partici-
    pants.' (Tripp, 1987, p. 11)
    To what extent can action research transform practices, understandings and
    situations?

5   'One of the characteristics of action research is that it is research which people
    get on with and do quickly . . . Academics are watchers of the world: teachers
    are actors in it. Teachers make decisions and search for "right" decisions.'
    (Bassey, 1990, p. 161)
    Comment upon how action research differs from traditional academic re-
    search. What are its strengths and limitations over academic research?

6   'Action research stands or falls by its demonstrable relevance to the practical
    ethic of education, as well as whether it is reliable, valid and refutable as a
    methodology.' (Adelman, 1989, p. 177)
    Have published studies demonstrated the relevance of action research? Is it
    difficult to prove the quality (reliability, validity) of action research? What
    solutions can you offer to this dilemma?

7   'Action research provides the necessary link between self-evaluation and pro-
    fessional development.' (Winter, 1989, p. 10)
    Explain why reflection and self-evaluation are so important to action re-
    search. Should action research lead to actual changes in practice? If so, does
    this provide professional development for teachers?

8   '. . . to place the teachers' classroom practice at the centre of the action for
    action researchers is to put the most exposed and problematic aspect of the
    teachers' world at the centre of scrutiny and negotiation.' (Goodson, 1991,
    p. 141)
    Do you agree that it could be undesirable to start a collaborative mode of
    research from a study of classroom practice? Are teachers sensitive to these
    studies? Are there advantages which outweigh the possibility of exposing
    teacher vulnerability?

9   'Teachers need time and resources to engage in action research.' (McKernan,
    1991)

Are these the major constraints? What additional factors can also have a constraining effect?

10   'Action research is where teachers subject themselves and their practice to critical scrutiny; they attempt to relate ideas to empirical observations; they attempt to make this process explicit to themselves and others through the written word.' (Hustler *et al.*, 1986)

Is this an accurate description of action research you have experienced or read about? Give examples to support your answer.

11   'Action research has the potential to merge and explore the nurturing, teaching, learning and curricular aspects of classrooms, schools and their contexts — major opportunities to hear the teacher's voice.' (Noffke, 1991)

Is this ideal or practicable? Give examples to support your stance.

References

ADELMAN, C. (1989) 'The practical ethic takes priority over methodology', in CARR, W. (Ed) *Quality in Teaching*, London, Falmer Press.

ANNING, A. (1986) 'Curriculum in action', in HUSTLER, D., CASSIDY, T. and CUFF, T. (Eds) *Action Research in Classrooms and Schools*, London, Allen and Unwin.

BASSEY, M. (1990) 'Action research in action', in DADDS, M. and LOFTHOUSE, B. *The Study of Primary Education, A Source Book, Vol. 4, Classroom and Teaching Studies*, London, Falmer Press.

BEATTIE, C. (1989) 'Action research: A practice in need of theory?', in MILBURN, G., GOODSON, I.F. and CLARK, R.J. (Eds) *Re-Interpreting Curriculum Research: Images and Arguments*, London, Falmer Press.

BELL, G.H. (1988) 'Action inquiry', in NIAS, J. and GROUNDWATER-SMITH, S. (Eds) *The Enquiring Teacher: Supporting and Sustaining Teacher Research*, London, Falmer Press.

BURNAFORD, G., BRODHAGEN, B. and BEANE, J. (1994) 'Teacher action research at the middle level: Inside an integrative curriculum', Paper presented at the Annual Conference of the American Educational Research Association, New Orleans.

CARR, W. and KEMMIS, S. (1986) *Becoming Critical: Knowing Through Action Research*, Geelong, Deakin University Press.

COCHRAN-SMITH, M. and LYTLE, S.L. (1993) *Inside Outside: Teacher Research and Knowledge*, New York, Teachers College Press.

DAY, C., POPE, M. and DENICOLO, P. (Eds) (1990) *Insight into Teachers' Thinking and Practice*, London, Falmer Press.

EBBUTT, D. and PARTINGTON, D. (1982) 'Self-monitoring by teachers', in BOLAM, R. (Ed) *School Focussed In-service Training*, London, Heinemann.

ELLIOTT, J. and ADELMAN, C. (1976) *Classroom Action Research*, Ford Teaching Project Unit 2, Norwich, University of East Anglia.

GOODSON, I.F. (1991) 'Teachers' lives and educational research', in GOODSON, I.F. and WALKER, R. *Biography, Identity and Schooling: Episodes in Educational Research*, London, Falmer Press.

GRUNDY, S. (1982) 'Three modes of action research', *Curriculum Perspectives*, **2**, 3, pp. 23–34.

HUSTLER, D., CASSIDY, T. and CUFF, T. (1986) *Action Research in Classrooms and Schools*, London, Allen and Unwin.

KEMMIS, S. (1991) 'Emancipatory action research and postmodernisms', *Curriculum Perspectives*, **11**, 4, pp. 59–66.

KEMMIS, S. and McTAGGART, R. (1984) *The Action Research Planner*, Geelong, Deakin University.

KEMMIS, S. and McTAGGART, R. (1988) *The Action Research Planner*, 3rd edition, Geelong, Deakin University Press.

LEWIN, K. (1948) *Resolving Social Conflicts*, New York, Harper and Row.

McKERNAN, J. (1991) *Curriculum Action Research*, London, Kogan Page.

McKERNAN, J. (1993) 'Varieties of curriculum action research: Constraints and typologies in American, British and Irish projects', *Journal of Curriculum Studies*, **25**, 5, pp. 445–57.

McTAGGART, R. and GARBUTCHEON SINGH, M. (1986) 'New directions in action research', *Curriculum Perspectives*, **6**, 2, pp. 42–6.

NOFFKE, S.E. (1991) 'Hearing the teacher's voice: Now what?', *Curriculum Perspectives*, **11**, 4, pp. 55–8.

STENHOUSE, L. (1975) *An Introduction to Curriculum Research and Development*, London, Heinemann.

THOMSON, M. (1988) 'The action research spiral as a model of curriculum change', Unpublished paper, Perth, Murdoch University.

TRIPP, D.H. (1987) 'Action research and professional development', in HUGHES, P. (Ed) *Better Teachers for Better Schools*, Melbourne, Australian College of Education.

WINTER, R. (1989) *Learning from Experience: Principles and Practice in Action-Research*, London, Falmer Press.

17 Curriculum Reform

Introduction

Proposals for reforms in education appear frequently in the literature and especially proposals for curriculum reform. Presumably this means that there are problems to be solved. Because of the frequency of reform proposals this would seem to indicate that previous reforms did not remove the problems they were intended to solve.

Curriculum reforms are typically top–down reforms but experience has shown that their impact is often very limited. To really bring about reform a massive system-wide effort is required that engages parents, and communities as well as policy-makers.

What Is Curriculum Reform?

Bourke (1994) notes that the term 'reform' is typically used to refer to changes instituted from above — 'the implication in much of the rhetoric is that only government decision-making can reform education' (p. 1). He questions whether governments are always able to reform (to make better) — on many occasions the changes implemented by a government are worse for at least some groups.

Kennedy (1995) asserts that curriculum reform is really about changes to the content and organization of what is taught, within the constraints of social, economic and political contexts. Curriculum content and organization is of central importance but unless a reform effort is consistent with the values of the wider society it is unlikely to be successful.

Hargreaves (1995) takes the issue further and notes the interconnectedness of curriculum reform in terms of societal change. For example, he argues that secondary schools are the prime symbols and symptoms of 'modernity' (for example, bureaucratic complexity, inflexibility) and that 'postmodern' conditions of the 1990s require very different principles (see also Chapter 44).

Lingard *et al.* (1993) refer to the reformation of schooling over the past decades. Some examples of reform include:

- devolution of responsibilities to school principals and school councils;
- school-based curriculum development within national frameworks;
- downgrading external support services for schools;
- increased school governance;

Table 17.1: Reform proposals in the USA during the 1980s

Core proposals
a   higher standards through mandates passed by state legislatures and state boards of education;
b   improved salaries for teachers to enable teaching to become more of a profession;
c   higher-order thinking skills;
d   reducing drop-out rates in high schools.

Ancillary proposals
e   performance incentives to 'quality' teachers;
f   removing state and federal regulations from schools;
g   increased use of standardized tests to make comparisons among schools and school districts;
h   school empowerment to empower other stakeholders such as parents and students;
i   to give parents greater choice over the type and location of schools they want for their children.

Source: Cibulka, 1990

- auditing of schools;
- centrally defined policy guidelines.

Sources of Curriculum Reform

There is an enormous array of individuals and groups who can agitate for and initiate curriculum reform. The local and national contexts often provide a 'window of opportunity' for visible leaders and also behind-the-scenes bureaucrats. Historically, individuals and groups have formed particular alliances but new advocacy groups are occurring in the 1990s, especially from business. Some typical sources include:

- governments;
- teacher unions;
- media;
- academics;
- industry.

Examples of reform undertaken by each of these groups are listed in Table 17.1.

'Governments' in many OECD countries have initiated curriculum reform in recent years. As an example, a major reform initiated by the then President Reagan in 1980 was to regain excellence for American schools. The publication of *A Nation at Risk: The Imperative for Educational Reform* led to a flurry of actions by states and especially by state governors, to implement major curriculum reforms. This in turn has led to states becoming far more dominant in curriculum decision-making, with an attendant erosion of power at the level of local school districts (Boyd and Kerchner, 1987).

'Teacher unions', especially in the UK and Australia, have been advocates of work place reform and especially changes (improvements) to school structures, pedagogy and professional development. For example, the Australian Education

Union has recently called for reforms in technology availability for schools. In a widely distributed paper, the AEU (1995) stated major priorities 'for a national technology strategy which will ensure that all schools and colleges are confidently placed to access information and construct and communicate knowledge irrespective of their location or the socio-economic status of the community they serve' (p. 5).

The 'media' can also be very influential, especially in highlighting problems in need of reform. Gill (1992) refers to a new secondary school curriculum developed in Victoria, Australia, which included many innovative features to increase school retention rates for all students. The Victorian press selected out particular stances and then took every opportunity to amplify them. Reform, in the eyes of the daily newspaper, was to eliminate and/or reduce the proposed new Victorian Certificate of Education 'by presenting a cumulative and consistent rhetoric of disruption — graphic slogans, headlines and bylines to establish a strident tone of attention-grabbing disaster' (Gill, 1992, pp. 3–4).

Over the decades 'academics' have been a major force in curriculum reform, especially in the post-Sputnik era of the 1960s, but their influence has been more sporadic in the 1990s. In terms of National Standards projects in the USA, academics are playing a significant role in subject associations, especially mathematics and science. For example, the National Council of Teachers of Mathematics included many academics (mathematics educators, mathematicians) to produce a new content framework for the K-14 mathematics curriculum.

'Industry' representatives are a relatively new but influential player in curriculum reform, especially at the secondary school level. For example, in Australia, the Business Council of Australia and the National Industry Education Forum addressed curriculum reform in several position papers and then distributed these widely, ensuring that politicians were well aware of their proposals.

There are also various combinations and alliances between the above groups and many others. For example, City Technology Colleges (independent schools) were initiated in 1986 in the UK, as a result of a partnership between government and industry. The sponsors own or lease the schools and run them. The colleges teach the full National Curriculum but emphasize technology and science and cater especially for students who are not well served by traditional school structures.

Yet, it should be noted that across all countries, reform efforts have been dismal failures. Sarason (1990) contends that schools have been intractable to reform — 'the failure of educational reform derives from a most superficial conception of how complicated settings are organized: their structure, their dynamics, their power relationships and their underlying values and axioms' (p. 4). Boyd (1988) maintains that 'changing schools is like punching a pillow. They absorb innovative thrusts and soon resume their original shape' (p. 299).

Internationalization of Reform

Since the 1980s, international organizations have been giving special priority to educational reform. For example, the OECD sponsored an International School

Improvement Project (ISIP) in 1982 involving fourteen countries and which examined the role of school leaders, external support, school-based review, research and evaluation and policy development and implementation. As noted by Papadopoulos (1987) the limitations in the availability of public resources and sharpened conflicts about priorities has led reform initiatives to be focused on the schools themselves. A consequence 'has been a realignment of educational reform partnerships and the forging of new alliances, both within individual national contexts and at the international level' (Papadopoulos, 1987, p. xi).

Kennedy (1995) refers to the similarities in reform efforts occurring in the UK, the USA and Australia since the 1980s. He concurs with Coombs (1985) that in all these countries there has been 'a crisis of confidence in education itself' (p. 9). No longer is curriculum decision-making the preserve of professional educators — governments are now playing a central role in terms of broad social, political and economic agendas.

Economic growth continues to be a major focus in many countries (Lane, 1995) and as a consequence, curriculum reforms focus upon the development of skills. New structures for education and training are being developed and new coalitions between government, unions and industry.

Ideology and Reform

It is very evident that reform proposals represent very different frames of reference about curriculum in schools. In the UK, the National Curriculum introduced in 1988 was based on the Right ideology of a market economy and a consumer-oriented emphasis. A number of schools have opted out of local education authority control, supposedly to allow parents more choice. A policy of open enrolment and local management of schools is now in place.

In New Zealand a massive restructuring of the education system occurred in the late 1980s. According to Peters (1995) the ideology for these reforms was based on neo-liberal principles of individualism, deregulation, corporatism and privatization.

There is currently in the USA a strong interest in national standards and the need to develop a core of knowledge and skills that all students should be taught. However the underlying ideology is about state-led standards, common practices for all students.

The ideology supports standard practices and uniform goals and tends to minimize the importance of equity issues and reduces the impact of local initiatives. Apple (1988) argues that reforms should concentrate on the relationship between schooling and the larger society and on the structure of inequalities in society — the deskilling of jobs, and the lowering of wages and benefits.

Categories of Reforms

In the USA over the last decade, various reforms have been advocated via official reports but also through state legislation. It is not all integrated into one major

Table 17.2: Reform proposals and their implementation in the UK during the 1980s

The following proposals were included in a series of Education Reform Acts passed by Parliament during the period 1987–8.

A National Curriculum will be introduced to achieve consistently high standards for students by providing:
a   a balanced and broadly based curriculum;
b   spiritual, moral, cultural, mental and physical development;
c   development in all the main areas of learning and experience (3 core subjects — English, mathematics, science; 7 foundation subjects — history, geography, technology, music, art, physical education, modern foreign language);
d   students with the opportunities, responsibilities and experiences of adult life;

The National Curriculum was implemented in 1989 using:
a   the core and foundation subjects;
b   four key stages have been used as phases of learning;
    key stage 1: the two infant years,
    key stage 2: the four junior years,
    key stage 3: the first three years of secondary schooling,
    key stage 4: the final two years of compulsory schooling,
c   attainment targets including up to ten levels of attainment cover the four key stages for each subject;
d   standard assessment tasks have been designed for each key stage and overall school results will be published.

reform policy, and in fact, some authors such as Cibulka (1990) argue that some of the reform proposals are not consistent and are even contradictory. Cibulka suggests that there are some major or 'core' proposals which have occurred in most states (for example, state mandates) and 'ancillary' proposals (for example, greater choice of schools) which have been advocated by some pressure groups in some states (see Table 17.1).

These proposals represent a 'pluralist' approach to reform and because of the inconsistencies between different policies there is little shared consensus over ends or means. These pluralist bargaining games may create a lot of media publicity but the lack of unity could mean limited chances of success. By contrast, reforms in the United Kingdom have 'coherence' and have been implemented as a total package of reform, despite widespread criticism. The ruling Tory party under the leadership of Prime Minister Margaret Thatcher produced reforms that were aimed at raising standards of all students. The creation of core and foundation subjects, key stages, attainment targets and standard assessment tasks were carefully orchestrated to achieve this end (see Table 17.2). Notwithstanding, it is far from clear whether these reforms have been accepted and implemented appropriately by teachers.

Plank (1988) suggests that there are four main types which he categorizes as 'additive' reforms, 'external' reforms, 'regulatory' reforms, and 'structural' reforms (see Table 17.3). By far the most difficult to achieve are the structural reforms.

'Additive' reforms are relatively easy to implement because they involve additional resources and do not affect the organizational character of schools. An example would be a fully-funded computer literacy programme.

Table 17.3: Types of curriculum reforms and examples

Additive	External	Regulatory	Structural
• increased salaries • pre-school initiatives • computer literacy programme	• preservice teacher tests • new high school graduation requirements • certification changes	• longer school day • longer school year • more basic skills • state-wide assessment	• smaller classes • vouchers/tax credits • merit pay plans • competency tests for teachers

Source: Plank, 1988

'External' reforms also have little effect on the structure of schools, as they concentrate upon teachers entering the system or students leaving the system. Examples include higher tests for preservice teachers or more stringent requirements for high school graduation. These types of reforms are typically welcomed by school boards and teachers' unions.

'Regulatory' reforms seek changes in schools but not necessarily affecting the basic structure. The emphasis is upon more time and effort to achieve higher student achievements. Examples include longer school days and school years, core curriculum, statewide testing.

'Structural' reforms require alterations to the structure and operation of schools. They question current school structures and have the potential to be extremely disruptive to teachers and students. Examples include merit pay plans and voucher systems for parents to use at schools of their choice.

Reform Reports

Reform reports are often a popular means of bringing a purported problem to the consciousness of the public. The reports tend to focus on one or two key elements, often dramatizing the problems so as to elicit the solutions. Examples include:

USA
National Commission on Excellence in Education (1983) *A Nation at Risk: The Imperative for Educational Reform*, Washington DC, US Department of Education.
The Holmes Group (1986) Tomorrow's Teachers, East Lansing, The Holmes Group.
UK
Department of Education and Science (1991) *Education and Training for the 21st century*, London, HMSO.
Dearing, R. (1993) *The National Curriculum and its Assessment*, London, SCAA.
Australia
Dawkins, J. (1988) *Strengthening Australia's Schools*, Canberra, AGPS.
Finn, B. (1991) (Chair) *Young People's Participation in Post-compulsory Education and Training*, Canberra, AGPS.

New Zealand
Minister of Education (1988) *Tomorrow's Schools*, Wellington, Government Printer.

Of these reports, one is selected out for closer scrutiny, namely *A Nation at Risk*.

The National Commission on Excellence in Education (1983)

Three university presidents, a Nobel Prize winner, distinguished corporative executives and other prominent educators, were appointed to this 'blue ribbon' commission in 1981 to complete a nationwide study of the quality of American education and to publish a report within eighteen months (Bell, 1993). Ronald Reagan, the President during this period, saw it was to his advantage to be portrayed as an educational reformer, and strongly supported the report.

A *Nation at Risk*, apparently, told the United States exactly what it was ready to hear, for public approval was instantaneous and overwhelming. The report identified a crisis that it alleged the nation was facing; its proposed solution was largely through the reform of the curricula of American secondary schools. In the post-Sputnik years, most Americans had believed the greatest threat to national security was military, but in the 1980s, most Americans believed it to be economic. The opening paragraphs of *A Nation at Risk* played heavily on this fear. In overblown language and metaphors borrowed from athletic competition and the military, it began as follows:

> Our Nation is at risk. Our once unchallenged pre-eminence in commerce, industry, science, and technological innovation is being overtaken by competitors throughout the world. This report is concerned with only one of the many causes and dimensions of the problem, but it is the one that undergirds American prosperity, security and civility. We report to the American people that while we can take justifiable pride in what our schools and colleges have historically accomplished and contributed to the United States and the well-being of its people, the educational foundations of our society are presently being eroded by a rising tide of mediocrity that threatens our very future as a Nation and a people. What was unimaginable a generation ago has begun to occur — others are matching and surpassing our educational attainments.

> If an unfriendly foreign power had attempted to impose on America the mediocre educational performance that exists today, we might well have viewed it as an act of war. As it stands, we have allowed this to happen to ourselves. We have even squandered the gains in achievement made in the wake of the Sputnik challenge. Moreover, we have dismantled essential support systems which helped make those gains possible. We have, in effect, been committing an act of unthinking, unilateral educational disarmament. (National Commission on Excellence in Education, 1983, p. 5)

This was indeed fine rhetoric and Reagan and his two Secretaries of Education made 'masterful use of their high offices as "bully pulpits" from which to sermonise about what needed to be done to improve public schools' (Boyd, 1988, p. 302).

The report captured the attention of the media and the public. In particular state governors rose to the powerful rhetoric and began developing state-level reforms. To sell the idea that states should take on the problem themselves was indeed a masterful and successful ploy.

The recommendations were remarkably prosaic given the crisis atmosphere and hysteria:

- high school graduation to be expanded to include four years of English, three years of mathematics, three years of science, three years of social studies and one-half year of computer science (The New Basics);
- schools and universities adopt more rigorous and measurable standards;
- more time to be devoted to learning the New Basics, including lengthening the school day and the school year;
- that salaries and working conditions be made more attractive to attract better quality teachers;
- that citizens hold educators responsible for providing the leadership.

There was a tremendous flurry of activity as states mandated new requirements for graduation subjects, for lengthening the school day and year and improving teachers' career ladders. There was also new partnerships with the business community. The US Department of Education reported significant gains in the percentage of high school graduates and almost all states had initiated state wide assessment programmes. Yet, it is also the case that these top–down initiatives by the states 'failed to meet expectations of those who sponsored the legislation' (Bell, 1993, p. 594). Boyd (1988) also notes the gross neglect of the federal government in minimal funding during this period, especially for the ailing urban schools.

Nation at Risk appears to exemplify many of the characteristics noted by Presseisen (1989) about reform reports — they may be high on rhetoric but they tend to be deficient in such matters as:

- including research data to support their assertions;
- providing reasoned consideration of options;
- presenting supporting evidence and argumentation for well-specified proposals.

Ginsberg and Wimpleberg (1987) refers to reform reports produced by commissions as being 'trickle-down reforms'. Pronouncements are made with sufficient strength and drama that they will survive in spirit, if not in letter, the filtering of trickle down — 'the "water" that leaves the commission pail is still "water" after it has filtered through the layers of sediment and reached the subterranean level of school and classroom. It gets there, however, as so many discrete drops and not as a stream' (p. 356).

Finally, it should be noted that making reform proposals is only part of the process and that there are many problems in getting reforms implemented. The factors affecting innovations and change, and implementation, as noted in Chapters 34 and 32 respectively, are most pertinent.

Reflections and Issues

1 'Educational reform cannot progress without financial resources. People, time and materials are necessary costs that are not considered to any great degree in most reform reports.' (Presseisen, 1989, p. 135)

   Why is it that reform reports rarely include detailed budgets? Who should determine priorities for finance for reform proposals?

2 Compare and contrast the following statements:

   'The school reform movement in the US has been the most sustained and far-reaching reform effort in modern times.' (Boyd, 1987, p. 28)

   'Most of the reforms that have been adopted in the US in the past five years have not significantly altered the traditional structure and functioning of American public school systems.' (Plank, 1988, p. 143)

3 Some of the most difficult dilemmas we face currently have been around for a long time.

   Give examples of reforms that have been proposed over the decades to solve a particular curriculum problem. Have any proposals been more successful than others? Give reasons.

4 'Do schools exist to increase the nation's productivity or for other equally important personal and social goals?' (Passow, 1988, p. 254)

   What is your stance on this matter?

5 'The reform proposals in the US reflect and help perpetuate practices that are at odds with equity and excellence goals.' (Cornbleth and Gottlieb, 1988, p. 11)

   Why do you consider that equity goals which were being advanced in the 1960s and 1970s are not being given a high priority in the 1980s and 1990s? Are equity and excellence diametrically opposed goals?

6 'Problems of logical consistency among the elements of American educational reform abound . . . If we ask how these all fit together, the answer is that they do not . . . What this analysis suggests is that a shotgun approach to reform, so characteristic of Americans in the past and once again being played out, is very risky, indeed. If Americans wish to succeed in their current reforms, their pragmatism must include more careful consideration of how to maximize the interdependent elements in these educational reform strategies rather than approaching them piecemeal.' (Cibulka, 1990, p. 108)

   Critically discuss.

7   'The agenda America should tackle if we want to improve schooling has nothing to do with national tests, higher standards, increased accountability, or better math and science achievement.' (Berliner, 1993, p. 640)
    Do you agree? What alternatives should be the main focus?

8   'The ongoing attempts to reform curriculum structures and processes at the national level may be more myth than reality and certainly are highly problematic in their intended outcomes to produce a more internationally competitive Australia.' (Smith, 1993, p. vii)
    Use examples to support or disagree with this statement.

9   'Schools, and especially classrooms, are remarkably resistant to change, much to the consternation of politicians, policy-makers and innovators . . . Professional and institutional structures are resilient: They withstand many an assault and have powerful capacities to maintain and reproduce themselves despite surface changes.' (Hargreaves, 1994)
    Can this claim be substantiated? Give examples to support your response.

References

APPLE, M.W. (1988) 'What reform talk does: Creating inequalities in education', *Educational Administration Quarterly*, **24**, 3, pp. 272–81.
AUSTRALIAN EDUCATION UNION (1995) 'National technology strategy for schools', Background Paper, Melbourne, AEU.
BELL, T.H. (1993) 'Reflections one decade after a nation at risk', *Phi Delta Kappan*, **74**, 8, pp. 593–7.
BERLINER, D.C. (1993) 'Mythology and the American system of education', *Phi Delta Kappan*, **74**, 8, pp. 632–40.
BOURKE, S. (1994) 'Some responses to changes in Australian education', *Australian Educational Researcher*, **21**, 1, pp. 1–18.
BOYD, W.L. (1987) 'Rhetoric and symbolic politics: President Reagan's school reform agenda', *Education Week*, March.
BOYD, W.L. (1988) 'How to reform schools without half trying: Secrets of the Reagan administration', *Educational Administration Quarterly*, **24**, 3, pp. 299–309.
BOYD, W.L. and KERCHNER, C.T. (1987) (Eds) *The Politics of Excellence and Choice in Education*, London, Falmer Press.
BOYER, E.L. (1983) *High School: A Report on Secondary Education in America*, New York, Harper and Row.
BRUNER, J.S. (1960) *The Process of Education*, New York, Vintage Books.
CIBULKA, J. (1990) 'American educational reform and government power', *Educational Review*, **42**, 2, pp. 13–29.
CONANT, J.B. (1959) *The American High School Today*, New York, McGraw Hill.
COOMBS, P. (1985) *The World Crisis in Education: The View from the Eighties*, Oxford University Press.
CORNBLETH, C. and GOTTLIEB, E.E. (1988) 'Reform discourse and curriculum reform', Paper presented at the Annual Conference of the American Educational Research Association, New Orleans.

DAWKINS, J. (1988) *Strengthening Australia's Schools*, Canberra, Minister for Employment, Education and Training.

DEARING, R. (1993) *The National Curriculum and its Assessment*, London, SCAA.

DEPARTMENT OF EDUCATION AND SCIENCE (1991) *Education and Training for the 21st Century*, London, HMSO.

FINN, B. (1991) (Chair) Report of the Australian Education Council Review Committee, *Young People's Participation in Post-compulsory Education and Training*, Melbourne, AEC.

GILL, M. (1992) 'A study in the politics of curriculum change: VCE and the press', Unpublished paper, Monash University.

GINSBERG, R. and WIMPLEBERG, R.K. (1987) 'Educational change by commission: Attempting "Trickel down" reform', *Educational Evaluation and Policy Analysis*, **9**, 4, pp. 344–60.

HARGREAVES, A. (1995) *Changing Teachers, Changing Times*, London, Cassell.

HARGREAVES, D. (1994) *The Mosaic of Learning*, London, Demos.

KENNEDY, K.J. (1995) 'An analysis of the policy contexts of recent curriculum reform efforts in Australia, Great Britain and the United States', in CARTER, D.S.G. and O'NEILL, M.H. (Eds) *International Perspectives on Educational Reform and Policy Implementation*, London, Falmer Press.

LANE, J.J. (1995) (Ed) *Ferment in Education: A Look Abroad*, Chicago, University of Chicago Press.

LINGARD, B., KNIGHT, J. and PORTER, P. (1993) (Eds) *Schooling Reform in Hard Times*, London, Falmer Press.

MINISTER OF EDUCATION (1988) *Tomorrow's Schools*, Wellington, Government Printer.

NATIONAL COMMISSION ON EXCELLENCE IN EDUCATION (1983) *A Nation at Risk: The Imperative for Educational Reform*, Washington, DC, Government Printing Office.

PAPADOPOULOS, G. (1987) 'School improvement in a broader context', in HOPKINS, D. (Ed) *Improving the Quality of Schooling*, London, Falmer Press.

PASSOW, A.H. (1988) 'Whither (or wither)? school reform?', *Educational Administration Quarterly*, **24**, 3, pp. 246–56.

PETERS, M. (1995) 'Educational reform and the politics of the curriculum in New Zealand', in CARTER, D.S.G. and O'NEILL, M.H. (Eds) *International Perspectives on Educational Reform and Policy Implementation*, London, Falmer Press.

PLANK, D.N. (1988) 'Why school reform doesn't change schools: Political and organisational perspectives', in BOYD, W.L. and KERCHNER, C.T. (Eds) *The Politics of Excellence and Choice in Education*, London, Falmer Press.

PRESSEISEN, B.Z. (1989) *Unlearned Lessons: Current and Past Reforms for School Improvement*, London, Falmer Press.

SARASON, S.B. (1990) *The Predictable Failure of Educational Reform*, San Francisco, Jossey-Bass.

SIZER, T.R. (1984) *Horace's Compromise: The Dilemma of the American High School*, Boston, Houghton Mifflin.

SMITH, D.L. (1993) (Ed) *Australian Curriculum Reform: Action and Reaction*, Canberra, ACSA.

THE HOLMES GROUP (1986) *Tomorrow's Teachers*, East Lansing, The Holmes Group.

18 National Goals and Standards

Introduction

Goals are often used by leaders as slogans for action. They can epitomize ideals and desirable directions but they are generally vague and global. Standards can also be slogans and general statements but they are being increasingly used as frameworks for student performance or school delivery.

Why Are National Goals and Standards Needed?

A major focus in many countries in the 1980s and 1990s has been the powerful thrust toward national goals and standards. Although the contexts are quite different it is no accident that the initiatives are interrelated — it is truly a cross-national phenomenon in the 1990s. Some of the common reasons *for* the development of national standards include:

- the need for students to have a higher range of skills;
- the need for a quality education (entitlement for all students);
- the need for an essential core of knowledge and skills for all students;
- the need for national assessment and reporting to ensure that standards have been reached;
- the need for the public to know how well schools are succeeding;
- the need for teachers to be aware of necessary knowledge and skills;
- the need for a common/national understanding and communication over curriculum matters.

Yet, it should also be noted that there are many critics of national standards. Some of the arguments *against* national standards include:

- it is not possible to create standards that apply equally to all students;
- schools don't have the capacity to help all students attain these higher standards;
- appropriate assessment methods are not available to measure whether students have attained the new standards;
- it will lead to unnecessary standardization and regimentation;
- it will reduce opportunities for the individual school to be the locus of accountability.

It is necessary to examine standards and goals in more detail — examples are included from Australia, Japan, USA and the UK.

Examples

Australia

The Australian Educational Council (AEC) comprising state and federal ministers of education produced the National Goals for Schooling in 1989. A working party of Directors-General laboured for almost eighteen months to produce a comprehensive set of goals which would be acceptable to all states and territories (Table 18.1).

The national goals have been cited by some writers as a remarkable achievement by the then Federal Minister John Dawkins to persuade ministerial colleagues from each of the Australian States and Territories to work toward and agree upon a set of common national goals for schooling in Australia — the Hobart declaration was a breakthrough — for the first time a set of national goals had been explicit and 'it represented the first step towards a shared understanding across education systems of the priorities for all Australian schools' (Kennedy, 1990, pp. 11–12). Yet, a closer analysis of these goals reveals that they are conservative and academic in nature, with some leaning towards general problem-solving skills in the environment.

The AEC and its Curriculum and Assessment committee appeared to use these goal statements (in some cases retrospectively) to justify their national curriculum development activities. For example an AEC paper (1992) concluded:

In recent years the Australian Education Council has taken steps to develop a more common view of the purpose of schooling and of the shape of the school curriculum.

This work began with the establishment of Common and Agreed National Goals for Schooling in Australia. It is continuing with the development of National Curriculum Statements and Profiles in eight learning areas through collaborative work between the States and Territories. Together, these documents represent national agreement on the purpose of the curriculum of Australian schools. The Statements and Profiles provide a description of commonly agreed areas of knowledge, skills and understanding and of learning outcomes within the eight areas of learning.

The Common and Agreed Goals also represent a broader consensus about the purpose of the curriculum. They reflect agreement about the value of excellence, the need for young people to be challenged by what they learn and the importance of improving standards of achievement and of providing for all young people a broad educational foundation. The goals state the expectation that schools will pursue broader personal goals, such as those concerned with physical and emotional health and the development of balanced judgement in matters of morality, ethics and social

Table 18.1: A summary of goals, learning areas, cross-curricular areas, groups with special needs

---

National Goals The Agreed National Goals for Schooling include the following aims:

---

1 To provide an excellent education for all young people, being one which develops their talents and capacities to full potential, and is relevant to the social, cultural and economic needs of the nation.

2 To enable all students to achieve high standards of learning and to develop self-confidence, optimism, high self-esteem, respect for others, and achievement of personal excellence.

3 To promote equality of educational opportunities, and to provide for groups with special learning requirements.

4 To respond to the current and emerging economic and social needs of the nation, and to provide those skills which will allow student maximum flexibility and adaptability in their future employment and other aspect of life.

5 To provide a foundation for further education and training, in terms of knowledge and skills, respect for learning and positive attitudes for long-life education.

6 To develop in students:

- the skills of English literacy, including skills in listening, speaking, reading and writing;
- skills of numeracy, and other mathematical skills;
- skills of analysis and problem solving;
- skills of information processing and computing;
- an understanding of the role of science and technology in society, together with scientific and technological skills;
- a knowledge and appreciation of Australia's historical and geographic context;
- a knowledge of languages other than English;
- an appreciation and understanding of, and confidence to participate in, the creative arts;
- an understanding of, and concern for, balanced development and the global environment; and
- a capacity to exercise judgment in matters of morality, ethics and social justice.

7 To develop knowledge, skills, attitudes and values which will enable students to participate as active and informed citizens in our democratic Australian society within an international context.

8 To provide students with an understanding and respect for our cultural heritage including the particular cultural background of Aboriginal and ethnic groups.

9 To provide for the physical development and personal health and fitness of students, and for the creative use of leisure time.

10 To provide appropriate career education and knowledge of the world of work, including an understanding of the nature and place of work in our society.

National Learning Areas
- English;
- science;
- mathematics;
- Languages Other Than English (LOTE);
- technology;
- studies of society and environment;
- the arts;
- health and physical education.

Special Areas
- English as a Second Language (ESL) band scales;
- Special education.

Table 18.1: (Cont.)

Cross-curricular Areas
• the environment;
• information technology;
• personal and interpersonal skills;
• career and work education;
• literacy;
• numeracy.

Groups with Special Needs
• girls;
• Aboriginal and Torres Strait Islander students;
• geographically isolated students;
• children in poverty;
• students who leave school early.

Source: AEC, 1989

justice. They also suggest broad social goals, notably the importance of understanding and respect for the cultural heritage and the promotion of active and informed citizens. (AEC, 1992, p. 1)

It is far from clear whether these national goals are being achieved. As indicated above, the goals are general and conservative and there are no performance indicator links with the national profiles apart from the exhortatory rhetoric.

Further, the trialing and implementation of the profiles is occurring at different rates and with different emphases across the states and territories during 1995 (Marsh, 1994). The profiles may be providing a common language for teachers, students and parents which could be directly linked to the national goals. It may increase the public accountability of schools. Then again the pressures could be so great upon teachers that changes are merely superficial.

At this mid-point in the 1990s it appears that the national standards and goals have had only moderate impact. Various writers such as Ellerton and Clements (1994) consider that the goals are 'prosaic and mundane' (p. 59). The goals were to be reviewed from time to time by the AEC but this has not occurred. The securing of an accord on common principles with the Hobart Declaration may have been an historic event but its impact since 1989 has been of little significance.

Japan

The Japanese Ministry of Education, Science and Culture establishes national standards and courses of study for K-12 students. There are various elements such as:

• national courses of study — specific details about content and teaching methods;
• regulation for textbook authorization;

- regulations for appointment of school board members;
- national regulations for the provision of instructional aids and equipment.

As noted by Abiko (1992) 'the national courses of study are not just guidelines but are statutory orders, which means that any school which does not follow them will be deemed to be breaking the law' (p. 138).

Various reform movements have occurred in Japan and since World War II there have been two, the enactment of the Fundamental Law of Education which set forth basic principles for education in the new democracy (Nakajima, 1990) and reports produced by the National Council on Educational Reform (1984) and the Curriculum Council (1958).

Eight basic principles for educational reform were identified, namely:

- the principle of putting emphasis on individuality;
- putting emphasis on fundamentals;
- the cultivation of creativity, thinking ability, and power of expression;
- the expansion of opportunities for choices;
- the humanization of the educational environment;
- the transition to lifelong learning;
- coping with internationalization;
- coping with the information age.

Of these the three highest priorities are:

- emphasis on individuality;
- transition to a lifelong learning system;
- coping with internationalization and the information age.

These goals are very laudable but quite difficult to implement. For example, the uniformity of content and methods and excessive competition in examinations creates difficulties for the encouragement of individuality.

In terms of internationalization Japan is widening the scope of some subjects such as social studies. A new, required world history subject is being introduced which 'will stress the diversity of history, lifestyles, customs and values of other countries in the world' (Nakajima, 1990, p. 113). Yet, various Japanese educators have been very critical of these national goals. Sasamori (1993) notes that 'in spite of submitting four reports relevant to all aspects of the future of education, only a few of the National Council on Educational Reform's recommendations were enforced, mainly because the Council itself has a strong tinge of politics' (p. 154). Abiko (1992) criticizes the political and economic motivations behind reform efforts in Japan. Marsh (1995) comments that the academic curriculum in Japan with a reliance on centrally provided syllabuses and textbooks emphasizing teacher-directed learning and leading to highly selective examinations, encourages and reinforces a narrow view of education and therefore reforms have difficulty in breaking this vicious cycle.

Table 18.2:   Goals 2000 sets into law the National Education Goals

By the year 2000 . . .

- **School readiness**: All children in America will start school ready to learn;
- **School completion**: The high school graduation rate will increase to at least 90 per cent;
- **Student achievement and citizenship**: All students will leave grades 4, 8, and 12 having demonstrated competency over challenging subject matter including English, mathematics, science, foreign languages, civics and government, economics, arts, history and geography.
- **Mathematics and science**: United States students will be first in the world in mathematics and science achievement;
- **Adult literacy and lifelong learning**: Every adult American will be literate and will possess the knowledge and skills necessary to compete in a global economy and exercise the rights and responsibilities of citizenship;
- **Safe, disciplined, and alcohol- and drug-free schools**: Every school in the United States will be free of drugs, violence and the unauthorized presence of firearms and alcohol and will offer a disciplined environment conducive to learning;
- **Teacher education and professional development**: The nation's teaching force will have access to programmes for the continued improvement of their professional skills.
- **Parental participation**: Every school will promote partnerships that will increase parental involvement and participation in promoting the social, emotional and academic growth of children.

Source: McKernan, 1994

USA

McKernan (1994) asserts that 'as recently as five years ago, the United States had no nationwide goals to provide focus and consistency in our teaching and no basis of determining whether we were internationally competitive or not'. In 1990 National Education Goals were developed by state governors and these were finally adopted in the Goals 2000 Educate America Act (see Table 18.2).

Substantial funding has been provided for state and local education improvement efforts, for a National Education Standards and Improvement Council, for a National Skills Standards Board and for parental assistance.

Further content and performance standards are being produced by national subject associations such as the National Council of Teachers of Mathematics and the National Council of Teachers of English. For example, mathematics teachers in the National Council of Teachers of Mathematics were the first group to produce curriculum standards in 1989 and these have been very well received, but as noted by Romberg (1993) only when they are being used in classrooms will real change begin to occur.

Core indicators have been developed to describe educational progress for each of the national goals and these are listed in Table 18.3. McKernan (1994) notes these indicators are not necessarily ideal measures of progress but they are the best of those currently available. McKernan concludes that over the period 1990–4 national performance has only improved on four indicators:

Table 18.3: Core indicators for each of the National Education Goals

The indicators are listed below for each goal:

Goal 1: ready to learn
1 Children's health index
2 Immunizations
3 Family-child reading and storytelling
4 Preschool participation

Goal 2: school completion
5 High school completion

Goal 3: student achievement and citizenship
6 Mathematics achievement
7 Reading achievement

Goal 4: teacher education and professional development
(No core indicators have been selected for this new goal yet).

Goal 5: mathematics and science
8 International mathematics achievement comparisons
9 International science achievement comparisons

Goal 6: adult literacy and lifelong learning
10 Adult literacy
11 Participation in adult education
12 Participation in higher education

Goal 7: safe, disciplined, and alcohol and drug-free schools
13 Overall student drug and alcohol use
14 Sale of drugs at school
15 Student and teacher victimization
16 Disruptions in class by students

Goal 8: parental participation
(No core indicators have been selected for this new goal yet. They will be addressed in future goals).

Source: McKernan, 1994

- general health and developmental status of infants has improved;
- mathematics achievement at grades 4 and 8 has increased;
- student alcohol use has declined;
- incidents of threats and injuries to students at school have declined.

Wide ranging collaborative efforts are already in place between federal, state and local agencies. Some specific initiatives include:

- legislative initiatives by the federal government (Safe Schools Act, School-to-Work Opportunities Act, Student Loan Reform Act, Elementary and Secondary Education Act);
- increased funding for early childhood programmes;

- substantial funding for educational improvement;
- funding of research to achieve national goals;
- establishing of voluntary national standards;
- extension of the collection of national assessment data.

United Kingdom

Prime Minister James Callaghan's speech at Ruskin College, Oxford in 1976 heralded needed change in education. Various problems were highlighted at this time including economic decline and a general decline in educational standards. Goodson (1994) considers that some of the major concerns were:

- that the curriculum had become overcrowded;
- variations in curriculum approaches in different schools;
- curriculum was not sufficiently matched to life in a modern industrial society.

A core curriculum was heavily promoted after the election of Margaret Thatcher in 1979. Following a third election success in 1987 the Government was determined to establish a new National Curriculum. Right-wing groups argued for the traditional grammar school subjects. Margaret Thatcher favoured a core curriculum in the areas of English, maths and science — 'the syllabuses should have a strong factual base and be rigorously tested' (Taylor, 1995, p. 13). Kenneth Baker, the Secretary of State, considered curriculum reform should be wider and wanted all students to have access to all ten subjects and to be subjected to uniform evaluation procedures. Ultimately, Baker's preference for ten subjects survived, and the Great Education Reform Bill (GERBIL) became law in 1988.

The goals of GERBIL are surprisingly few in number, namely:

- the curriculum should be balanced and broadly based and should:
  * promote the spiritual, moral, cultural, mental and physical development of pupils at school and of society; and
  * prepare such pupils for the opportunities, responsibilities and experiences of adult life.
- It is intended that the curriculum should reflect the culturally diverse society to which pupils belong and of which they will become adult members. It should benefit them as they grow in maturity and help to prepare them for adult life and experience — home life and parenthood; responsibilities as a citizen towards the community and society nationally and internationally, enterprise, employment and other work. (DES, 1989)

Far more significant were the structural details of the National Curriculum included in the Bill, namely:

- core and other foundation subjects to be studied by all students;
- attainment targets (knowledge, skills and understanding) to be used at the end of each of four key stages;
- programs of study, defined as the matters, skills and processes which must be taught during each key stage;
- assessment arrangements for assessing students at or near the end of each key stage.

Specific regulations were also included about:

- the role of local education authorities;
- local management of schools;
- 'opting out' provisions for LEA schools to become grant maintained schools.

In the case of the UK, the goals of the National Curriculum were few in number but the specific values, priorities and standards permeate a wide ranging number of regulations and requirements. Whitty (1995) points to the dangers of the over-regulation of GERBIL. Goodson (1994) is also critical of the detailed control exercised over the school curriculum — 'this would seem a late and somewhat desperate attempt at nation-building, in terms of both nation-state governance and the partial propagation through curriculum of national ideologies, selective memories and images' (p. 110).

Some interesting similarities and differences can be noted between the UK and the USA. The goals and standards developed in the UK 'have been far more politicised and ideologically charged than in the USA where similar market-oriented reforms have enjoyed considerable bipartisan support' (Boyd, 1994, p. 2).

Whitty (1995) considers that the devolution and centralization goals and practices of GERBIL have had more destructive than productive effects. Goodson (1994) notes how both countries have used the perception of nations at risk and social groups at risk to justify increasing the powers of central government over the school curriculum.

Reflections and Issues

1 'The agreed goals for schooling in Australia can only be effective if they are linked to concrete action plans and resources.' Were the national goals developed in 1989 little more than rhetoric?

   What resources have been forthcoming since the goals were announced in 1989?

2 'The national goals in Australia signalled an intensification of collaborative effort between states and territories.'

   Do you agree? Give details to support your stance.

3 'In the UK the competitive market is seen as the best system to give consumers freedom of choice — the ideology as applied to education seeks to enhance freedom of choice for parents as consumers over their children's education.' (Saron, 1988)

    To what extent is this ideology reflected in the National Curriculum? Give reasons.

4 The subjects included in the National Curriculum in the UK are 'largely to be viewed as purveyors of factual knowledge and the technical skills of knowledge acquisition rather than as sources of values.' (Elliott, 1991, p. 22)

    Are values minimized in the National Curriculum? Discuss.

5 'Japan has provided its people with equal educational opportunity but neglected giving genuine value to children's spiritual and cultural development.' (Sasamori, 1993)

    Discuss in terms of educational goals and recent reform practices.

6 'Major issues for Japan in the 1990's are the difficulties of coping with rapid social changes, especially internationalisation and the information age.' (Nakajima, 1990)

    How do these issues impact upon schooling and the curriculum? Are they being addressed by current reform programmes?

7 'In the USA there is a pervasive feeling that educators need to be monitored, if not managed, and that our schools are in a state of crisis.' (Eisner, 1990, p. 1)

    Is this the major factor behind the National Standards initiatives? What are some other factors? Compare these with factors responsible for the National Curriculum in the UK.

8 'Higher standards are necessary and important as replacements for the current de facto, low-level standards implicit in most textbooks and tests.' (Alexander, 1993, p. 9)

    Do textbooks and tests have a significant influence on teaching in the USA? How can higher standards provide a solution?

9 The Goals 2000 Act in the USA provides for $400 million for new standards (content and performance, and assessment standards) and could be as significant as Britain's 1988 GERBIL Act.

    Examine the main features of each Act and their respective influence to date.

References

Abiko, T. (1992) 'Accountability and control in the Japanese National Curriculum', *Curriculum Journal*, **4**, 1, pp. 137–46.

ALEXANDER, F. (1993) 'National standards: A new conventional wisdom', *Educational Leadership*, **50**, 5, pp. 9–10.

AUSTRALIAN EDUCATION COUNCIL (1989) *Common and Agreed National Goals*, Canberra, AGPS.

AUSTRALIAN EDUCATION COUNCIL (1992) *General Issues in Curriculum*, Melbourne, AGPS.

BOYD, W.L. (1994) 'National school reform and restructuring: Parallels between Britain and the United States', Paper prepared for the British Educational Management and Administration Society Conference, Manchester.

CURRICULUM COUNCIL (1985) *First Report*, Tokyo, NCER.

DEPARTMENT OF EDUCATION AND SCIENCE (1989) *The Education Reform Act 1988: The School Curriculum and Assessment*, London, DES.

EISNER, E.W. (1990) 'Should America have a National Curriculum?', Unpublished paper, Stanford University.

ELLERTON, N.F. and CLEMENTS, M.A. (1994) *The National Curriculum Debacle*, Perth, Meridian Press.

ELLIOTT, J. (1991) 'Disconnecting knowledge and understanding from human values: A critique of National Curriculum development', *Curriculum Journal*, **2**, 1, pp. 19–31.

GOODSON, I.F. (1994) *Studying Curriculum: Cases and Methods*, New York, Teachers College Press.

KENNEDY, K. (1990) 'Strengthening Australia's schools as a blueprint for national efforts at curriculum reform', Paper presented at the Annual Congress of the Australian and New Zealand Association for the Advancement of Science, Hobart.

MARSH, C.J. (1994) *Producing a National Curriculum: Plans and Paranoia*, Sydney, Allen and Unwin.

MARSH, C.J. (1995) 'School education and economic development in Asian countries', Paper presented at the Annual Conference of the Japanese Society for Curriculum Studies, Fukuoka.

MCKERNAN, J.R. (1994) (Chair) *The National Education Goals Report*, Washington, DC, Government Printer.

NAKAJIMA, A. (1990) 'Education for the twenty-first century: A Japanese perspective', in WILSON, D.C., GROSSMAN, D.L. and KENNEDY, K.J. (Eds) *Asia and the Pacific*, Calgary, Detsilig Enterprises.

NATIONAL COUNCIL FOR EDUCATIONAL REFORM (1984) *The First Report*, Tokyo, NCER.

ROMBERG, T.A. (1993) 'NCTM's standards: A rallying flag for mathematics teachers', *Educational Leadership*, **50**, 5, pp. 36–41.

SARON, R. (1988) 'Education policy under the Thatcher government', *Australian Education Researcher*, **15**, 2, pp. 55–63.

SASAMORI, T. (1993) 'Educational reform in Japan since 1984', in BEARE, H. and BOYD, W.L. (Eds) *Restructuring Schools*, London, Falmer Press.

TAYLOR, T. (1995) 'Personality, policy and the process of curriculum change: The United Kingdom 1902–1988', Paper presented at the Biennial Conference of the Australian Curriculum Studies Association, Melbourne.

WHITTY, G. (1995) 'School-based management and a National Curriculum: Sensible compromise or dangerous cocktail', Paper presented at the Annual Conference of the American Educational Research Association, San Francisco.

19 Vocational Education and Curriculum

Introduction

Many countries are currently reconsidering their education and training arrangements in the light of economic, social and personal factors. For too long vocational education has been a poor second to general/academic education. Ellis (1995) notes that 'the talents of thousands of young people are being wasted because educational systems measure only academic success and not practical, creative or interpersonal skills' (p. 84). Contemporary efforts to develop vocational education are emphasizing access, flexibility and relevance. To date, the endeavours are very encouraging and warrant close examination.

Some Definitions

'Vocational education' has always been a major thrust in education but its impact has varied over the decades. The current emphasis in vocational education is upon broad, experiential schemes and the world of work rather than directed toward occupational training or recruitment. Vocational education is characterized as:

- experientially based in terms of content and teaching method;
- directly relevant to student needs;
- emphasis upon core skills.

In different countries there are a multitude of awards and certificates which have emerged in the 1980s and 1990s and which address vocational education. Jessup (1995) describes the General National Vocational Qualifications (GNVQs) which were introduced in 1991 in the UK to provide a broad-based vocational education — 'in addition to acquiring the basic skills and an understanding of the underpinning principles in a vocational area, all students awarded a GNVQ will have achieved a range of core skills' (p. 37).

Moore and Hickox (1994) emphasize that vocational education is all to do with raising the general skill level in society in order to improve economic performance and international competitiveness. They stress that new vocationalism in the UK is:

- directly and explicitly related to skill requirements in the labour market;
- uses an industrial skills training model based upon competencies;
- promotes entrepreneurial attitudes.

'Competence': Competency-based standards are the lynch-pin of most contemporary vocational education programmes. Competency-based 'units' consist of units of work which contain elements of competence and associated performance criteria (NCVQ, 1991). An 'element of competence' is a description of an action, behaviour or outcome which a person should be able to demonstrate. 'Performance criteria' are statements against which an assessor judges the evidence that an individual can perform the activity specified in an element. Evidence of performance is required in respect of each element of competence (see also Chapter 10).

The Need for Vocational Education

Many countries are grappling with developing education and training systems that can produce an educated, skilled and flexible workforce so that industry can be competitive in domestic and international markets. Unemployment levels loom large in a number of countries and it is crucial that programmes are introduced which provide some chance of future employment for unemployed youth.

Ellis (1995) criticizes the monoculture of academic measurement of achievement. Hargreaves (1984) is critical of the sharp contrast between the 'academic' and the 'vocational' — all 'academic' courses should in our view contain practical and applied features, and all 'vocational' studies should have academic elements.

Carnevale (1995) argues that the new standards of industry in the 1990s will rely on three factors which are critical to success:

- information-based technologies — customizing services, monitoring outcomes, getting consistency of standards;
- high performance organizational formats — the use of worksite teams, networks, dynamic elements of goal setting, communication and involvement;
- more highly skilled and autonomous workforce — higher levels of basic skills, adaptability skills, interpersonal and communication skills, team work skills, technology skills.

Curriculum Elements

Because vocational education has an occupational or employment base, rather than a subject base, it is not unexpected that the curriculum orientation is quite different.

Outcomes

The vocational curricula tend to be very explicit as to their intentions. Explicit statements of intended outcomes, along with competence standards and performance criteria are commonly used. Justifications for this high level of specificity include:

- education and training programmes should be transparent and accountable;
- explicit statements encourage clarity and student ownership — learners take charge of their own learning to a much greater extent.

Yet there are educators who are critical of the large number of outcomes/units and elements in vocational programmes. For example Walker (1994) and Cairns (1992) are critical of the emphasis upon standardization and uniformity and minimum standards.

Content

The selection of content for vocational curricula requires input from a wider range of sources including industry, government and community as well as educators. Eraut (1989) cites four categories for the selection of content objectives:

- occupational practice: justified in terms of national manpower needs;
- roles in society: in terms of citizenship and local community;
- cultural and academic knowledge: in terms of domains of knowledge;
- interests of the learner: interests and needs.

Core skills are a major element of the content in vocational programmes. Jessup (1995) refers to the high priority given to the core skills of communications, application of number and information technology. Oates and Harkin (1995) refers to the high level of demand for core skills units in the GNVQs in the UK whereby teachers provide learning settings which contextualize the core skills in ways which are meaningful to students.

Learning Experiences

This element can be interpreted in quite different ways. Jessup (1995) argues that an outcomes approach defines the performance criteria and competencies and that 'any' processes of learning can be used to achieve these ends. Yet it can also be inferred from published accounts of outcomes approaches that certain learning experiences are given higher priority than others. For example, a major emphasis is upon student-centred learning — students are encouraged to take increased responsibility for their own learning (Nash, 1995).

Another distinctive aspect is that the curriculum is typically based upon small units or modules — each of which can be separately assessed and certificated. This aspect is often highlighted as a major feature because:

- it enables students to concentrate upon manageable units of work and thus they are likely to be more highly motivated than working on a year-long subject;

- small units facilitate credit accumulation and credit transfer;
- each unit is a unit of assessment and not a unit of instruction;
- it provides maximum flexibility to students because various combinations of units can be used to meet the requirements of the qualification;
- enables the assessment in each unit to be more directly related to the learning experiences of the students.

Yet there are also a number of educators who are highly critical of the use of modules. Smithers (1994) and Young (1995) argue that modules are not of themselves an alternative curriculum framework. They don't address the basis for breaking up a subject into parts and there can be problems of lack of coherence. Young (1995) sums up the issue as follows — 'Alone they treat learning as if it was like shopping in a supermarket — no system or relationship with sellers is required to shop in a supermarket except at the cash till' (p. 178).

Assessment

Assessment is a major feature of many vocational programmes — the bedrock of a valid system of employment relevant qualifications (Steadman, 1995). To a large extent assessment activities are based upon summative/certification and accountability purposes. The modules/units have clearly established criteria of competence which indicate to the student what is to be learnt and also indicate to the assessor what can be assessed.

Jessup (1995) argues that assessment in vocational programmes can be more flexible because it can allow different kinds of evidence in real-life situations (workplaces) as well as instructional centres. Assessment practices can also be used to recognize prior learning.

Yet, Steadman (1995) cautions that assessment of modules can be very complicated. For example, if assessments are too specific the areas covered are too small and possibly inconsequential. How many times does a candidate need to demonstrate a satisfactory performance? Should assessments be low-inference or high inference? What are some of the difficulties in collecting assessment evidence in workplace settings?

Certification

Contemporary vocational programmes place a considerable emphasis upon certification. There are sound reasons for this. There continues to be considerable prejudice about vocational qualifications compared with traditional, academic qualifications.

Curriculum developers of vocational programmes, must of necessity, show parities between their units and other academic units. In the UK, the National Council for Vocational Qualifications have provided full details of the interlinked

Table 19.1: *Pathways for post-16 students*

Academic	GNVQ	NVQ	
		Description	Level
		Professional qualifications. Middle management	5
Degree	GNVQ Level 4	Higher technician. Junior management	4
A/AS level	GNVQ Advanced	Technician. Advanced craft supervisor	3
GCSE (grade C or above)	GNVQ Intermediate	Basic craft certificate	2
GCSE (below grade C)	GNVQ Foundation	Semi-skilled	1

Source: Hodkinson and Mattinson, 1994

pathways between GCSE, A levels and GNVQs (Table 19.1). The New Zealand Qualifications Authority has produced a single qualifications structure which links the school certificate, sixth form certificate, trade certificates and degrees. The Australian Standards Framework provides eight levels of achievement and all accredited education and training courses, ranging from certificates and diplomas to degrees, fit within the framework.

Examples

General National Vocational Qualifications (GNVQs)

The GNVQ was a government initiative in the UK in 1991 to establish parity of esteem between academic and vocational education — 'to produce a broad-based vocational qualification which could be delivered through full-time programs in schools and colleges' (Jessup, 1995, p. 37).

A major objective is to encourage a far higher proportion of young persons to stay in full-time education beyond the end of compulsory schooling at age 16. It is proving very popular with 16-year-olds but also with the 14–16 age group and adults — the concept of a single national system does appear to be working. Some major characteristics of the GNVQ include:

- GNVQs are available at three levels, Foundation, Intermediate and Advanced. The advanced GNVQ is equivalent to two A levels (see Table 19.2);
- over forty GNVQs are now available (for example, Leisure and Tourism; Health and Social Care);
- each GNVQ has a number of units (twelve to fifteen), a number of sub-elements (over fifty) and a large number of performance criteria (200–300);

Table 19.2: Qualification Pathways (UK)

Qualification Pathways		
Academic	GNVQs	NVQs
Higher Education		5 (Professional, Managerial)
		4 (Higher technician, Junior management)
2 GCE A-Levels	Advanced	3 (Technician, Supervisor)
5 GCSEs, Grades A-C	Intermediate	2 (Craft)
Other GCSEs	Foundation	1 (Foundation)

Source: Smithers, 1995

- there is a requirement to complete core skill units in communication, application of number and information technology;
- there is no fixed time for students to complete each unit but schools are making decisions based upon limited resources (eight to twenty-six hours a week);
- internal and external forms of assessment are used.

Reactions to the GNVQ have generally been positive. Harrop (1995) notes 'that GNVQs are providing a way of meeting the growth in staying-on rates. Schools and colleges are promoting the advantages of diversity they can offer and take pride in meeting the varied needs of their students' (p. 128).

Jessup (1995) is very positive about the GNVQ noting that students take greater responsibility for their own learning and that it establishes national standards through the specification of outcomes. Yet, various critics have noted problems with the GNVQ. Hodkinson and Mattinson (1994) conclude 'our analysis questions the feasibility of two or three parallel post-16 tracks of equal status in the British context. The tensions identified suggest that earlier failures to develop a distinctive, high status vocational pathway may be replicated' (p. 333). Ainley (1993) suggests that such a three-track model no longer reflects employment needs, if it ever did.

National Qualifications Framework (NQF)

The New Zealand Qualifications Authority (NZQA) was established in 1990 as part of a range of educational reforms and an ideology of hierarchical managerialism (Codd, 1994).

The National Qualifications Framework (NQF) was designed to simplify a confusing system of qualifications and to provide incentives for people to continue learning. Eight levels in the NQF were established, ranging from the equivalent of senior secondary education through to degrees (see Table 19.3). The high school certificate has been the 'gold standard' for academic entry into university up until recently but it is envisaged that the new national certificate will gradually replace

Table 19.3: NQF levels

1 2 3 4	National certificate

5 6 7	National diploma Initial degree

8	Other degrees, Higher certificates and diplomas

it. Under NQF, qualifications have been packaged into flexible modules termed 'unit standards'. These units are of different sizes depending upon the amount of work needed to complete them but they all use a standards-based assessment which measures performance against clearly defined standards.

The unit standards are currently being offered in schools, private and government training establishments, colleges of education, polytechnics and the workplace. Details about the unit standards are provided through the National Catalogue of Units which lists:

- title of the unit;
- purpose statement;
- entry information;
- learning outcomes and assessment criteria.

Providers of the unit standards are accredited by NZQA. Accreditation is an evaluation of the provider's ability to deliver the unit standards. Moderation requirements have been established. Providers use their own methods to teach each unit but there are standards required, as part of accreditation procedures to ensure quality levels of:

- learning and teaching approaches;
- content and context;
- resources;
- range and number of assessment.

The Framework was introduced progressively and will be in place by 1996. Various qualifications use common units. Hood (1992) notes that the big advantage of the new framework is that it offers flexibility of learning — industry and enterprises can package the units that make up qualifications in the way that best suits their needs.

Merits and Demerits of Vocational Education

Vocational education initiatives have been many and varied within and across countries. Yet, contemporary initiatives are not only distinctive but appear to be quite successful. In general terms the major merits can be characterized as:

- emphasis on student-centred learning;
- emphasis on skills which can be practised in the workplace as well as in schools;
- assessment is based on real-life situations;
- provides flexibility of choices for students;
- the curriculum is more relevant for students;
- modules permit cross-transfers and credit recognition.

Some of the major problems yet to be resolved include:

- a variety of modules limit the coherence of a programme;
- lack of rigour in assessment requirements;
- professional development demands on vocational teachers are very heavy and have not been given a high priority;
- the performance criteria and indicators are creating an excessive work load for students;
- there is insufficient quality control of standards between institutions;
- vocational units still lack status compared with academic subjects.

Reflections and Issues

1   'If current academic examinations at the end of secondary school were broadened to include vocational skills many of the current problems relating to education and training would be solved.' (Marsden and Ryan, 1991)
    Explain.

2   'The introduction of GNVQ has, as we had hoped, contributed to the achievement of our curriculum goals. There has been an increase in the impetus towards cross-curricular projects, the integration of core skills, modularization of courses, experiments with teaching and learning styles and resource-based learning. GNVQ has without doubt contributed to, and accelerated, the changing culture of our institution both for staff and students.' (Jackson, 1995)
    Explain why the GNVQ appears to have been very successful in a number of UK colleges.

3   'The model (Jessup's Outcomes Model) does not assume that there is only one way to learn or even that there is necessarily a best way. It recognises

individual differences and individual preferences and opportunities. Above all it does not prescribe the form of learning.' (Jessup, 1991, p. 138)

What are the implications of this model for undertaking curriculum planning? Use examples to illustrate potential, benefits and problems.

4   Explicitness and clarity of intended outcomes is not a characteristic of many teaching institutions. Vocational qualifications do achieve this end and this is a major advantage over many traditional academic qualifications.

Do you support this statement: Use examples to illustrate your position.

5   'GNVQs have an important function for students in providing choices within the full-time and part-time education system for the type of course they want to take and for progression beyond the course they choose.' (Harrop, 1995, p. 117)

Is this in fact occurring in the UK? Give examples.

6   'The separation of outcomes from processes encourages colleges to concentrate on assessment and leaves it up to them whether to invest time in devising new learning strategies.' (Young, 1995, p. 174)

Is there too great an emphasis upon assessment? How might new learning strategies be linked to assessment?

7   'What is certain is that if the full potential of GNVQs is to be achieved, teachers need to be comfortable and familiar with the student-centred flexible learning philosophy and methodology.' (Sutton, 1994, p. 351)

What are some of the assumptions of a student-centred methodology? What implications are there for teacher planning and modes of instruction?

8   'The forces impelling change in education and training have been largely economic and social — on upskilling and improving the educational base of all employees.' (Merson, 1994)

Have educational and pedagogical factors been considered sufficiently in the structures and qualifications produced? Give examples to illustrate your case.

9   'The vocationalist stress on experiential or real life learning echoes, as we have suggested, many of the themes of the progressivism of the 1960s. But it is open to some of the same objections. By combining a crude experiential philosophy of learning with an equally crude behaviourist definition of "competency" and "outcomes" vocationalism risks ignoring the deeper intellectual competencies that, it can be argued, are necessary to create the truly "flexible" workers which the occupational structures of post-industrial societies will demand.' (Hickox and Moore, 1992, p. 290)

Critically examine the statement. Adopt a position in favour or against using examples to illustrate your case.

References

AINLEY, P. (1993) *Class and Skill: Changing Divisions of Knowledge and Labour*, London, Cassell.

CAIRNS, L. (1992) 'Competency-based education: Nostradamus's Nostrum', *Journal of Teaching Practice*, **12**, 1, pp. 1–31.

CARNEVALE, A.P. (1995) 'Education, training and the economy, keynote', Paper presented at the Victorian Association of Directors of TAFE Colleges, Melbourne.

CODD, J.A. (1994) 'Managerialism, market liberalism and the move to self-managing schools in New Zealand', in SMYTH, J. (Ed) *A Socially Critical View of the Self-managing School*, London, Falmer Press.

ELLIS, P. (1995) 'Standards and the outcomes approach', in BURKE, J. (Ed) *Outcomes, Learning and the Curriculum*, London, Falmer Press.

ERAUT, M. (1989) (Ed) *The International Encyclopaedia of Educational Technology*, Oxford, Pergamon.

HARGREAVES, D. (1984) (Ed) *Improving Secondary Schools*, London, ILEA.

HARROP, J. (1995) 'GNVQs phase one', in BURKE, J. (Ed) *Outcomes, Learning and the Curriculum*, London, Falmer Press.

HICKOX, M. and MOORE, R. (1992) 'Education and post-Fordism: A new correspondence', in BROWN, P. and LAUDER, H. (Eds) *Education for Economic Survival*, London, Routledge.

HODKINSON, P. and MATTINSON, K. (1994) 'A bridge too far?: The problems facing GNVQ', *The Curriculum Journal*, **5**, 3, pp. 323–36.

HOOD, D. (1992) 'Qualifications framework', *The Executive Secretary*, 8 October.

JACKSON, T. (1995) 'Piloting GNVQ', in BURKE, J. (Ed) *Outcomes, Learning and the Curriculum*, London, Falmer Press.

JESSUP, G. (1991) *Outcomes: NVQs and the Emerging Model of Education and Training*, London, Falmer Press.

JESSUP, G. (1995) 'Outcome based qualifications and the implications for learning', in BURKE, J. (Ed) *Outcomes Learning and the Curriculum*, London, Falmer Press.

MARSDEN, D. and RYAN, P. (1991) 'Initial training, labour market structure and public policy, intermediate skills in British and German industry', in RYAN, P. *International Comparisons of Vocational Education and Training for Intermediate Skills*, London, Falmer Press.

MERSON, M. (1994) 'Post-16 education and training: Agendas and structures', *The Curriculum Journal*, **5**, 3, pp. 295–305.

MOORE, R. and HICKOX, M. (1994) 'Vocationalism and educational change', *The Curriculum Journal*, **5**, 3, pp. 281–93.

NASH, C. (1995) 'Flexible learning and outcomes', in BURKE, J. (Ed) *Outcomes, Learning and the Curriculum*, London, Falmer Press.

NATIONAL COUNCIL FOR VOCATIONAL QUALIFICATIONS (1991) *Guide to National Vocational Qualifications*, London, NVQ.

OATES, T. and HARKIN, J. (1995) 'From design to delivery: The implementation of the NCVQ core skill units', in BURKE, J. (Ed) *Outcomes, Learning and the Curriculum*, London, Falmer Press.

SMITHERS, A. (1994) 'The paradox of A levels', *The Curriculum Journal*, **5**, 3, pp. 355–63.

SMITHERS, A. (1995) 'Britain's education and training revolution, keynote', Paper presented at the Biennial Conference of the Australian Curriculum Studies Association, Melbourne.

STEADMAN, S. (1995) 'The assessment of outcomes', in BURKE, J. (Ed) *Outcomes, Learning and the Curriculum*, London, Falmer Press.

SUTTON, A. (1994) 'NTETs, GNVQs and flexible learning', *The Curriculum Journal*, **5**, 3, pp. 337–53.

WALKER, J. (1994) 'Competency-based teacher education: Implications for quality in higher education', II R Conference, Canberra.

YOUNG, M. (1995) 'Modularisation and the outcomes approach: Towards a strategy for a curriculum of the future', in BURKE, J. (Ed) *Outcomes, Learning and the Curriculum*, London, Falmer Press.

Concluding Issues

It is important to reflect upon what has been achieved by reading about these nineteen concepts. Some relevant questions which might be asked include:

- To what extent did the information provided about each concept add to your understanding of curriculum matters?
- Were there matters left unstated that troubled you? Were you unable to follow-up these unresolved aspects in the references supplied?
- Has a reading of these concepts added to your understanding of what should be taught, to whom, when and how?

Schools are very complex organizations. Over recent years we have gained a number of insights about the processes and factors involved in curriculum planning and development and this has been due in no small measure to our use of conceptual structures and particular concepts. Concepts are powerful tools for exploring and reflecting upon relationships between major actors and events in the school environment.

There are no 'right' answers in curriculum. Analyses of events and problems using appropriate concepts is certainly preferable to a slavish rendering of factual accounts and the reproduction of particular recipes of action.

Curriculum workers need to develop balanced, informed and justifiable answers to major curriculum issues which they are prepared to uphold and value. If readers are even beginning to reflect and develop along these lines then the key concepts approach to curriculum is vindicated.

References

DERRIDA, J. (1972) 'Discussion: Structure, sign and play in the discourse of the human sciences', in MACKSEY, R. and DONATO, E. (Eds) *The Structuralist Controversy*, Baltimore, John Hopkins University Press.

DOLL, W.E. JR. (1987) 'Foundations for a postmodern curriculum', Paper presented at the Annual Conference of the American Educational Research Association, Washington, DC.

DOLL, W.E. JR. (1993a) *A Post-modern Perspective on Curriculum*, New York, Teachers College Press.

DOLL, W.E. JR. (1993b) 'Curriculum possibilities in a "post"-future', *Journal of Curriculum and Supervision*, **8**, 4, pp. 277–92.

DUKE, 1984 *Teaching: The Imperilled Profession*, Albany, New York, SUNY.

Foucault, M. (1972) *The Archaeology of Knowledge and the Discourse on Language*, New York, Pantheons.

Giddens, A. (1990) *The Consequences of Modernity*, Cambridge, Polity Press.

Giroux, H.A. (1992) *Border Crossings: Cultural Workers and the Politics of Education*, New York, Routledge.

Graham, R.J. (1991) *Reading and Writing the Self: Autobiography in Education and the Curriculum*, New York, Teachers College Press.

Griffin, D.R., Cobb, John B., Ford, M.P., Gunter, P. and Ochs, P. (1993) *Founders of Constructive Postmodern Philosophy: Peirce, James, Bergson, Whitehead, and Hartshorne*, Albany, NY, SUNY Press.

Habermas, J. (1970) *Knowledge and Human Interests*, Boston, Beacon.

Hargreaves, A. (1995) *Changing Teachers, Changing Times*, London, Cassell.

Jencks, C. (1986) *What Is Post-modernism?*, New York, St Martin's Press.

Jencks, C. (Ed) (1992) *The Post-modern Reader*, New York, St Martin's Press.

Kincheloe, J.L. (1993) *Toward a Critical Politics of Teacher Thinking: Mapping the Postmodern*, Westport, Bergin and Garvey.

Lather, P. (1991) *Getting Smart: Feminist Research and Pedagogy with/in the Postmodern*, New York, Routledge.

Miller, J.L. (1987) 'Women as teacher/researchers: Gaining a sense of ourselves', *Teacher Education Quarterly*, **14**, 2, pp. 52–8.

Naisbitt, J. and Aberdene, P. (1990) *Megatrends 1000: Ten New Directions for the 1990s*, New York, Avon Books.

Rhedding-Jones, J. (1995) 'What do you do after you've met poststructuralism?', *Journal of Curriculum Studies*, **27**, 5, pp. 479–500.

Schon, D.A. (1983) *The Reflective Practitioner: How Professionals Think in Action*, New York, Basic Books.

Slattery, P. (1995) *Curriculum Development in the Postmodern Era*, Garland, New York.

Sloan, D. (1993) *Insight-imagination: The Recovery of Thought in the Modern World*, New York, Teachers College Press.

Spivak, G.C. (1985) Strategies of Vigilance, *Block*, **10**, 9, pp. 12–17.

Swanson, A.D. (1993) 'A framework for allocating authority in a system of school', in Beare, H. and Boyd, W.L. *Restructuring Schools*, London, Falmer Press.

Toffler, A. (1980) *The Third Wave*, New York, Bantam Books.

Index

CPSIA information can be obtained at www.ICGtesting.com
Printed in the USA
BVOW040128051011

272589BV00003B/2/A